PRAISE FOR LEGS ASTRIDE THE WORLD

"Mary Susan Heath tells the story of the young man before the uniform, the older man in the uniform of World War II and Korea, and the aging man after the uniform was retired, questioning why he survived, and others did not. Johnson's stories related to his devoted niece are of lessons learned, loss, destruction, and death, but never defeat."

— **Katherine Wolfe**, author of *Time that Has Gone*,
and coauthor of *Savannah on My Mind*

"Here are stories many soldiers would never tell. We witness the tears in 'Legs' Johnson's eyes and his inability to speak any more. You will set aside what you don't know, or never knew, and simply listen and marvel at what two determined human beings can do."

— **Judy Hogan**, Writer, Poet, Publisher, Teacher,
author of the *Penny Weaver Mystery* series

D1300558

"Ms. Heath's strong prose balances 'Legs' Johnson's storytelling. But she never forgets her subject and enhances his life with rich sensory images, such as the meals they enjoy at Legs' favorite southern restaurants, the Blue Ribbon Diner and Huey's in Mebane, NC."

—Margaret Boothe Baddour,
author of *Easy Magic,* and *Scheherazade*

LEGS ASTRIDE THE WORLD

LEGS ASTRIDE
THE WORLD

Mary Susan Heath

"Let Valor not Fail!"

Mary Susan Heath

Deeds Publishing | Athens

Published by Deeds Publishing in Athens, GA
www.deedspublishing.com

Printed in The United States of America

Cover design by Mark Babcock.

ISBN 978-1-950794-25-6

Books are available in quantity for promotional or premium use. For information, email info@deedspublishing.com.

First Edition, 2020

10 9 8 7 6 5 4 3 2 1

To all the Soldiers and Family members of the 187th Airborne Infantry Regiment, past, present, and future.

Contents

Foreword   xi

Preface   xiii

Acknowledgements   xvii

Almost a Violation   1

The Fun of It All   5

Getting There   11

Defying Authority   15

Having the Last Word   21

Walking the Dogs   29

Pulling Rank   37

Second Interview   43

Road Kill   51

A Close Call at Powhatan   57

A New Broom   63

Coming Up in the World and Back Down Again   71

Back to the Farm   77

Outclassed in Clayton   83

Falling Down and Getting Up as "Legs"   89

Sweet Genevieve   97

Launching from Oak Ridge Military Institute   103

Courtship and Marriage   109

The Bombing of Pearl Harbor   119
Preparations and Delays   125
A Warm Welcome to Mebane United Methodist Church   133
Kicking Ass and Saving Face   139
Delegating Authority   145
Jump Training   153
Chilling in New Guinea   159
Delivered from the Enemy   165
Survival   169
Grace   177

Photographs   181

The Death of Joe Rangel in Leyte   235
Expediency in the Field   241
Planning for Survival and One Who Did Not   247
Giving Orders like Papa and Loving like Mama   253
Food in the Field and on the Farm   259
Letters from Home   263
The Protection of Rank   273
Being Careful Not to Rankle Rank   279
Of Morals and Manners   285

Contrasts and Contradictions   291
A Daring Rescue   299
Feeling Small and Walking Tall   309
Occupying Germany   315
Getting Picked and Getting Bill   323
Lessons from Landsberg   331
Landsberg and the Press   343
Observations at Landsberg Prison   349
Bill's Death   353
"Kiss My Ass Goodbye" in Korea   359
Getting the Call   371
My Last Close Call   379
Church at Home   383

Afterword   391

Author's Notes   397

Bibliography   401

About the Author   403

Foreword

My lifestyle to date has been one of joy, happiness, and fellowship with family and friends. As a matter of record, I wanted to share with them the specifics of my service to my country and tell the personal stories that are not part of my official record. This thumbnail sketch of my life includes memories of growing up during the Depression, as well as previously untold experiences of my military career.

I chose my niece, Mary Susan Heath, to write this book because of our shared love of family, as well as her educational background. She has my permission to share these stories with others who may be interested in their historical or philosophical perspective. I have been blessed with the joy of family and with these experiences, as my niece has told them in this biography.

Remembering where I came from has helped me to determine why I am where I am today. It is my hope that my grandchildren and their generation can better understand their heritage by knowing these details about my life.

Lehman H. Johnson, Jr.

Preface

*"People do not die for us immediately, but remain bathed in a sort
of aura of life which bears no relation to true immortality but
through which they continue to occupy our thoughts in the same
way as when they were alive. It is as though they were traveling
abroad."*

— **Marcel Proust**

My Uncle Legs, Lieutenant Colonel (Retired) Lehman H. (Legs) Johnson, Jr., was in his eighties when he summoned me to hear and record his story—one that began on a farm during the depression of the 1930's and journeyed through World War II, Korea, and almost to Vietnam, when it was cut short by a premonition, in his words, a sense that "there was a bullet out there somewhere with my name on it."

We did not begin at the beginning because memory doesn't work that way. Instead, it picks up a thread and then catches another to bind it. So for more than a decade, my favorite uncle and I wove those threads together into a tapestry of his life. For the purposes of this book, that time has been compressed into approximately a year and a half.

It was clear and cold in December of 1997, when I drove up the one-way road to 856 Knollwood Falls, in Mebane, North Carolina. Uncle Legs met me at the side door, his blue eyes steely in the harsh light of a winter day. He was a tall, slender man, who stood with the military bearing of a soldier, even though he now walked with a cane.

"Why, it's Mary Susan!" My uncle spoke as if my coming were not entirely expected, even though, in fact, he called me after decades of avoiding all attempts by various parties to get him to tell his war stories. Uncle Legs welcomed me into the kitchen with a hug and then motioned toward the adjoining room.

"After you." He tapped his cane for punctuation and then stood aside for me to go first. At the entrance to the den, he ducked his head to avoid the door frame, the hair still full, a salt and pepper gray, just as I remembered, trimmed in a military "high and tight."

"How's the family?" he asked, gesturing toward the couch as he settled himself in his familiar chair, the one that I knew had to be his. The brown leather of the overstuffed rounded back was soft in the place where I would come to expect him to lean back in thought. The matching ottoman was way out in the floor to accommodate the length of those legs that had given him the nickname.

Uncle Legs stretched them out across from me, the khaki pant legs stiff from heavy starch. Bright orange and blue plaid socks peaked at the end of single creases. The toes of his polished loafers pointed sharply to the ceiling, the ankles taut over the footstool. He was all spit and polish, the uniform of the day completed by a sweater.

"They're fine," I replied. Perched on the edge of the couch, I leaned forward, notebook in hand.

He sighed heavily and pressed his lips into a thin line. "This is not going to go well," I thought and flexed my own ankles. He waited some more and then cleared his throat.

My family patriarch would not begin to talk at all about his own life until he had received a satisfactory answer to the query that opened almost every succeeding interview. The question was a basket to be filled with all the eggs I could gather, stories about my mother, my sisters, their husbands, and their children, as well as any news that I might have of his own sister, Sulou Wagstaff. It was also understood that I was to add anything I knew about our other relations, especially his cousin, Betty Johnson Toler, who was born and raised on the farm adjoining his family's homeplace.

He looked intently at me over his glasses while I spoke haltingly of every detail I could recall. Occasionally, he crossed and uncrossed his long legs, running slender fingers through his thick hair, all the while intoning "I'm so sorry," when there was bad news.

Always the family. I was to fill the pause following the question with information that would bathe us both in a sea of shared recollection. Recent family doings would prime the pump. Then my uncle could draw up the stories from his own well of memory. I was not in charge of this interview, nor would I ever be during the ones that followed.

I would be better prepared in that respect next time. For the moment, I did the best I could, and then sat rapt, almost at attention, hands folded in my lap, and listened.

"I do not have what the Army psychologists call 'survivor guilt.' But I have questions," he began. "I have lived many of the answers, but I want to sort out some things for anyone who might be interested in learning about a particularly interesting time and place in history.

"These questions are different from the ones I had when I was growing up at Powhatan, near Clayton, North Carolina. Those had to do with things like, did we have enough wood for the cook stove, and would we be warm that winter. We were always hot in the summer. Everybody was. That was just the way things were, and I never questioned that."

His eyes met mine. "The valedictorian of my high school class never left his family farm until his children moved him to a rest home. I imagine Paul Otto had questions too as he got older, but I suspect they were of an entirely different nature than mine.

"Except for the wars, I would have had other questions. But I have been in war, and I have seen men die. I have heard them plead with God to let them live and beg Him to let them die. I remember that most died bravely, and some just died, instantly. For others, it was an agonizing death. It's true what they say that there are no atheists in foxholes, and that those who have no religion find it there.

"I had religion before I ever saw a foxhole, but being in one deepened my faith and changed the way I viewed my life before and after the war. When I was in combat, I asked myself, as I do today, 'Why did I survive, and so many others didn't. For what reason was I somehow set apart?'

"I'm still here, and when I do leave this earth, it will be under different circumstances." My uncle's voice trailed off into a sigh, and he crossed his legs.

"So we need to talk about these things now?" I asked.

"We do."

Acknowledgements

To Katherine Wolfe, poet and priestess of prose, I thank you for always encouraging me and for believing in the value of the story.

To my friend, Margaret B. Baddour, for critiquing the manuscript and for helping me find my narrator's voice, as my uncle's confidant and kinswoman.

To my friend, Judy Hogan, for encouraging me to seek an audience for my uncle's memoir and for helping me to understand the nuances of the genre.

Cindy Brookshire, editor extraordinaire, thank you for lending me your professional editorial skills and your invaluable insight as a writer.

Annie Berger, thank you for being the best audience ever, as this process of writing and publishing *Legs Astride the World* played itself out and came to fruition.

To my mother, Mary Johnson Simmons, thank you for being a wise and wonderful primary source for the early years, second only to your brother, who is the subject of this book.

For Lee Holstein, (now deceased) my uncle's faithful mortarman and friend, I am so grateful. Uncle Legs would have been so pleased about your serving as my primary source for the World War II years, after his death. It was a privilege to have known you.

Uncle Legs, you thanked me many times for writing your story. The pleasure and the privilege were mine. I think you made me the family griot.

To my uncle's wife, Jane Johnson, thank you for letting me into your lives and for sharing in this project. Your warm and gracious hospitality provided us with the privacy Uncle Legs needed to "tell me things he hadn't told anyone else before."

Much appreciation is due my uncle's children and their spouses for their support, for providing photographs, and for helping me transcribe my uncle's handwriting. They are Lee and Mary Deane Johnson, Jule (deceased) and Mary Jo Johnson, Steve and Connie Johnson, and Robert and Candy Arey.

Special thanks to Lee Johnson, my uncle's oldest son, and Evie Johnson, great granddaughter, for their tireless research on the military awards and medals.

A debt of gratitude is owed to Scott C. Woodard, Historian, US Army Medical Department Center of History and Heritage, for reading the memoir from a military perspective. Scott added valuable information concerning my uncle's career, his awards and the medals.

Many thanks to Marty Tschetter, local history librarian, for his assistance early on in this project with scanning and cataloging the photographs from Uncle Legs' life and career.

For my husband Tom, now deceased, I am grateful for his unwavering support and for always telling me that it was important for me to write this book.

Finally, thank you to Bob Babcock and to Deeds Publishing Company for appreciating the value of my uncle's story as a World War II veteran and for guiding me, gently and professionally, through the publishing process.

Almost a Violation

*"How did I come to be at this place in my life,
and why am I still here?"*

— Lieutenant Colonel Lehman H. (Legs) Johnson, Jr.
(January 12, 1916-May 1, 2009)

My uncle recalled a recent discussion in his men's Sunday school class in Mebane, when he told those present that he knew exactly what it felt like to execute someone. The lesson had been about the remorse Paul felt after having held the robes of the Pharisees while they were stoning Stephen.

Before church, a child, whose father had been in the class, came up to him to ask about that story.

"I didn't think it was a good idea to tell him about my experience executing Nazi war criminals at Landsberg Prison." His eyes left me for a moment and veiled a scene from memory that was not to be replayed that first Saturday of our interviews. Taking a deep breath, my uncle shifted his weight in the chair, and the leather crackled. He laced his fingers together and placed his palms against the back of his head, as if it hurt. His eyes narrowed, and for a moment, I glimpsed the pain that shadowed the answer.

I squirmed on the couch; feeling as though I had witnessed a private act, opened a door on someone who was undressing. "First of all, the child would not have understood. He was too young, and second, I was in church at the time, about to enter the sanctuary. Answering his question then and there would have been almost a violation of the worship experience." My uncle paused and glanced sideways at me before staring straight ahead.

"You see, Mary Susan, sometimes it's hard for veterans to talk about some of the experiences they've had. Some won't discuss them at all. In a sense, discussion violates the trust of the other men, what they've been through together, and what they might have said to each other at the time. As long as they are alive, sometimes it's best not to talk. One man's memory of a specific event might be very different from what another man remembers."

Most of the people who were part of my uncle's stories were deceased by the time I began interviewing him. There would be no betrayal of a confidence. His storytelling to me could become an unraveling of the questions he wanted to answer before his own death, without that consideration.

The answers would come from the fabric of his life, and the memoir would become the pattern into which we would stitch his stories, like one of his mother's quilts, one event leading to another by association that had nothing to do with chronological order. When we finished, there would be a pile of what my grandmother called scraps.

My uncle raised his eyebrows, locked his hands behind his head, and looked somewhere way past me.

"How did I come to be at this place in my life from my upbringing on a farm at Powhatan in Clayton, North Carolina? Why am I still here when there were so many others who died in World War II? How did I deal with that knowledge then and how do I deal with it now? I still question that," he said. "It's with me every day."

In the sharing of his stories, my Uncle Legs taught me much about the history of the times, about human nature, and indirectly, he taught me about myself. He was and is, even more so now, a part of who I am.

The Fun of It All

"Do you know what a cow pie is?"

—Lieutenant Colonel Lehman H. Johnson, Jr.

I glanced out the window in time to catch the winter sunset, the day's last rays reflecting orange against unnaturally green grass. It was Saturday night, and Jane, my uncle's wife, and her son Warren had worked during the warmest part of the day to manicure the lawn in time for Sunday. We didn't hear the mower anymore, but I could still see the tracks.

Uncle Legs followed my gaze and picked up the glass of red wine that was on the table beside him, but did not drink. "Jane still wants to do most of the yard work," he said, "with Warren's help. She did it before we got married, and her way of doing certain things hasn't changed. There's a man in our church who comes twice a year and puts out chemicals to keep the grass looking like that."

I stretched and waited, knowing that my favorite uncle would come back to the little boy, whose name was Bobby, when he was ready, since we had left the child waiting for a story. I was waiting, too, but I was also beginning to understand that prompting would not get us there any faster. If the blood was flowing from a wound, I didn't need to put a bandage on it. It would seal itself.

Uncle Legs smiled, not at me, but at the memory, and spoke again. "I was on my way to service, hefting the pack of memories the morning's lesson had reminded me I was still carrying, a load that seemed to get heavier every time I tried to unpack it, when there was Bobby. His eyes were wide open and he had the same curious expression that I had seen many times on the faces of adults asking about my war stories. This child, who appeared to be about eight, had planted himself right in my path, in the hall that led to the main part of the church. I was marching on, and he, by virtue of his position, was demanding that I halt.

"'What does it feel like to ex-e-cute somebody?' His face was white as a sheet except for the freckles. He was shifting back and forth from one foot to the other. I knew he was waiting for the guts and gore that came with bragging rights for his little friends. So instead, I told him a different story.

"'Do you have any friends?' I asked. He nodded up at me. I guess he thought maybe that I was like one of those superheroes that are so popular today in cartoons and movies.

"You know, Mary Susan, the children in this church call me 'Chicken Legs.'" He shook his head bewildered.

I laughed. "I don't think they are going to get you mixed up with Col. Saunders," I said to him. "The danger, I think, is that they will think you are like one of those larger than life characters who spring onto the stage of life, with no existence before or after their heroic moment. Then the curtains close."

He looked directly at me. "Since the child had asked, I wanted to clear up that misconception. There's a lot that happened to me before the war, and I've lived a lot since." He leaned back, sighed, and the chair exhaled a stream of air with the movement. I nodded in understanding, making a mental note to guard my own expressions during future interviews. He drifted off into his own thoughts.

"Friends that I remember from that time in my life include Hugh Paige, Jr. who lived about three blocks from the house. I remember him as being a smart young man in school. He later became an F.B.I. agent. As far as I know, he was never in the war. He returned to Clayton to live.

"Then there was Sam Robertson, who still lives there. His college education at what was then known as Trinity College was interrupted by the war. Sam's father owned the livery stable across the street where he bought and sold mules. His family, like mine, had left the farm to become part of a different class of people—merchants, townspeople in the big city of Clayton. The difference was that his family stayed. Mine did not."

He gazed at the wall directly in front of him, at the pictures of his and Jane's respective children when they were growing up, and the shelves of war novels. Then he leaned toward me and came back to his story.

"I asked the child another question. 'Do you have a BB gun?'

"He drew his brows together and answered quickly. 'Oh, no. My parents don't let me play with guns. Did you have a real gun?'

"I laughed, patting him on the head. 'As they say on television, don't try this at home. Sam and I spent hours playing among the bales of hay stored in the loft of his daddy's mule stables. Although we played hide and seek sometimes, the bales made great forts. We would stack them, hide behind them, and then run between them, ducking for cover.'

"'What do you mean, ducking for cover?' asked the child innocently. 'Did you take blankets up there and make tents?'

"'No,' I said, a bit uneasily, not so sure that this was a story his father would want me to tell. 'We had BB guns, and we shot back and forth at each other as we ran, lickety split, between the bales of hay. Sam had his side of the barn and I had mine.'

"'Did you ever hit each other?' Bobby asked.

"'Yes, we did,' I replied, becoming more and more uncomfortable with where this conversation was taking me, so I said to him, 'We're going to be late for church.' I heard Jane opening the 11:00 service with an organ prelude, and I moved to push past him.

"When he did not retreat, I decided Bobby would make a good soldier. He countered my position. I shifted my weight and sighed, leaning on my cane, and Bobby continued, 'Didn't that hurt? What if you had shot each other in the eye?' He was positively dancing.

"'Well,' I said. 'It never occurred to us that we might actually get hurt. We were about your age, and our parents already allowed us to go hunting. We knew what we could hit and what we couldn't. We were playing at war, and, of course, it stung when we got hit. We usually tried to hit each other on the legs of our overalls. I don't recall ever having to dig any BB's out of my skin, and we never aimed at each other's faces. It's not like we were playing with shot guns or air rifles.'

"Bobby was beside himself, and since I had already let the proverbial horse, or in this case, the mule, out of the barn, it was too late to shut the door on his curiosity. So I ran after it, hoping to catch it and at least corral it. I did not wish to become a curiosity myself in the church I now called home. I plowed on, more than a little concerned about what kind of seeds I was planting in this child's mind."

My uncle drew his shoulders up around his ears, and I could imagine how he must have looked to this little boy. "Mind you we were still standing there as the church service was starting. I said to him, 'Bobby, one of our favorite activities was to jump down from the loft, into the hay that had been pushed below for feeding the mules.'

"By way of explanation, I added, 'The mules would hear us playing upstairs and they would become restless from hearing the ping of our BB guns, stomping their feet and moving around in their stalls. We liked to jump down when they were like this, surprising them and us sometimes with what we landed in.' The child's face was blank.

"'Do you know what a cow pie is?' I asked Bobby. He nodded solemnly. 'Well, mules make these as well. Let's just say the mules did not use the privy that was outside the stables as a courtesy for the customers, the farmers who would come to town once a week to buy the things they didn't grow and to conduct business. You can go to Clayton and see Sam Robertson's Mule Stables any time you want to. They're on Main Street and you can still see that printed on the building.'

"'Pe-euw!' Bobby said.

"Lest he think that my childhood was all fun and games, I thought I better tell him how these sessions usually ended. 'How does your mother call you in for supper?' I asked.

"'I'm usually in my room playing video games before we eat dinner.'

"'Really,' I said, realizing I had lived a life that is just as foreign to that child as if I were on another planet.

"I told him that when it was time for my supper, or maybe when my mother discovered that my chores had not been completed to her satisfaction, she would call across the street from the front porch of our house, 'Lehman Johnson, Jr., get in this house this minute!' She always got the 'Jr.,' in there out of respect for Daddy.

"I told Bobby, 'She wasn't worried about me. Mabel Johnson was calling me to come home because she needed me to fall in line with whatever the executed plan of action for the family was to be at that given moment.'

Bobby blinked. I knew he would ask me again about the Nazi war criminals, but for the moment, he was distracted by the story I had just told him. I took his hand and steered him through the heavy door into the church sanctuary. His dad spotted us and lifted his hand. Bobby ran to his father, and I took my usual aisle seat, third row to the right and leaned back.

"Mary Susan, because of that child's question, I had been transported somehow to a mule stable in Clayton, North Carolina. I don't think I heard a word of the sermon. In my thoughts I went back to jumping out of a mule stable to the jungles of New Guinea, in 1944, where I was falling again, falling from a jump station this time that we had built to practice our parachuting in preparation for entering combat in WWII.

"Then Jane was playing the postlude, and the congregation stood. I didn't get up, but at that time, it wasn't because I couldn't stand for long periods of time, like now. I was thinking, 'Praise God from whom all blessings flow' because the doxology was really the only thing I remember hearing in that service. Indeed. I have much to be thankful for." My uncle looked at me to see if I was following his associations in time.

Indeed, I thought. *Indeed, you do — and so do I. I am thankful for you.*

Getting There

"We weren't playing at war, but yet we were."

—Lieutenant Colonel Lehman H. Johnson, Jr.

Dinner at my uncle's house was always precisely at 5:00 p.m., 1700 military time. About 4:30, Jane would inquire delicately from another room, "Legs, what time did you say we were going to dinner?" Of course. she knew. It was always the same.

Uncle Legs would glance at his watch, the Rolex that matched Jane's, and keep on talking. When he decided we were at a good stopping place, he would suggest that we pick up there when we returned. It was a pattern that we began that day. Of course, it was not a suggestion. As my grandmother would say, he had chased that rabbit as long as he was going to, without a bone. It was time to eat.

"We weren't playing at war, but yet we were," he said, running his left hand through his crew cut that was still more gray than white. "We'll get back to that." He drew himself up to his full height and shuffled off to the back of the house, ducking his head under the door frame, and leaving the cane right where it was, propped against the brown leather chair.

I was left looking at his ramrod straight back and facing the conclusion of our first interview. Memory is a magic carpet ride, connecting long buried associations. I was not to be a passenger this time. He was falling into space and time, and I wanted to know where he had landed, so I could go with him.

But for the moment that was not to be. Hopefully, we would pursue that line of thought during dinner or at some other point in the weekend. We were on his time. It was futile to pursue the point. I put my notebook down and went to what he referred to as "the little girls' room" down the hall "to freshen up." When he met me back in the den, Uncle Legs had added a yellow plaid cardigan sweater to his already well-coordinated attire.

"Daddy always said that being well-dressed helps make an impression and whenever possible to match my socks and handkerchief," he said, lifting his left pant leg, revealing fresh, argyle socks and a lean muscular calf. A handkerchief peeked out of his shirt pocket, like a spring daffodil. I smiled, thinking that you could take the boy off the farm, send him all around the world, but there would always be a certain protocol. It was as rooted in Johnston County soil as what he called the "veggies" his Mother had served with every meal.

"After you," he said, using his cane to wave me in front of Jane, down the carport steps to her car. He followed her, the cane hooked over his right forearm, for just in case. Our faces were reflected in the polished surface of his blue Jaguar, that was reserved now for daytime driving, with Jane most often at the wheel.

"I always did like speed," he said, nodding toward the car as we settled ourselves into Jane's sedate white Acura. "One year after I got out of service, I got three speeding tickets — had no idea I was going so fast — just enjoying the ride. Genevieve kept telling me to slow down—lucky I didn't lose my license. My insurance premiums got pretty high. But you know, I had been in Germany, where there was no speed limit. I drove as fast as I wanted on the Autobahn, and there were many things I had to adjust to when I got home. Speed was just one of them."

We were headed out of town down Highway 70 into Orange County and out of Alamance. Jane was driving the speed limit, 55 mph as soon as we left the city limits. There was no train, just the tracks that paralleled Center Street and brought the slow lumbering freight trains through Mebane.

I gazed out the window, thinking, *I'll bet you're not the only one who had some adjustments to make,* remembering visiting him with my mother, his sister, in Raleigh and how his sons had double timed it out of the house to meet us at the curb and take in our luggage. It was during that visit that my Aunt Genevieve had told the story of Uncle Legs' return from World War II. My cousin Jule, who must have been about two at the time, stood between his parents and pointed his finger at his father. "Who's that man?" he had asked.

He and Aunt Genevieve, my uncle's first wife, had complementary personalities. I imagined that their parenting styles had been equally complementary. It must have been a jolt, especially to his sons, when Daddy came home from the war.

"You're on my dime," my uncle stated firmly, as we settled ourselves in a booth at Huey's. "A local watering hole," he called it. "You can get everything here from fried oysters to fried pork chops and fried chicken." We studied our menus and then ordered.

"Well, then," I said, "I guess that means that when you come to see me, you'll be on mine."

"Yes," he said, "except that I won't be coming, at least not for these interviews. I want you to come here."

"All right," I said, "how often do you want me to come?"

"How often can you come?"

"About once a month," I replied.

"Once a month, it is," he concluded. The food arrived, and I was hoping I would not be called upon to serve up any more family lore. I was as dry as a bone in that respect, having had all the marrow sucked out of me by our opening conversation.

Dinner was another telling story, and I was wishing that I had a tape recorder, or at least my notebook. Fortunately, it was etched in my memory and retold many times in the months to come, and then finally with the layers of reserve that covered his feelings pulled back. "I wish everyone could grow up with the advantages I had," he began, after he had blessed the food and checked his chicken.

Defying Authority

*"It's too bad that children today can't experience some
of the things that I experienced and that they can't enjoy their
childhood like I did."*

— Lieutenant Colonel Lehman H. Johnson, Jr.

Uncle Legs went on sawing on his golden fried, crackling chicken, and I put down my fork to focus on what I would have to remember. My first impulse was to write on my napkin. Yet I sensed that had I started taking notes, the dinner conversation would have dried up faster than a mud puddle on a hot July day. Jane continued eating. Her blue eyes were pools of understanding, but she neither commented nor interrupted the story flow that had been primed before our meal.

Our waitress, who called them by name, hovered nearby, but even she maintained a respectful distance. Everybody within earshot was listening. It was evident to me that in his adopted hometown, my uncle maintained a quiet kind of celebrity status.

"There was a railroad track—it's still there—close by our house at Powhatan. There was a place where the train had to go up a 5% grade, and where it slowed down considerably as it climbed the hill. I knew exactly where that was and exactly when that would occur, based on the train schedule. I frequently jumped into an open box car and rode the train from Wilson's Mills to Clayton. Either I would walk back in time for supper or hitch a ride with somebody who might be coming my way. It was quite a lark. If they knew it, my parents weren't concerned, as long as I did my chores and showed up on time for meals. They did not bother themselves with my whereabouts in between times. They figured I had the good sense to go where I needed to go and do what I needed to do.

"This time, however, I was determined not to come back. I don't recall exactly what the disagreement was about, but I do recall my intention to run away from home. It might have been the privy hedge that surrounded our yard. A privy hedge was common landscaping at the time—Ligustrum is the proper name I believe—for privacy and to separate the yard from the field. Either I gapped it or I didn't get it even enough. I never could do that clipper thing well enough to satisfy my dad.

"I don't remember exactly why I did what I did, but I waited for the train and hopped on at just the right time. Of course, I made it. It wasn't the first time I had jumped that same train, and I settled in for the ride, not sure exactly where I was going, except that it would be past Clayton. I did not know what I would do when I got there, but I was very pleased with myself, at the moment.

"It didn't take long for me to have second thoughts. The train was gathering speed, and I'm thinking now that there must have been something I was supposed to have done, or done over again, before supper that was the cause of my dissatisfaction. It wasn't fear of punishment that made me jump out into the briar patch that lined the train tracks from Wilson's Mills to Clayton because my parents didn't really punish me. I jumped because even at that age, I had a sense of responsibility to my family."

"How old were you?" I asked.

"Probably about ten or twelve," he said, draining his tea glass and glancing toward the young, pretty waitress, who appeared at our table.

"What can I get for you, Legs?" She drawled out his name.

"I need unsweet this time. Thanks, honey," he smiled appreciably at her. "Doctor's orders."

His glass filled, Uncle Legs turned back to Jane and me across the booth. "You see, there was no sense of entitlement whatsoever in my family—not like it is today. Whatever job I had to do was for the benefit of the entire family, and I certainly didn't expect to be paid or get an allowance. We knew that we needed each other, so I had to do some things I didn't want to do. But I did them. For the most part, I did what my mother and dad told me to do.

"Anyway, the train was going full throttle when I jumped, so I got all scratched and bummed up when I fell. I ran back home, bleeding and crying, my clothes torn—another problem. My legs were especially all scratched up—they were just horrible. It was dinner time when I ran into the kitchen, all out of breath. The family was sitting there, calmly eating and talking among themselves. The kitchen was warm from the woodstove where Mother had just taken up the food, but the atmosphere was chilly.

"If I had been missed, no one made any reference to my absence. Certainly no one had looked for me. All Mother had to say was, 'Just go wash your hands and face.' The conversation ceased immediately. I washed up as best I could and returned to the table and sat down in my accustomed place. No one spoke to me or passed me any food. They continued eating. My sisters, Sulou and Mary, followed the lead of my parents and said nothing. No one called on me to give an account of where I had been or asked if I was hurt. It was apparent that I was now excluded. There was nothing for me to do except get up and leave the table, which I did. There was nowhere for me to go, so I went and lay on my back in my bed. Later Daddy opened the door and got me up. He didn't whip me or punish me. My family not talking to me at all—that had been my punishment, and he had given me awhile to think about that—to get a bellyful as he might have said. Instead, 'I hope you've learned your lesson' was all he said when he came in my room. I had."

Uncle Legs glanced over at Jane and then at me. "Are you two ladies done?" he asked. When we nodded, he said to our waitress, "Check please, Judy."

She returned to our booth, bill in hand. "Did you enjoy your meal?"

"Oh, yes," Uncle Legs answered. "Your fried chicken here is almost as good as my mother's. I've never eaten fried chicken like hers anywhere. But then y'all probably don't use a cast iron skillet and cook on a hot wood stove—or fry your chicken in lard."

My uncle took out a tip card from his wallet and laid it on the table. When he found the appropriate column for calculation, he stabbed it with his pen and added the decreed amount. He grinned. "I never was very good at math." Jane discretely looked the other way.

Uncle Legs stood and made his way to the door without looking back, occasionally touching the backs of the booths as he passed. He waited there like a sentinel while Jane and I scrambled out of our seats to follow. Standing aside for Jane and me to precede him, he opened the door and held it, his cane providing the balance required for this courtesy.

The wind swirled inside when another patron entered the small foyer and deposited a few brown leaves inside on the mat where my uncle was standing. I looked down at his feet and read, "Y'all come again." The cold came in as more people entered the restaurant, some through the door my uncle was still holding.

I hesitated. "Go ahead! Ladies first." He hit the end of the cane on the floor for emphasis. "I've just thought of something else I wanted to tell you. That lesson came in handy later on. I'll tell you in the car."

We settled in, Jane at the wheel, Uncle Legs beside her in the passenger seat, and me in the back. I looked out the window as the same scene from before—trees that had undressed for the winter—played itself out in reverse, except this time it was almost dark.

The transition into a more recent past was as seamless as one of his mother's quilts. You know the stitches are there, but they are so tiny as to be almost invisible. "I had a son that did that to me once—Jule wanted to leave the family and run away from home. After my retirement, he decided that he was not going to move with us to Raleigh. Genevieve and I had made the decision to move there based on the quality of the schools that would be available for Candy and Steve, the two younger children, and because that location was close to both our families. We had closed on a house.

"Jule, however, had decided that he was going to stay in Clarksville, Tennessee, that summer rather than move with the family. He was to go off to college in the fall in Tennessee, and I guess this was his way of declaring his independence. I'm not sure where he had planned to stay, but I didn't argue with him. Instead, I helped him pack his bag, and then I set it out on the porch. He soon changed his mind. I wonder where he got those kinds of ideas." My uncle did not turn around.

I smiled, thinking, *yes, I wonder about that myself.* We made a right turn at Sneed's Grocery and Hardware onto Cook's Mill Road. Then we crossed the bridge and went past the old mill, to make another right turn onto Knollwood Falls Road, up to Jane's home. I remembered that she had said her first husband had designed that house to take advantage of the view, and to give each of their four children their own bedroom. Coincidentally, my Uncle Legs also had four children. As we climbed, I looked out the back window, appreciating the remaining colors of the last leaves still clinging to the trees and the old mill, no longer operational, that was still visible in the dying light.

"The apple doesn't fall too far from the tree," Uncle Legs said, glancing back at me and winking, as Jane wheeled us expertly into the garage.

Having the Last Word

"Part of my punishment was that I was not allowed to finish the plowing..."

—Lieutenant Colonel Lehman H. Johnson, Jr.

Jane got out of the car and went on up the steps to unlock the door. "Wait," Uncle Legs said to me. "I'm coming." I had my hand on the door handle, but I removed it just in time. Balancing on his cane, my uncle was out of the car and opening my door before I could protest. "Ladies first." He said it like it was law.

Uncle Legs sat in the same place in the den, and I resumed my seat on the couch at the angle where I could look at him without staring.

"Jane," he called, and waited briefly before he called again, "Jane! Can I get my nightcap please?"

"Of course you can," she said, disappearing into the kitchen.

To me, he said, "Will you join me?"

"No, thanks," I replied. "I don't drink."

"Will it offend you if I do?" He frowned, concerned, but took the glass Jane offered. We both knew that my mother, his sister, was offended by the use of any alcohol in her presence. I assured him that I was fine with his evening ritual.

"My doctor says one glass of red wine a day is good for me. It helps regulate blood pressure." Taking a sip, he leaned back in his chair. "I need to elevate this leg," he said, lifting his pant leg to reveal an angry blue web of veins radiating from a knot on his calf. "The doctor says it's a blood clot. I was cleaning off some undergrowth on that slope beside the house, and I slipped and got poked in the leg on the way down. Couldn't get up until Jane and Warren heard me. I might have to stop doing that, at least for awhile." He stretched the bum leg over the foot stool and covered his lap with an afghan that was always draped behind him for easy access.

"That and you probably need to stay off that ladder," Jane added as she left the room. "We can get somebody to clean out those gutters. What if you fell?"

"I know. I know. I just like to do it myself." Jane had already disappeared and did not hear his response.

"I grew up that way at Powhatan. We did our work ourselves, and my parents taught me to work. Before we had mules on the farm, we had a horse. Even after we moved up in the world and got the mules, we kept the horse. He was older, but he could still work. It was spring and Daddy and I were plowing the fields, getting them ready to plant the corn. Sweat was dripping down my collar, and I was thinking about how much I would like to go fishing. I was not concentrating on what I was doing, and to tell you the truth, I was deliberately breaking the rows. Corn rows are supposed to be straight. I was not holding the plow steady, so mine looked more like a worm in hot ashes than one stretched out full length and fried in the sun.

"As soon as Daddy noticed the difference between my rows and his, he called my attention to what he assumed was my carelessness. 'You're making it hard on that animal,' he said.

"I did not have the good sense to keep my mouth shut, and I sassed my father. 'You think more of this horse here than you do your own son.'

"Daddy stopped dead in his tracks, and the mule he was driving in front of him responded immediately to the slight pressure he applied to the bit. The mule was wiser than me. Instead of plowing on, the mule stood patiently in the long pause that followed without even stomping his feet. I watched that mule switching his tail from side to side to fan the flies that were now attempting to bite and waited for my daddy's reaction."

My uncle's legs were stretched out in front of him, and he crossed his feet at the ankles as he waited for the irony of the situation to sink in. From what I had heard about my grandfather when he was younger, I expected his reaction nipped any future rebellion in the bud.

"He did not let go of the lines nor come close to me. He didn't have to. I could see the anger in his eyes. Sparks were flying from them as sure as if I had struck an ax against a flint. I could smell the fresh turned dirt on which we were both standing."

Strange how memory returns with the smells, I thought.

Uncle Legs gave me a long, intense look. Then he breathed in and held it for a few seconds before he continued.

"'This mule and I'll finish the job,' my daddy said to me. 'You take the horse to the barn and wait for me behind the shed.'

"I immediately clicked the reins across the back of the horse and drove him very carefully to the end of my row, this time holding the riding plow steady, and around the edge of the field, so as not to make any unnecessary furrows in what had already been done, and through what was probably going to be done over again. The horse was delighted to be going back to the barn early. He pawed the ground with his front feet and snorted at the door, knowing that he would soon be fed. I knew I had something coming too, but I was not looking forward to it.

"Being sent to the woodshed meant that something else other than your fireplace was going to be warm."

In my uncle's day, corporal punishment did not usually take place in the house, requiring instead a larger arena for the taming of an unruly spirit. 'And so the twig would be bent,' my grandmother was fond of saying.

Yes, bent, I thought, *but not broken.*

"This was not something that occurred regularly in my household," he continued. "I had never answered my father that way before, and I never responded to either of my parents that way again.

"Part of my punishment was that I was not allowed to finish the plowing. Being allowed to have that kind of adult responsibility was a privilege, not a deprivation. I was being allowed to do a man's work. The girls certainly weren't allowed to plow. I was ashamed of myself long before Daddy got to the woodshed. But I knew better than to leave my post. Apologizing would have no effect on the consequences.

"The rest of my punishment came when Daddy joined me. He didn't say a word, or take off his belt. His face was as red as a tomato, and I was not sure if that was from the sun or whether his anger had ripened. He did not hesitate. I could smell his sweat at the same time that he caught me across the mouth with the back of his hand. Then he turned on his heel and was gone without further directions. None were needed. I was left to nurse the sting and stare at the footprint where my father had turned away from me.

"Mary Susan, I knew that I would be expected at supper like usual. I knew that my father would never mention this incident again to me or anyone else. I doubt if he even told Mother. No one would know, except that I'm telling you. It was over and done with, and there was nothing for me to say or do, except do better next time. We would go on, and I would pick up my share of the load without resentment next time."

My uncle looked sideways at me to see how I was taking his story of what might be considered child abuse today. He smiled and struck his left knee for emphasis.

"Parents today worry way too much about their children's self-esteem. I knew I was loved and that my father believed in me and respected me. He was confident that I could earn my way in life, and as a result, I came to that conclusion as well.

"Are you sleepy?" he asked, stretching himself from the shoulders up.

I shook my head. "No."

"Good. Then let's end on a high note.

"Someone had to cut the wood that heated the stove, as well as for the fireplaces that heated the house. That was, of course, me. We used pine for the cook-stove because it burned hotter and was easier to split. Oak was for the fireplace. The wood smelled different when it was burning. The pine was sweeter. The oak smelled more like burning leaves. I could have walked through the house blindfolded and told you which room I was in just by the smell." He breathed deeply in and out, and then continued.

"We had plenty of woodland. I would go out in the woods and cut down smaller trees or pick up wood that had fallen and bring it back to the woodshed behind the house. I split the logs with an ax and made a pile that would last for three or four weeks.

"The wood that I cut for the kitchen had to be exactly eighteen inches long and one and one half inches wide. I would hold the split pieces with my left hand and use my right to make another cut with a hatchet in order to get the stove wood just the right width."

I nodded.

"A stack of stove wood was as big as this room, so it was a motion I repeated often. Because it was dangerous and I was the oldest, I was the only one of the three children allowed to cut wood, although Mary's job was to bring in the small pieces and fill the box that sat in the kitchen, convenient by the stove.

"I remember when the inevitable happened. I missed my aim and cut my thumb badly. I was bleeding like a stuck pig. Mother heard me holler. She came out with a dish towel in her hands and wrapped my thumb up tight until the bleeding stopped. It's a wonder I didn't cut my thumb off. I didn't cut any more wood that afternoon, but I did the next.

"There was no change in my responsibilities. I don't recall Mother even saying, 'Be careful.' Things still needed to be done. If there was no stove wood, she couldn't cook. If there was no wood to heat the wash pot, there would be no clean clothes. Without firewood, there would be no heat in the house in the winter. No one had to spell that out for me.

"My parents were not physically affectionate at all, and I don't remember them telling us as children that they loved us very often. They lived it. The necessities they provided for us were handmade or homegrown with the utmost care and concern for our comfort and well-being.

"Just any old thing and any old way wouldn't do. You showed your love and respect by doing your best for each other. As the only boy, and the oldest child, I knew without being told that it was my responsibility to make sure we were supplied with wood. I would be more careful next time. My family would be warm and well-fed that winter because of my efforts."

Jane came up from the basement and entered the room. "Sunday School is at 9:45, and I need to be there an hour early for choir practice. Legs usually comes just in time for Sunday School. Do you want to go on with me or come later with him?"

"I'll wait for him." *I guess that would mean I'd be riding in the Jag*, I thought. *What was that he said about liking speed?*

"Can you stay for a while after lunch?" My uncle lifted the wine glass that he had been holding up to the light. I realized he had never set it down. The glass was still nearly full.

"I'm on your time." I thought to myself, *none of us, including you, knows how much of that we have. I think you've had an awareness of that fact for some time now.*

"I think I'll go on up now." I stretched, not realizing until that moment how long I'd held one position. I went upstairs, and Jane went down the hall to their bedroom, but not before dimming the light. Uncle Legs was left to finish his wine in the soft glow where memory had held us.

Walking the Dogs

*"Major, I did not join the Army to walk dogs.
I joined the Army to fight the Japanese."*

—Lieutenant Colonel Lehman H. Johnson, Jr.

The church service at Mebane United Methodist Church was over promptly at noon. We would have been out in time to beat the Baptists, who were not so prompt, to be first in line at the Blue Ribbon Restaurant, except that Uncle Legs was unwilling to leave his Jaguar at the church unattended. We would have to drive back home first, then go to the restaurant in Jane's car.

"Why don't you follow me, Legs?" Jane suggested, as she glanced at me.

I understood. If Uncle Legs and I were following, then our speed would be regulated by hers. He would not pass her. Having gotten to church that morning in record time, I hoped he would agree.

"All right," he said. "After you." He slid under the wheel of the low-slung car and tossed his cane into the back seat. I got in on the passenger side and buckled up for the ride. He turned the key in the ignition. The engine purred and then made the sound that a cat makes when it pounces. His foot caressed the accelerator. I held onto the door handle and applied my feet to the floor.

Jane was already on Center Street, an extension of Highway 70, and we slipped out behind her, down South Fifth Street, following closely. It was a straight shot downtown, and Jane was gaining momentum. We were about to be in her trunk. There was no conversation. My uncle was enjoying the feel of the car's power, and I was riveted by the ever-decreasing space between our car and Jane's.

After what seemed like a very long time, although it was not, we arrived at the right turn in front of Snead's West-70 Grill and Grocery, where I caught a glimpse of a sign on the front of the building that read NO PANHANDLING (bumming), among other admonitions. We were going too fast on Woodlawn Road for me to read the rest of them. Uncle Legs barely slowed down for the left onto Mebane Rogers Road. I caught a glimpse of the sign for Rich's Lawn Care, but if I had blinked my eyes, I would have missed it.

Then almost immediately we turned back right onto Cooks Mill Road. My uncle accelerated in the half mile that brought us to the foot of the hill where he and Jane lived, and we came to an abrupt stop in front of the *In* sign. I lurched against my seat belt while my driver leaned forward and found the button for the power window on his side. He cocked his head to the left, listening.

When we could no longer hear the sound of another car, Uncle Legs leaned back against the blue leather seat and explained, "It's safer if only one car goes up at a time, just in case somebody gets their directions mixed up." The road to their home, Knollwood Falls Road, was a single-lane paved road, so narrow that there were signs posted, pointing to the way in and the way out. I looked up but could not see their house through the trees.

When he was satisfied that Jane was there, Uncle Legs gunned the engine and we began the climb. We were going up with no strain whatsoever on the engine, and we were gaining speed. The drive around the hill to their home is scenic, and it is sometimes possible to see deer and other wildlife in the woods. I didn't look this time.

I felt as if I were in the last car of a roller coaster, and we were climbing to the pinnacle, after which there would be a sudden plunge. There was no bar for me to hold onto, but my hands were clenched tight in my lap. My nails bit into my palms. Then at last, the Jag's tires crunching on the gravel that marked Jane's driveway allowed me to open my eyes and relax my hands.

Uncle Legs whipped the car into the double garage beside Jane's usual parking place. I noticed when we got out that some of the molding around the garage door on his side was damaged. He followed my gaze as we walked toward Jane's car. She was waiting a little further down the circular drive, already headed out in the right direction.

"I've got to get that fixed," he said. "I backed into that last weekend and had to get the bumper fixed. Haven't gotten around to the garage door yet."

* * * * *

Our arrival at the restaurant my uncle always called "the blue top," was more like a community meet and greet than a meal out. Everyone, including our waiter, was on a first-name basis. Calls of "Hi, Jane. Hi, Legs, Who's this you've got with you?" greeted us as we made our way past the working juke box to a recently vacated booth, upholstered in blue vinyl so as to match both the roof and the blue ribbon at the entrance. The patrons looked at me knowingly, and I wondered what they had been told about this project. I was the niece visiting here for an interview with Legs Johnson and that fact, in itself, made me interesting.

At Jane's suggestion, we ordered the chicken pie from the list of 'blue plate' specials. Before we committed, however, Jane explained that the specialty of the house was not chicken pie in the usual sense. It was more like a thick chicken soup with a huge puff pastry on top. But if I liked chicken pot pie, she assured me, I would not be disappointed.

Our steaming orders were delivered by a young man who addressed my uncle as "Col. Johnson." Jane, Uncle Legs, and I held hands around the table, and Uncle Legs blessed the food. "Dear Lord," he prayed, "we are truly and humbly thankful for this food we are about to receive. Bless the hands that prepared it. Bless it now to the nourishment of our bodies, and us to Your service. In Jesus' most holy and precious name, I pray. Amen."

"Amen," Jane and I repeated together as we released each other's hands. The three of us picked up our spoons and hit the tops of our pastries, in unison. The crusts cracked wide open, and we mushed the crispness into the chicken broth, bits of tender chicken, and vegetables that had supported it. I savored the smell of paprika and celery salt when it was all combined.

"I don't have a problem with authority," Uncle Legs said as he fished out a hunk of chicken from his pie and took a bite. "I did what my parents told me to do, and I respected them. There was no question about who was in charge and as children, we were secure in that. We understood that they knew what was best for the family. We could ask questions, but for clarification only.

"That part prepared me for following orders in the military. I had already learned to listen carefully and to follow directions. It turned out to be a very valuable skill since, during the war, orders were not written down. That was in case you were captured. Certainly, you could be tortured, but at least the enemy would not have a specific written plan of action. You could always lie, and it was presumed that you would—if you said anything under those conditions."

Trying the chicken again, he chewed thoughtfully. "There are all different kinds and styles of leadership. Some people know how to use their authority, and others abuse it. My parents were fair. Since I had never been exposed to the second kind, I had to learn in the military how to deal with people who thought their position put them above everybody else. It was a hard lesson, and I almost didn't get a second chance.

"I dreamed about this last night. It's a story I hadn't planned to tell you because I'm not proud of it."

Memory is a busy spider, I thought, *spinning and threading your associations together to make a web of its own.* "So you'll tell me?"

He nodded. "Yes."

"I got into trouble. I brought that trouble on myself in the same way that I got myself dismissed from the corn field."

I waited and laid down my fork. I considered once again trying to take some notes at the table but thought better of it. A story when it is told is a living, breathing thing. But each time it's told, the story changes, and it may be connected to different stories. Sometimes it's a very painful thing. Sometimes the speaker is changed by the telling. But once it's written down, none of that transformation happens anymore. There would be a time for writing later.

"I was stationed at Camp Mackall, North Carolina in 1943. As a newly minted captain, I was looking for a chance to prove myself, and I was, of course, hoping for a promotion.

"My assignment was to act as the division headquarters commander, although this position is not recorded on my official record. It didn't last long, due to the fact that I had not yet learned the lesson I mentioned earlier." He drained his tea glass, and paused, gathering the details that would provide the presentation for his story.

"Part of my job at Camp Mackall was to see that the commanding general and all his staff were taken care of when they were on post. I was to make sure that they had a place to sleep, hot water for shaving, etc., etc., etc. Anything they needed, anything they wanted, I was supposed to get." He snorted.

"It was a tissy boy's job," Uncle Legs said, striking the table with his open palm. The silverware clattered. "That's the best way I can express it."

In the hush that followed, I realized he was still angry decades after this incident happened. *Imagine that*, I said to myself. I glanced over at Jane to see if I could read her thoughts. She was covering a smile with her napkin.

Uncle Legs continued indignantly. "With the general was this major who was one of his staff officers, and as a major, he outranked me. I had fetched and carried and fetched and carried some more."

"One morning he came out with his dogs on their leashes, all ready to go. 'Captain, I want you to walk my dogs,' he said. I can see him right now holding the leashes out to hand the dogs over to me.

"Without any hesitation whatsoever, I said, 'Major, I did not join the Army to walk dogs. I joined the Army to fight the Japanese.'

"The major's response was swift—'Captain, you are impertinent and insubordinate.'

"'Yes, sir,' I said, and made an about face and walked away. That was very poor behavior for a junior officer," Uncle Legs said, looking at me and shaking his head.

"What happened?"

"I overheard the major talking to another officer. 'Why don't we just go ahead and try the idiot,' he said." My uncle's eyes were blue saucers. "That was me they were talking about! That statement will always stay with me. Until this incident, I had no idea that officers in the U.S. Army talked about other officers like that. But, of course, he outranked me.

"Later, I learned from another of the general's staff officers that there had been serious discussion of my being court-martialed. I was most fortunate that this did not take place. However, I was transferred down to the 187th Parachute/Glider Regiment as service company commander. This was not a very good place for a promotion, and I knew that. There was to be no major's leaf for me, at least not yet."

"That must have been a bitter pill to swallow," I said, scraping the last of the chicken pie from my bowl. "Was part of your punishment that you didn't get to walk the dogs?"

He ignored me. "I did not dwell on my losses," he said, crossing his knife and fork across his plate. His tone did not invite further probing. The ability to move on past a mistake was something he had learned behind the woodshed on a farm in Johnston County.

Our waiter, who had been listening from a distance, appeared at our booth with the check. "Thank you for your service, Sir," he said.

The young man bowed slightly, his left hand behind his back, and handed Uncle Legs the bill. The fact that he was about the same age as the Legs in the story we had just heard was not lost on us.

My uncle smiled and left a generous tip. "You are more than welcome." We were past this little hitch in Uncle Legs' career and back in the Blue Ribbon Diner, among the memorabilia from the 50s and 60s, a collage of pictures from the Eastern Alamance High School football teams, and the poster of a red 1955 Chevy. I was relieved for Uncle Legs and thankful for the waiter whose words had brought us back to the present.

Pulling Rank

*"This was the first and only time I ever pulled rank
on any junior officer, but that day I pulled rank
on Lieutenant George Ister."*

—Lieutenant Colonel Lehman H. Johnson, Jr.

Back in the den, Uncle Legs eased himself back into his accustomed
seat, and I took up my post on the couch.

"Do you have time for another one?" he asked.

"I do." The day's light was beginning to fade behind the slope of hill
that we had just climbed to get to his and Jane's home. Even the grass
was a little less green, and the trees stood out in sharp relief against the
dying light. I would be driving home in the dark, but it didn't matter.

My uncle cupped his chin in his left hand and gazed at the soft
glow produced by the pilot light for the gas logs in the fireplace. "Jane,
can you give us a little more heat in here?" he called.

"Helps to take the chill off," he said. "It seems like I'm cold a lot
now, and my left shoulder still gives me a fit." He massaged the offending joint with his right hand. "I spent many a night sleeping in the
cold on damp ground, beside the road or in a field, and this shoulder
has never quite forgiven me. I've lived under some conditions and done
some things that wouldn't even cross my mind now."

"I appreciate the fact that you are willing to tell me about them." I wondered if my uncle didn't have a problem with authority in the same sense that he didn't have survivor guilt. *Does memory deny even as it recalls?*

Jane appeared and turned up the logs, and he warmed to his story.

"This was the first and only time I ever pulled rank on a junior officer, and I'm not proud of this story either. After many delays, we had finally gotten our orders and were on our way to California."

"Was this before or after Pearl Harbor?" I needed the timeframe.

"After Pearl Harbor. We didn't know exactly where we were going, but we knew we were going to the South Pacific—for training."

He rolled off the details like it was yesterday. I understood that we had gotten to this juncture by way of his refusal to walk some dogs that belonged to an officer who outranked him. What would link the events was a lesson learned about the tenuous balance between being your own compass and when to take direction from others.

"From Camp Mackall, I finished up my training at Camp Polk, Louisiana, along with the rest of the 187th Glider Infantry Regiment. We were a two-battalion glider regiment, but we were also trained as paratroopers. We staged at Camp Stoneman, California, on April 29, 1944, but it took us a week to get organized and loaded. We got a crash course in how to live aboard a ship and how to deploy a lifeboat, should that skill be needed. However, we weren't in the Pacific Ocean yet when we were practicing.

"We cruised from Suisan Bay to San Pablo Bay in river boats. Then we moved on through San Francisco Bay and under the Oakland Bridge to Oakland Mole. There the Red Cross treated us like heroes and served us coffee and doughnuts. We boarded the transport ships, sailed back under the Oakland Bridge, through San Francisco Bay, and under the Golden Gate Bridge. On May 6, 1944, we sailed out into the open Pacific on our way to parts unknown. There had been several false starts, so I was relieved to finally be on my way, and I was very anxious to prove myself.

"We were a cocky bunch, and the Army tried to make sure we stayed that way. At some point during the first part of our long trip to the Pacific, we passed through a shed before boarding. Over the shed was a sign that read: 'Through These Portals Pass the Best Damn Soldiers in the World.' We were sure we were all that and more.

"We still weren't told what our destination was to be, and there were certainly no landmarks in the middle of the ocean. News about the war came from a bulletin that was printed on ship every day. We eagerly anticipated its publication and passed it around from man to man. There was only one copy, so there was no possibility of anyone keeping it and later sending it back home.

"At the time we felt that these newspapers, which were published by the Pacific Command, were an accurate reporting of the news. We were anxious to know what was going on out there in the world outside, and we did not concern ourselves with questions about censorship or raise issues about our purpose."

"What do you think about that now?" I asked.

He thought a moment. "Now I think the Army told us what they thought we needed to know to keep morale up. We also received information by radio communication. I imagine we got the same selective version there as well.

"At some point, we knew that we were headed for an island in the South Pacific and that we would be going into combat, again, at some point. That was enough. It was not ours to question the when, how, or where. We didn't know it at the time, but General MacArthur had told our commander, General Joseph May Swing, that we were his 'secret weapon,' in that we were also trained as paratroopers, as well as infantry men. To keep that secret, all of our paratrooper gear was hidden, and very little information about us was given to the press. Just exactly how

MacArthur planned to use us remained a mystery. Our division was a division in reserve, which meant that we could be deployed at any time. We wouldn't know what time that would be until it came. We explained to our men that we were doing this — carrying out our mission, that is — one day at a time."

"Did that bother you?" I asked. I was just beginning to understand that I was to remember my uncle and articulate his stories, recall his history, and explore it with him, if that was what he wanted. My uncle would never write anything down himself, and that was why he had tapped me. I felt like a griot. Real griots are born into the family, and they inherit their position. I was deeply honored.

He answered me. "No, it did not, and if it did, it wouldn't have mattered. It took us approximately three weeks to get to our stopping point, which turned out to be New Guinea, an island in the South West Pacific. It was a calm ride. The ocean was a glassy blue as far as you could see. It was so calm, peaceful even. The trip over would have been boring except for the fact that I got seasick every day.

"We hadn't even gotten out of the swells of the bay when I first got sick. Like I said, our training for ship life didn't take place on the ocean. It was mentioned almost in passing that we might be a little seasick at first, but that we would get used to the motion of the ship. I never did. Unfortunately, many others were similarly affected to the point that the stench infiltrated our sleeping quarters. We had to mop out the hole every morning where the guys had thrown up during the night.

"I didn't think I was going to live to fight a war. I was 28 years old and this was the first time I had even been out of the United States. It was also the first time that I had been out in a boat on the ocean or in a boat of any kind where I couldn't see the shore. It was the same for most everybody else. We were all in the same boat, both literally and figuratively. For me, this was quite a contrast from being on the farm where I put my feet on the ground every day. I knew then exactly where I was going and how to get there at all times.

"Finally, I couldn't take it anymore. There had to be some way that I could improve my circumstances. When I began to take notice of my surroundings, I realized that there was this young lieutenant who had a top bunk. Where he slept, there was fresh air coming in from a port hole. Where I slept on a bottom bunk, there was no ventilation.

"'Lieutenant, trade bunks with me,' I said.

"This was the first, and only, time I ever used my rank on any junior officer, but I pulled rank on Lt. George Ister that day. He was one of the extra lieutenants that we had working in the S-3 section (the section for training, plans, and operations.) I was just beginning my career, and I was yet to be tested in battle. Perhaps my thinking was that someone else could do his job if he were unable and that my job as a captain was more important. I don't remember. At any rate, I was certainly practicing self-preservation.

"Lieutenant Ister was wiser than I had been in similar circumstances. His only response was, 'Yes, Sir.' He moved his things.

"Needless to say, he was not very happy. I can't say that how he felt made a gnat's difference to me, but at least I was finally able to get my sea legs. I don't know what happened to him or how he got along for the rest of the trip."

He paused and shifted slightly in his chair. By telling me these stories in such close proximity to each other, my uncle must have seen some similarity in Major Porter's attitude and his own perspective. But none was admitted.

"Finally, we survived seasickness and landed in Dobodura, New Guinea, on May 29, 1944. We made camp there with our whole division and started our jungle training. We hadn't been in any jungles before, so that's why we were training there. I know that now. I didn't know it then. Those above us expected that we would be in similar terrain, so we were being sent into that environment to prepare ourselves. We were in New Guinea for approximately five months.

"It was while we were there and during a training exercise that Company B's commander, Captain Franks, dropped his grenade. It killed him instantly. Company B was without leadership. The man who was over Captain Franks was Lt. Col. George Pearson, Commander of the 1st Battalion, 187th Regiment. He asked me to come over and take over Company B. Career-wise, I was back on track."

"Very good," I said. "Did you in any way feel guilty about that promotion?"

He paused. "It's always nice to have some friends in high places. Sometimes you make your luck and sometimes you fall into it. In this case, I fell into it. When he promoted me, Col. Pearson never mentioned the walking the dogs' incident, the one that had almost derailed my career. We laughed about it though after we both retired. It would not have been like him to badmouth the major any more than that.

"I will say, however, that Major Porter was a horse's ass, and no one liked him." Uncle Legs crossed his legs, at the knees this time, left over right. The toe of his suspended shoe snapped up and down from the ankle.

I stood up. Major Porter had been dismissed, and I thought this might be a good time for me to leave while my uncle was obviously savoring the fact that he had been vindicated. Circumstances had intervened to set things right, and I thought it might be best if we ended there.

"I got pretty sure of myself after that," he said. "I never became a 'yes' man."

"I could not imagine that you would have." This time I let myself out.

Second Interview

*"The kitchen was always the center of activity in the house, and
between the fireplace and the woodstove, it was always warm there
in winter."*

— Lieutenant Colonel Lehman H. Johnson, Jr.

"Legs! It's Mary Susan!" Jane called from the kitchen. She announced
my arrival this second time as though I were royalty. The side door
under the carport was left open for me, for family. Company used the
front door.

I heard the cane tapping as Legs unfolded his six foot, four-and-a-
half-inch frame from his chair and rose to greet me. He was coming to
the kitchen to hug me. I was to wait there.

He stooped slightly to accommodate the cane, which, even when
fully extended, was not long enough. He bent to envelop me in a hug
of deep and abiding affection.

Uncle Legs gestured toward the den, insisting that I go first. I hesitated, and he tapped his cane again. I wasn't sure whether he was main-
taining his balance or wanting me to go in ahead of him. This time I
moved, and he followed me into the den.

"What's this?" he asked, pointing to the tape recorder I carried.

"Do you mind? I want to be sure I get every word you say. I'm not sure I can take notes fast enough. The tapes are sixty minutes long, and that timing should work well for our sessions."

I wanted to be able to hear his voice when he no longer had it, when I no longer had him, and I had another reason. I wanted the backup for proof that he had said these things.

"Okay. We'll just sit here together on the couch with your machine between us and record this interview." He balanced himself on the edge of the sofa instead of sinking back into it. He eyed the recorder, his breath hissing like a cat that stares into the eyes of a dog and dares it to come any closer. The month before, when he had sat in his chair, there had been physical distance between us.

Being over there had allowed him the space to retreat into the past and relive it. He had been able to block out the present and my presence along with it. Now with his wiry frame seated directly across from me, he reminded me of a praying mantis, watchful and waiting. His arms were folded across his chest, but I was glad he was willing to humor me.

"Let me tell you what it was like, growing up at Powhatan." He started speaking before I could turn on the tape recorder and launch my first question. His voice was loud and he directed it to the tape recorder rather than to me.

I hit the start button.

"I was born in 1916, this month in fact—January 12, 1916. My family was living on a farm in a little area called Powhatan, just outside of Clayton, North Carolina."

I relaxed, no longer feeling like I had to follow the thread of his conversation. I would have the tape, and I could always listen to it and untangle the associated memories. "As a boy growing up, I don't recall making demands on my parents. They had gone through so much. I didn't want to add anything to what they were already dealing with by asking for things I knew we couldn't have. We were poor, but so was everybody else around us. Poverty is relative, and as a child, I didn't know we were poor. I had to get a little older to develop my class consciousness."

He glanced at me to see if I was listening. I realized then that I was there not only to record his experiences, but to distill their meaning. He was giving me grapes, but I was to make wine. He wanted me as an audience and my attention was to be my offering to him. The stories were his gifts to me. He would never know his readers.

"Why was the area called Powhatan?" I asked.

"Supposedly the farm was located on the campground of a tribe of Indians, who were known as the Powhatan. That was probably true because I found arrowheads all the time out in the field when I was plowing."

He stopped talking, and the only sound in the room was the hum of the tape recorder. His long, slender hand reached out to swat the stop button. "We don't want to waste that." Waste was not something that people of his generation took lightly.

My uncle stood and stretched, taking his seat in his chair, rather than returning to the couch. He eyed the recorder.

"The farm," I prompted.

"Oh, yes. I was born there. My parents, Lehman Holson Johnson and Mabel Jones Johnson, were living there with her parents on the family farm at Powhatan. It was not unusual at the time for young couples to live, at least for a while, with one set of parents or the other, while they got on their feet."

I pressed the start button on the recorder and turned up the volume as loud as it would go, hoping he would not be distracted again. Uncle Legs clicked right along with his story although I had missed the first part.

"What was unusual in our situation was that brothers had married sisters. This other set of Johnsons also lived on the Jones farm. You know Betty, don't you?" he said to me.

"Yes." I realized that we had not yet done the family inquiries.

"We are double first cousins. Betty's mother, Mildred Jones, was my mother's sister. Betty's father, Leslie Jones, was my father's brother. Until his death, William Jones, Jr. and Elizabeth (Bet), commonly known as Mammy Jones, owned the farm and headed up the family farming operation. By the way, how is Betty?"

"Her husband Delton is not well. He has Alzheimer's and is pretty much confined to the house. I usually take Betty one of our family calendars, so I've seen them recently. I don't think Delton knew who I was. There was no conversation or response from him at all when I spoke to him. He just sits in his recliner all wrapped up. Betty is determined to care for him at home. They have been inseparable their entire married life."

"Yes." He rubbed his forehead with the tips of his fingers. "Alzheimer's disease is a thief. It robs a person of both their past and the present. It's a terrible thing to see someone you love deteriorate right before your eyes. The last time we went to see my sister Sulou, she called me 'Daddy,' and Jane was 'Mother.' I can't stand it. That's why I don't visit her more often. She thought we were back on the farm when, in fact, we were right there in the living room of Croasdaile Retirement Village. That living room doesn't look anything like our parlor did."

I waited, and the tape recorder whirled on.

"The house at Powhatan was made up of seven rooms: a kitchen, dining room, three bedrooms, a parlor, and a big storeroom off to the back that was used as a bedroom at one time. When it was cold, we normally built a fire in just the kitchen and mother and daddy's bedroom. We would stay there until we went to bed, and we dressed there. My sisters slept on another double bed in the same room as our parents, but as the only boy, and the oldest, I had my own bedroom.

"I had a big double feather bed all to myself, as well. Mother made each of us one by sewing two sheets together and stuffing it with feathers. When there was an electric storm, mother would put us all on her and Daddy's feather bed and we would stay there until the storm passed. There was no real protection, but we felt secure and no one was ever struck by lightning.

"As children, reading was our main entertainment. I remember Mary, my baby sister, your mother, curling up like a little cat in the wood box beside the stove in the kitchen with her books. She was too young to have chores yet, but she loved to be there during the day while mother cooked. Sulou and I were busy working, so our reading was done at night.

"We used oil lamps at night for reading and to light the house. I was allowed to have one in my bedroom, so I could read and do home-work. The light was not good, but that didn't stop me. It was cold, too, because there was no fireplace in that room. At night I would snuggle down in my bed and read Zane Gray novels. They were my favorite. I got one out of the library each week, and I read every night."

He gazed across the room at the gas logs that glowed like the flames of memory, flickering and throwing shadows on the wall. He stared into the fire that was not real and recalled scenes in his child-hood home that warmed him even now.

"I still remember when we finally got an Aladdin lamp. People who bought them to replace their wick lamps exchanged a twenty-five-cent lamp for one that cost approximately four dollars and fifty cents — a huge amount of money during the 1920s and 1930s. Door to door salesmen called on families like mine and offered them an Aladdin lamp with fuel to use free for one week. At the end of the week, they could return the lamp, with no questions asked, or they could buy it. Those that could afford them generally bought the lamps.

"Having one was definitely an upgrade. The light from an Alad-din lamp was so much brighter than a kerosene lamp. I could read as long as I could stay awake at night with no eye strain. Using a gallon of kerosene, the Aladdin lamp produced four times more light than a wick kerosene lamp. Besides, they were cheaper to operate and safer than the traditional kerosene lamps. They used the same principle of incandescence as electric light bulbs today. You can still buy them."

"Did you say that there was a fireplace in the kitchen?"

"Yes, there was, but there was also a woodstove. The kitchen was the center of activity in the house, and between the fireplace and the woodstove, it was always warm in the winter. Mother cooked on that stove, and I have never tasted food like that again. It had a smoky flavor. The same foods do not taste the same when they are cooked in a conventional oven.

"We had biscuits every morning for breakfast. Biscuits and cornbread baked in a woodstove are out of this world. To this day, I love cornbread. Mother made hers from cornmeal with a little salt, baked in the oven or fried on top of the stove. There was never any left on the table." He smiled, remembering the family and a mother whose love was seldom expressed in words. Instead, she served it up three times a day in delicious meals made from scratch.

"What did the stove look like?"

"The stove had four eyes, and under these was the oven. Mother kept a pot of coffee on the stove all the time. That was the first thing you smelled when you came in the house. It was pretty strong coffee, and it got stronger as the day went on because the same pot simmered on the stove until it was gone. We did not waste it. Both of my parents drank coffee, and I remember that Daddy liked his very sweet—three teaspoonfuls of sugar to a cup. That was quite an extravagance, considering the price of sugar. We had to buy it, as opposed to most everything else we ate, which we grew on our own. It was a standing joke that Daddy liked a little coffee with his sugar."

I remembered this as a habit my grandfather practiced at the breakfast table long after he and my grandmother had bought the house in

Kenly, North Carolina, where they retired. Their coffee was made daily in an electric percolator. Their lifestyle remained frugal but not stingy. My eyes met my Uncle's and we smiled at the shared recollection, although I did not know its origin until now.

The tape recorder clicked. "What's that?" he asked.

"We have to turn the tape over."

"Let's don't do that. I've worked up an appetite." He stood up and slapped the stop button on the offending machine. "If you don't mind, don't bring that thing back." The formal interview of the evening was over, and I was once again following his line of retreat as I watched him go down the hall to his bedroom. He returned with his jacket and cane looped over his arm. "Jane," he shouted down into the basement, "Chow time!"

"Is Huey's all right with you again?" He headed toward the kitchen and then stood aside for Jane and me to catch up.

That moment in time was suspended, and we could not get back to exactly that place when we returned. But we would go on to another in the way that memory makes inroads and then connects them, building bridges between the past and the present.

I did not bring recording devices or my video camera to any more of the sessions that all took place in my uncle's home and in the small-town restaurants there. To have done so, after his directive, would have been like taking too many pictures during a live performance and missing the opportunity to engage in the experience.

There was an unwritten and unspoken contract drawn up between us during the time that I was privileged to share my uncle's confidences. These were to be family visits. I was to be both the repository and the translator of what he told me. I knew now that he wanted more than a simple retelling and recording of his words.

Road Kill

"If I killed it, we ate it or gave it to somebody else to eat."

—Lieutenant Colonel Lehman H. Johnson, Jr.

At Huey's, Uncle Legs checked his fried oysters for appropriate dry-ness by slicing into one. The oyster milk squirted out into his plate. He frowned. "They're not there yet," he observed and sent them back.

I thought, *I bet you didn't complain about the food at home when you were growing up*—But then again, since I was also familiar with my grandmother's cooking, I knew my uncle had high standards. I had ordered the fried chicken this time since it came highly recommend-ed, according to my uncle, second only to Mabel Johnson's lard-fried chicken. While we waited for his order to return, he began again.

"I don't remember Mother having any trouble with any of the chil-dren eating. She was very matter of fact about the food, as she was with everything else. She fixed the meals and put them on the table, and we ate it all. There was no waste.

"She could do more with cheese and eggs than anybody I ever saw, and she didn't fool around with recipes either. She added a pinch of this and a pinch of that until she got whatever she was cooking like she wanted it. We were never hungry because Mother was such a good cook. She could make anything taste good, and she didn't throw much stuff away in her kitchen.

"Remind me to tell you about eating possum. I'll save that one until we get back home. It really was delicious, but you might lose your appetite when I tell you how we acquired this delicacy."

I took a bite of my crisp, golden fried chicken. "Thank you." I was glad that story would be reserved for later.

Our waitress returned with a new plate of oysters. This time the test was by taste. "Delicious." He bit into one and pronounced them fit.

He glanced at my plate. "When I was growing up, chicken was for Sundays and special events. Mother would say, 'Lehman, Jr., come help me catch this chicken.' Since the chickens were right there running around convenient in the yard, we would catch one any time we wanted fried chicken, wring its neck, and watch the bird flop around until it died. Then Mother would stick it in a pot of water boiling in the yard to loosen the feathers. That would take a few minutes. Then she'd pull him out by the feet and pick him clean. Mother liked a good clean chicken."

So that's why we do it, I thought. When I was growing up, my mother always meticulously examined the processed chicken that we bought in the grocery store for feather nodules. I do the same thing. It was a collective memory, but I had no awareness of it until that moment.

Uncle Legs closed his eyes and savored the taste of his now just right oysters. Then he studied my half-eaten chicken.

"The chicken that mother fried in that iron frying pan was like none I have tasted before or since then."

"Yes, I know," I agreed. "I still have her iron frying pan, but evidently I lack the other 'ingredients.'" I remembered that fried chicken as a child, although by that time, my grandmother was cooking on an electric stove. I can't imagine how she ever got the grease hot enough and maintained an even temperature on a wood stove. As an adult I have tried to fry chicken in that skillet on an expensive, glass-topped stove. "Mine has never tasted like hers."

My uncle smacked his lips. "We had chicken or pork from the farm. We raised hogs along with the chickens. With the meat, Mother always put three veggies on the table with cornbread. The beets, peas, beans, and corn came from our garden and had to be picked, of course. The 'extra' was canned and put away for the winter.

"We also ate what Daddy and I killed when we went hunting."

"And what was that?" I wondered if I was about to get the possum story. I was glad I had finished eating.

"In the car."

In the back seat I gazed out of the window at the railroad track that splits Main Street. Huey's was maybe a mile outside of town. I thought about how my uncle had gotten back to Powhatan since our last visit. I think he will always return. Downtown, we passed a mural painted on the side of the old White furniture factory. Next block down was The Mebane Mural, circa 1929, given to the people of Mebane by James Rice, and dedicated to Milton McDade, town historian.

Was there anybody left who remembered working in the furniture factory or were the apartments that had been created out of the old, decaying building the monument to their experiences?

Did people still talk about James Rice or Milton McDade? McDade was a local photojournalist who had given the town his Mebane memorabilia, with the stipulation that his collection would one day be housed in a museum. Rice Jewelry Store was printed on a dark blue box above the buildings in the mural. Both of these men had done their best to assure themselves of a place in posterity.

But what of my uncle? He stitched one story to another, like cross stitch, and then provided the context to frame his narrative. That was the pattern. Some of the stitches were still ragged beneath the seams. His questions had come at the beginning, and I wondered would there still be questions at the end.

"Road kill," he said from the front seat.

"What?" Startled, I was brought back to the present. It was almost dark, but I strained to see if there was a raccoon or maybe a possum that had been run over and left in the road.

He grinned and looked back at me to see how I was taking the pronouncement.

"Daddy believed hunting was a sport. That meant you gave the target a chance, and that you put food on somebody's table. Once I shot a rabbit with a BB gun when he was sitting still, and Daddy saw me. I remember he told me, 'Don't ever shoot a rabbit unless he's running.' I didn't, after that one incident."

"How old were you?"

"I was hunting with a shotgun by myself when I was twelve years old. I had a 20 gauge Browning, that I won at the county fair for having the prettiest cow. That was thanks to Betsy, the Guernsey cow that we kept for milking.

"Anyway, after school, I'd always go out and shoot me a rabbit, and I'd usually get one or two. When I got home, I'd skin it and throw the entrails to the dogs. Mother had a rule. Nothing with fur or feathers came into her kitchen. She would always clean the rabbit up some more after me and then barbecue it. It was delicious. The front shoulders are the most delicious, tenderest meat.

"We did the same thing with the squirrels I killed. We ate them. We also ate the catfish we caught in the pond that was on the farm. Sometimes, I gigged frogs there, and Mother fried the legs. If I killed it, we ate it or gave it to somebody else to eat. Meat was not wasted.

"This was true of even the possums that we sometimes killed when we were hunting other game. Once in a while, the dogs would tree a possum when they were supposed to be chasing a rabbit. Daddy would shake the tree, and the possum would then fall out. We tried to keep the dogs away from him because if an opossum got hold of a dog, he would just strip him. A possum could literally skin a dog alive. You didn't stick your hand out either to touch that possum because its teeth were poison, and you didn't want the same thing to happen to your hand.

"Daddy would put his foot on the animal's head, and it would immediately relax and pretend to be dead. That's where the expression 'playing possum' comes from. I bet you didn't know that." He waited and looked back at me to measure the effect of his story. I shook my head.

"I had no idea."

"I would get a stick or a broom handle, if one was handy. This stick was then placed behind the possum's head. Daddy would break his (the possum's) neck by putting his foot on the broomstick and yanking the tail up. You could hear it snap."

The sound I made when I drew in my breath was an "S," sucked back against my teeth. Uncle Legs was not distracted by my reaction, and if he heard it, he ignored me.

"Most of the time, Daddy put the possums in a bag and gave them to Paul Dennis and his wife Lottie, the black family who lived in a tenant house located there on the farm. They were always glad to get them or anything else we gave them."

"Did you ever eat possum?" We were now in the garage, but neither Jane nor I made a move to get out of the car.

"Yes, we did. I remember once that Daddy brought a possum home in a sack alive and kept him in a pen. I'm not sure why he did it that way this time, but that's what he did. We fed that possum sweet potatoes and corn bread to clean his nasty body out. Daddy called opossums the buzzards of the woods because they would eat anything.

"When he was fat enough, daddy broke his neck, just like we would do when we were hunting, and Mother barbecued him. It was delicious, like everything else she cooked. The meat was very clean with no blood in it." He paused for effect.

"Did everybody eat?"

"They did." There was laughter in his voice. "Nobody complained, and nobody called it road kill."

A Close Call at Powhatan

"Punishment was unnecessary, and I did not fear it."

— Lieutenant Colonel Lehman H. Johnson, Jr.

"It's a wonder I'm still alive but it's just as miraculous that I survived my childhood with all my members intact." He held up both hands and wiggled his fingers in the air.

We were back in the den, and Jane came in with my uncle's glass of wine. "I'll be down here in the basement working on my Sunday School lesson but will come up just before bedtime for a chat. He's telling you things I never knew, and I've been knowing Legs Johnson since 1983." I heard Jane's retreating footsteps.

When we didn't hear her anymore, he spoke. "This is new material." He leaned back, relaxed, and sipped his burgundy. His eyes were clear, blue like a summer sky undisturbed by clouds. I waited.

"When we lived in Clayton, Daddy and Lanelle, his youngest brother, would go hunting, mostly small game like rabbits, squirrels, and foxes. Birds like dove, pheasant, and quail were also fair game. Sometimes they invited me to go along.

"I haven't told you yet, but we didn't always live at Powhatan. There was a move to Clayton and then another one back to the farm when I was about twelve years old. I'll tell you about how that came about another time. Right now, I want you to appreciate how lucky I am to be alive.

"Once we moved back to Powhatan, Daddy let me go hunting by myself. I would come in from school and hang my book bag on a peg. It was one of those rectangular, over-the-shoulder bags balanced by the books you put on each side. Like everything else we had, Mother made it. There were many afternoons that I provided the meat for the evening meal — supper. Dinner was something we had in the middle of the day, usually on Sundays. Lunch was what mother packed for us to take to school.

"Anyway, if we had it, I would enjoy a cool, delicious glass of buttermilk, what we called clabber, and maybe a left-over biscuit after school. It was thanks to Betsy, our Guernsey cow that I had both the buttermilk and the shotgun. Did I tell you that I won that gun for having the prettiest cow at the county fair?"

"Yes, you did." I smiled. He was still proud of having won a contest with a well-groomed cow.

"My use of that gun was almost the source for the end of this book." He stopped.

"I had raised a litter of beagle hounds there on the farm, and they were the best rabbit dogs. They knew when I was home. They would start barking as soon as I got in the yard because they knew they were about to be let out. It was that way on this day.

"We were in the woods, and the dogs were running ahead. I could hear their howling, like they had already picked up the scent of a rabbit, and I was following their direction. It was easy because not only could I hear them, but I could also see where the underbrush was disturbed where they had created their own path. These hunting dogs and I worked together. We had a job to do, and they were bred and trained to do their part.

"Suddenly, I heard the awfullest noise and yelping coming from my dogs. We spent hours out in the woods, just me and these dogs, and I knew their voices. What I was hearing now was their particular howls of distress. These beagles weren't like pets, but I took good care of my dogs, and I was attached to them, as they were to me. The briars and brambles were grabbing at my clothes and scratching my face and hands, as I ran to find them. But I didn't pay any attention.

"When I caught up with them, I saw that some bigger dogs were tearing mine to pieces. My little pack was outnumbered. Mr. Archie Jones had dogs in the same area, so it was probably his that were attacking mine. Several of them already had my dogs by the throat and were shaking them.

"I ran into the middle of the fight, and without thinking, I used the butt of the gun like a hammer to hit the dog closest to me on the head. It was loaded, of course, and when I did that, the gun went off. The shell tore a hole in my jacket right under my arm, just missing my chest by an inch or two. Of course, the dogs scattered, and I went home. My dogs got there first.

"When I told my parents what had happened, there was very little said, just not to ever do that again. Punishment was unnecessary, and I did not fear it. I was never afraid to tell my parents when I made bad decisions. In return, they expected me to learn from my mistakes. I was still allowed to go out hunting by myself, no questions asked."

"What's that?" Jane asked, returning from the basement. "Did I overhear you say that you sometimes made mistakes?" She smiled, and his face lit up.

"Did I ever tell you that I have never understood how one man could be so lucky twice?" The question was directed at me, but he was looking at Jane.

"Yes. You've told me," I said. He adored Jane, this second wife who answered, "Sir?" when he called.

"I think about that every day, too. I will probably tell you that again because it's on my mind. Some of these stories I will repeat. I remember more as we go along."

"That will be just fine," I said. Memory covers things up, and sometimes the blankets need to be pulled back one layer at a time. If they are snatched off all at once, the storyteller can be left shivering in a room, alone and exposed to the cold before the fire is built. My uncle told me on more than one occasion that his mother got him up to do chores before he went to school just like that. "Mother knew how to get me up!" he had said. I wanted his awakening through this process to be gradual and gentle.

"Mistakes? Bad decisions?" Jane prompted, sitting down in her chair, the one closest to him.

"That definitely wasn't you," my uncle said, gazing into the fire. He reached to pat her hand.

Uncle Legs stretched and yawned, then stood up. "Jane, would you cut the logs back on pilot? I don't think it's safe to burn them while we're asleep. I don't think even that sleep number bed we have now is as comfortable as that feather bed Mother made for me, but I'm ready for it. Do you know what a sleep number bed is?"

I shook my head. "No. You're about to tell me?"

"You get fitted for this bed. There's a factory show room right here in Mebane. Jane and I went in before we bought it to find out what our sleep numbers are. It's very comfortable, but not like the bed I had when I was growing up."

"That probably has something to do with the fact that your feather bed was made by Granny Johnson just for you," I observed.

"Speaking of our bed," said Jane. "I need to get in it. Good night, you two."

Uncle Legs got up to follow her and steadied himself on the arm of his chair as he looked down at me. "My mother and I enjoyed a very special relationship. Tomorrow, I'll tell you more about that."

"I'll look forward to it. Sweet dreams." They had left the lights on in the room for me to turn out when I went to bed, although nothing was said about that. There was no need.

A New Broom

"Her hand bled through the ribbon, and I remember seeing the drops of blood there on the ground."

— Lieutenant Colonel Lehman H. Johnson, Jr.

After church the next morning, Uncle Legs and I waited in the sanctuary for Jane to get out of her choir robe and join us. The congregation of Mebane United Methodist Church was milling down the red-carpeted aisle and leaning over pews as neighbor greeted neighbor and caught up on what had happened since last week. A stylishly dressed older woman approached as we waited there on the pew. I stood up to greet her.

"You must be Denise!" she said and extended her hand. "I'm Alma. Jane has told us you are writing a book about Legs, and I just wanted you to know that when you get through, I want you to present it to my book club. Legs is like a celebrity here." She said all that in one breath, and I was speechless.

I took her hand. *Who is Denise*, I wondered.

Before I could introduce myself, Jane came up in front of us on the next pew. "I see you've just met Mary Susan. This is Legs' niece. She's visiting us this weekend, and they are working on his book."

Alma looked puzzled. "I thought you said Denise was coming when I saw you in the grocery store."

Jane didn't miss a beat. She was smooth as silk. "Alma, what I said was 'the niece is coming this weekend, and I'm getting some food for us.' Mary Susan is Legs' niece. She's here to interview Legs for his memoir." Jane's tone was loud and distinct.

"Oh! I misunderstood you. I've told a lot of people about Denise. What did you say her name is?"

Jane leaned slightly to Alma's right. "Her name is Mary Susan Heath. This is Legs' niece. She will be coming once a month, so you'll see her then."

Alma recovered. She was still holding my hand. "Then I hope you'll visit us here at Mebane United Methodist Church."

"It will be my pleasure," I said. "This will take a while. We'll talk about that book club when I finish."

"Oh, yes, I'm counting on it." She waved as she backed down the pew. "Bye, now!"

"Alma is hard of hearing," Jane explained, when she was out of ear-shot. "We'll try to clarify, but you may always be 'Denise,' here."

"No problem," I said. "I certainly feel welcome."

* * * * *

"How does Denise feel about barbecue for lunch?" Uncle Legs teased on the way to the local Smithfield Chicken and Barbecue.

"I'm sure she likes it fine," I said from the backseat of Jane's car. "We have these back home, but the closest one is in Smithfield. Denise doesn't get there very often."

The red brick building looked familiar. We drove past the drive-thru sign advertising a 10-piece family pack and a gallon of tea, sweetened unless you specified differently.

The mural on the side of the building was distinctively Mebane. To get to the entrance, we walked past a giant yellow roadster painted on the brick wall. The car was full of stylishly dressed people. Black letters over their heads asked, "HUNGRY NOW?" Below the car was the solution: "WE'RE JUST AROUND THE CORNER."

Once inside, I noticed that unlike other restaurants in that same chain, this one had posters all over the walls advertising classic movies and Hollywood stars from the '50s: seductive Rita Hayworth in *Lady from Shanghi*, Marilyn Monroe's skirts swirling up in *The Seven Year Itch*. We seated ourselves at one of the shiny Formica tables, and our waitress came out from behind the counter that was lined with their brand of hushpuppy mix and barbecue sauce.

"What would youse Sweeties like?" She did not call Jane and Uncle Legs by name, and she didn't know any of their preferences, like the waitresses at Huey's sometimes did.

We placed our order and Uncle Legs picked up the thread of conversation that he'd dropped the night before. "I thought about taking y'all to Cracker Barrel because they have such a nice porch and all those rockers that remind me of our front porch. We'll go there next time."

You don't have a front porch, I thought. "Do you mean the enclosed porch off the den of Jane's house?"

"No! I mean the porch around the front of the house at Powhatan where I grew up." He frowned. He was there. Where was I?

I realized he was tossing me the ball of thread that he had started winding up the day before. "Tell us about the porch." As it turned out, it wasn't the porch that was so important, but his mother, who kept the yard and the front porch just like she kept house.

My uncle leaned back in his chair. His voice carried over the din of Sunday diners, who were now filing in. Some of the parties were large, and they pushed the tables for four together themselves to make room. No one here turned around when he spoke. "Mother was just as proud of the front porch as any other part of the house. She swept it just as often." He smiled and took a sip of his sweet iced tea.

"The porch went half-way around the house on three sides, and there were wisteria vines growing up the banisters that shaded the porch, like a gazebo. The porch and the banisters were painted white, and we had nice rocking chairs and lattice chairs to sit in and enjoy the cool of the evening."

Our plates of barbecue, golden fried chicken, Brunswick stew, and boiled potatoes were delivered by our waitress. Uncle Legs blessed the food. He never lowered his voice when he said the blessing, and that Sunday was no exception. I could still hear him over the piped-in music of the 50's and 60's.

Between bites, he continued with his story. "We enjoyed some good visits with our neighbors and kinfolks on that porch. We all worked hard, but we knew the value of life and enjoyed what we shared of it." His eyes took on the dreamy quality of a blue sky over the ocean just before sunset. My uncle was enjoying the food before us, but he was savoring the taste of memory even more.

"Our relations with our neighbors were such that they would do whatever you asked them to do, and we would do the same. It was the same with the other set of Johnsons who lived there on the farm. The only other place I've experienced anything like that is in the military. None of us had our families nearby, so we became that to each other."

Uncle Legs looked out over the crowd of people now lining up at the door because all the tables were full. When it was clear that one group was leaving, the next party came over and hovered over the almost vacated table. He waved his fork at the scene. "I don't know half those people."

"A lot of them are probably stopping in to eat off the interstate," Jane observed.

"Your mother…," I prompted. I hoped we would not come here to eat again. Too many distractions for storytelling.

But if he heard the metal pan that had been dropped in the kitchen area, my uncle ignored it. "There was no grass around our house. People didn't want that back then. In fact, if grass grew there, we chopped it out. Mother swept our yard just like the porch and the house. Her yard broom was a bunch of small dogwoods I had cut and bound together and wrapped around with a string. The kitchen broom was made out of what we called broom straw.

"When it wore out, she and I would go down to the railroad track together to get straw for a new broom. It grew there. This was just one of the many chores that Mother and I shared. She depended on me to do the work that was either too dangerous or too difficult for the girls. I suppose they could have done this — cut the broom straw that is — but she asked me to go along."

There was definitely a pecking order in your house, I thought, while he continued. *The memory of your mother is bound up in the work she did, work that you and she usually shared.*

"One time when we were breaking the reeds of straw, Mother cut her hand. Maybe she had tried to break too much of it at one time. Anyway, she wrapped her hand up with ribbon she had in her apron pocket. The ribbon was probably there for binding up the broom. Her hand bled through the ribbon, and I remember seeing the drops of blood there on the ground. It looked like it was sprinkling rain, but of course it wasn't.

"She couldn't stop the bleeding, but Mother kept on breaking the straw that she needed anyway. I remember she was careful not to stain the straw with her blood. She was a very hard worker and very precise about everything she did. But she was not one to share her feelings. She didn't say anything at all this time.

"I remember I cried when I saw my mother's hand bleeding, but I tried not to let her see. I turned away from her and pretended that I was looking for straw a little further down, but I kept hearing the straw crack behind me. Today, I have this very strong emotion, thinking about what she was going through to make a broom to keep that house clean. We didn't have any money to spend for a store-bought broom."

Uncle Legs wiped his eyes with his napkin. This time I looked away. Our waitress had appeared at our table unnoticed.

"Can I get you gentlemens and ladies anything else?"

"I'd like some banana pudding, please ma'am," Uncle Legs said, "and some for them, too." The pudding was served up promptly in little plastic cups with plastic lids on top.

Uncle Legs eyed his dessert. It was a thick yellow custard surrounded by vanilla wafers. No meringue. No cool whip on top. He tasted it, and we all began to eat.

Suddenly, my uncle laid his spoon down with more force than was necessary and raised his hand to call the waitress back to our table. She was at his elbow before he could turn around to see if she was coming. She was an older African American woman, wearing a khaki ball cap with Smithfield Chicken and Barbecue stenciled on the front. It was hard to tell how old she was, but she was no spring chicken, for sure.

"Is everything all right, sweeties? What 'bout for this here sweet gentleman?" Her forehead wrinkled with concern and the corners of her mouth turned down, although her eyes were expressionless.

When he spoke, my uncle's voice was softly even. "There are no bananas in this banana pudding."

"Naw, Suh. This here 'naner puddin' ain't like that your mama made. Mine neither. It's bah-naner flavored pudding with a few 'nilla wafers thrown in fer good measure. We's make it fresh ever' mawning, but there ain't no naners in this here naner puddin'."

"Then it's not banana pudding."

"Naw, Suh, it ain't real naner puddin', and I's sorry. Is thar anything else I can git fer y'all?"

"My check, please."

When she brought the bill, Uncle Legs kept his eyes focused on it and added in a tip. Then he stood abruptly, took his cane and started striding toward the door. Looking at his retreating back, I thought about how these childhood stories provide the yardstick by which all subsequent pleasures and pain are measured. Banana pudding was supposed to have bananas in it and real meringue on top.

Jane and I looked at each other. Uncle Legs was waiting for us at the door, and we had our cue to leave. He was jabbing the tile with his cane. *So this was the way things were to be*, I thought, sliding back from the table. *Advance and retreat. Take cover if the memories overwhelm.*

Jane and I got up and followed him. There was no conversation in the car as we drove home, and I left early that weekend. But before I left, I had come to believe that past pleasures have no equal in the present and to understand that suffering does have memory.

Still, I knew I was not the enemy and that my uncle knew that, too. What I could see was a woman holding the broom straw in her left hand, because the ribbon that was supposed to have bound it was wrapped around her right hand—and soaked with blood. In the telling I hoped my uncle could sit back and view that scene, and others, with empathy for those involved—the child that he had been at the time, as well as his mother. It was from her that he had acquired this interesting combination of sensitivity and a rock-hard sense of survival. I would wait until he was ready to talk about her again.

Not even Jane could make a banana pudding like his mother did. I'm sure, although I never asked her, that Jane was wise enough not even to try.

Coming Up in the World and Back Down Again

"The flames were so high that I could see them leaping up in the window of my second story bedroom." (October 8, 1926)

— Lieutenant Colonel Lehman H. Johnson, Jr.

February was a cold month, but there were heralds of spring. The daffodils nodded their heads in greeting, and the first robins hopped from branch to branch of the still bare trees. At the door I looked back down the winding drive up Knollwood Falls that I had just made to Jane and Uncle Legs' house. I saw a promise of new life.

The stories of that weekend would hold that same promise. I would hear of loss and destruction, death and destitution, but not defeat. A quiet acceptance of destiny would rise from the ashes of a fire.

As Uncle Legs and I sat in the den, we passed through the preliminaries of recent family lore and caught up with what everybody was doing. He and Jane played a lot of golf, and he was looking forward to spring when they could resume their normal rounds. He tossed aside the statements from his stockbroker that he had been studying when I came in. "I don't fool with this stuff. I pay somebody else to look after it. Leaves me time for chasing that little white ball."

Golfing had not been an activity that had been part of my uncle's

71

growing up, but it gave me an opening. "Why do you think your Dad wanted to leave the farm?"

He hesitated before continuing. "Daddy liked salesmanship, not farming. But farming was what he had been born into. It was also what he had married into."

"Neither he nor Leslie, Betty's father, liked farming, but when Grandpa Jones died at age 44, on March 4, 1913, somebody had to head up the family farming operation. It is unlikely that there was any competition for the job. Other family members have said that Leslie disliked farming even more than Daddy. Leslie found work off the farm as a prison guard at the Johnson County Prison Camp shortly after my grandfather's death. Daddy wasn't far behind in leaving. When I was seven, we moved to Clayton.

"We lived in a big old red brick house across from the livery stables, one block off from Main Street. Mother took in two teachers as boarders to help pay the rent. Daddy bought the hardware store on Main Street from a Mr. Pope. That made us part of a different class of people, and I enjoyed my new status, along with the indoor plumbing and electricity that came with city living. Clayton wasn't much more than a wide place in the road then, but it was definitely a move up from the farm.

"Leonard, Dad's youngest brother, lived with us during the summer and worked in the hardware store. He had played baseball there in Clayton and had gotten an athletic scholarship to Oak Ridge Military Institute. Oak Ridge was a junior college at that time. It was and still is located about eight miles northwest of Greensboro, North Carolina. I was impressed by Leonard's uniform when he came to our house. I saw how other people treated him and looked up to him.

"Leonard and his uniform were 'the cat's meow' in Clayton. I'm sure that was part of the reason I was attracted to a service career. I wanted that same respect. It came with the uniform. It did not come with wearing overalls."

Uncle Legs crossed and uncrossed his long legs. Looking into his eyes was like looking into two cesspools that had clouded over. I couldn't read his expression. "Mary Susan, this may be hard for you to understand. Even though the merchants depended on the farmers as customers for their living, most of them felt that they were a cut above that cloth. Like my daddy, most of them were fresh off the farm themselves. It didn't make sense, but that's the way it was." He sighed.

"For a while life as we were living it was good. About the only thing that we still did like when we were living on the farm was to keep a cow. Mother wanted us to have our own fresh milk, so when we moved to Clayton, Betsy came, too. We kept her in a little shed behind the house, and I had to milk that dadgum cow every morning before I went to school. We lived in town, but I still had chores.

"Mother would let the milk I brought in sit for a while and then skim off the cream that literally rose to the top. Her whipped cream desserts were the best I've ever tasted. The rest of the cream went into a five-gallon churn, where it remained until I got home from school. I would come in and have a delicious glass of cold buttermilk, maybe some cornbread.

"Then I would sit there and pump until the butter was made. It usually took twenty to thirty minutes. Mother would skim the butter from the top and put it in a mold. We didn't have a refrigerator, of course, so she would wrap the butter up and put it in a pail that we lowered down into the well. The buttermilk that was left might be used in cooking that night or it might be stored in the well, too.

"The butter was rich and fresh. To this day, I still eat hot biscuits with butter.

"We didn't need all the butter that got made, so Mother, who was very enterprising, sold the extras through Daddy's store. Her little side business was prosperous. Business in the hardware store was also good.

My parents bought a lot there in Clayton, and they were making plans to build Mother her dream house.

"Then there was the great fire in Clayton. I remember it like it was yesterday. The town was almost burned up on October 8, 1926." Uncle Legs leaned forward in his chair and looked expectantly toward the stairs.

"All this talk about butter and biscuits has made me hungry. Where's Jane? It's supper time."

I wondered if this was the way it was to be each time. Would he stop talking when it hurt? Then I remembered that as a boy, my uncle chopped wood the next day after almost cutting off his thumb. He would come back to it although he might sand down to the layer of feelings past the details through several versions of the same story.

At Huey's, our waitress asked if we wanted biscuits or hush puppies with the meal. I ordered beef tips over rice with hush puppies.

"Biscuits, please," Uncle Legs smiled across the booth at me. "I'll have a steak with a baked potato, and bring me some butter. Real butter. I don't want any of this margarine stuff."

"I'm not sure what your cardiologist would say about that." Jane scolded. She ordered a salad.

"He's not here," Uncle Legs replied. "Now, where was I?"

"Clayton was burning," I prompted.

"Yes. Some people called it the Great Fire of Clayton."

He drifted off in thought and concentrated on buttering a biscuit from the steaming basket that was now before us.

"It was a Friday morning and we were in the kitchen having breakfast. Biscuits, I'm sure. The phone rang and Daddy answered it. The phone box was mounted on the wall with the receiver hanging by a hook. To talk on the phone, you leaned toward the wall to talk into the mouthpiece. You could balance yourself against the wall with one hand and hold the receiver up to one ear with the other.

"When Daddy heard that Main Street was on fire and that several businesses were burning, including his, he just dropped the receiver and ran to the hardware store. We could hear the caller still talking. 'It must have started during the night. It's already fully engaged,' the caller said. 'The Clayton Fire Department is there. Raleigh is on the way.'

"Mother, Sulou, and I sat there in shock. Mary, who was only about three years old, didn't understand what was going on, but the rest of us certainly did. The fire burned on during the day and throughout the night. The flames were so high that I could see them leaping up in the window of my second story bedroom. We heard the pop, pop of the police shooting holes in the fifty-gallon oil drums stored in a nearby service station. This was done so that they would not explode from the intense heat. Daddy didn't come home the whole time, and I don't remember Mother saying much."

He stopped talking and deliberately buttered another biscuit. Another pat of butter went on the potato. I waited.

"I don't remember being really afraid at the time. Our house was a block away from the actual fire and two fire departments were there. They were containing the blaze. I do remember being worried about money. I was only ten years old at the time, but Mother and Daddy talked about things in front of me that they did not discuss when the girls were around. I knew Daddy had gone into debt buying the hardware store." Uncle Legs took a bite of the steak and chewed thoughtfully. His ribeye might as well have been old shoe leather from the length of time that passed before he swallowed it and spoke again.

"The next day, when Daddy came home, he slumped in a chair at the kitchen table. His shoulders were rounded with exhaustion and discouragement—like a worn-out horse collar. I sat down across from him and asked, with no preliminaries, 'How much insurance did you have on the store?'

"Daddy shook his head wearily. 'Not, enough, son. Not nearly enough.' I remember feeling like someone had knocked the breath out of me. He had around $35,000 in insurance, and the hardware store and the contents were worth at least $100,000."

Uncle Legs swallowed hard and signaled to our waitress. Mine and Jane's plates were clean, but his was not. He had eaten only half his steak. "Check, please."

His family's dream was in ashes. The telling of it had given the loss renewed power. No one spoke of it, or anything else for that matter, on the way home.

Back to the Farm

*"Even the feed sacks became something else —
maybe a dress for one of the girls — or an apron."*

—*Lieutenant Colonel* Lehman H. Johnson, Jr.

In the den the silence lay between us like a trench. Then Uncle Legs
took several deliberate sips of the red wine that was part of the evening
ritual and continued.

"Dad's store and the grocery store next door were both destroyed.
People said that the cause of the fire was faulty wiring or some shortage
in the electrical system. There was a newspaper article printed in *The
Smithfield Herald* four days after the fire, October 12, 1926.

"The article said that the beginning of the fire was 'in a pile of rags
caused by spontaneous combustion' in the L. H. Johnson Hardware
building. Whether or not that was actually true, I don't know. That
same article stated that there were four 'losers' from the fire: Charlie Horne, who owned the building; the Clayton Department store,
managed by W.I. Whitley; the L.H. Johnson Hardware Company; and
Owen Gulley Company, general merchandise. You can still read that
article in the archives at *The Smithfield Herald*. Both Mr. Ivan Whitley
and my father were stripped of their livelihoods.

"There was nothing in Clayton for us then, but my parents were not ready yet to move back to the farm. Instead, Daddy got a job selling Chevrolets for a Mr. Holleman, who owned a dealership in Smithfield. We moved to Smithfield right after the fire.

"The timing for such a move was right. Daddy was a natural born salesman, and it looked like we had landed on our feet. Due to the Highway Act of 1921, many new hard-surface roads had been built, linking North Carolina's county seats, including Smithfield, the county seat of Johnston County. These included N.C. 10, which later became U.S. 70, and N.C. 22, which is now N.C. 301. There was great demand for new automobiles.

"Business was booming, but our prosperity was short-lived. On October 29, 1929, the day that came to be known as 'Black Thursday,' the stock market crashed. Suddenly, there was no demand for new cars, and General Motors halted production. There was no job. The Great Depression had begun. We went back to the farm because there was nowhere else for us to go.

"We children were told one morning at breakfast that we were moving back to Powhatan. I was not upset and neither were Mary and Sulou. I accepted the fact that our parents knew what was best for the family, and Mary, of course, had never lived on the farm. She had been born in Clayton. It never occurred to any of us children to question our parents' judgment. A question like 'How much insurance did you have?' was acceptable. 'Why didn't you have more?' was totally unacceptable.

"Farm prices were already at a very low point, and most farm families were already feeling the pinch. When the stock market crashed, it wasn't big news in Johnston County. In fact, *The Smithfield Herald* didn't even carry the story. Cotton, which was the main cash crop in the area at the time, had sold for twenty cents a pound in 1925. In 1926, it brought only twelve cents a pound. Supply far exceeded demand. The goods produced from cotton, like cloth, also fell in value because no one was buying. No one had any money, but my parents knew we wouldn't be hungry. The best that we could do was to become as self-sufficient as possible, and that's what my family did.

"We moved back to the farm in January, 1930. Everything we needed was there. Our car that we still owned was set up on blocks and parked in the barn because there was no money for gas or for tires either. We walked to the nearby three-room school-house and to Powhatan Free Will Baptist Church, instead of driving to the Missionary Baptist Church in Clayton where we belonged. Both the school and the church were about 700 yards from our corn fields — within spitting distance of the farm.

"It was quite a change in lifestyle. Even in Smithfield, and before that in Clayton, we had gas lights, indoor plumbing, city water, and city sewer. At Powhatan, we had a pump and a privy or outhouse. Still, there was no time that I remember on the farm that I was hungry or went anywhere improperly dressed.

"I was not to wear overalls to school. Mother had an aversion to these although I don't know why for sure. Maybe she felt that dressing like that denoted that we were a different class of people. I had to wear a pair of pants, a shirt, and a sweater to school. I wore the same blue sweater with my basketball letter on it every day and black shoes that were always shined. I had two pairs of pants — a blue pair and a black pair — corduroy in the winter, and Mama would rotate them, so they could be washed. I had one change of clean clothes. She made all of our clothes.

"Even the feed sacks became something else — maybe a dress for one of the girls or an apron. There was no waste in our household. Remember me talking about the butter Mother made in Clayton and the fresh milk?"

I nodded.

"That cow went with us to Smithfield and then back to the farm as well. When we got there, Mother added chickens. The little extra cash we had came from the butter and egg money. The difference was that now we had to go to our customers, instead of having them come to us. It became my job to go into town once a week and sell the extra eggs and butter and do our grocery shopping. I looked forward to the trip, but at the same time, I was also aware that my social standing had changed.

"I still visited some of my old friends from Clayton, and nobody did or said anything specific to me. But I was different. That was just the way people looked at things at the time. I had once stood behind one of those counters. Now I drove around town in a wagon pulled by our mules, Maude and May, and took care of my family's business. I knew all the merchants, and they remembered me from the hardware store. Almost all of them bought something. I don't know if they actually needed to or not. Some would use the butter and eggs themselves. Others would resell to their customers.

"Handling family finances was not the only skill I acquired at Powhatan. When we moved back, I was a small-town boy who didn't know which end of the hoe to pick up. At the end of our time there, I could milk not one, but two cows before I went to school. I knew how to kill hogs and hang up the meat. I knew how to hand up clothes from a wash pot, rinse them in the cold pot, and hang them on the line."

There was pride in his voice. "I had become a farm boy. There were many advantages that I enjoyed as a result of that fact. I learned to respect myself, and to have self-confidence. I learned to be independent when I was very young. I was doing a man's work but didn't mind it. I did not miss the amenities of city life so much, and my parents never complained. So I didn't either."

He caught my eye. "Yes, I know—feelings again. I felt that people looked down on me as being a farm boy. It was the loss of social standing that bothered me the most." He drained his glass and set it down with finality. His eyes twinkled. "But I still dated the prettiest girl in town—Alice Barbour, whose father owned Barbour's Dry Goods store."

He stood up abruptly, and so I did the same. "Good night," he said. "Did I tell you yet how I got my nickname?"

"Chicken legs?"

"No. Just Legs."

"You haven't told me about that yet," I said.

He yawned. "This story tonight reminded me of that. If I forget, will you remind me?"

I nodded. "After church?"

"After church."

Outclassed in Clayton

"I never questioned him, or asked him about the cross that lit up the dark that night or the sheets the men were wearing."

—Lieutenant Colonel Lehman H. Johnson, Jr.

We were back in the den in our accustomed places. The rituals of the Methodist service had been comforting, and lunch had been, in his words, "satisfying." Nothing unusual or "out of the way" had happened that Sunday morning. We settled in for the afternoon.

"I've told you about the house we lived in at Powhatan, but I haven't told you about any of the outbuildings there on the farm or anything about the people who lived there.

"There was an empty pack house there on the farm that doubled as a store for the tenants. Daddy kept sugar, salt, cornmeal, and other staples in there that the tenants might need while they stayed to help us get in the crops. After the tobacco was cured, we sometimes graded it in that building. I can still smell the tobacco now. It never went away, and the mellow, musty scent mixed with the odor of the dry goods Daddy kept for the tenants. He kept a ledger of what they got, and they settled up at the end of the crop season.

"There were two tenant houses on the farm, each with an outhouse. Daddy would go and get these black folks from South Carolina, who didn't have anything to do, and they would stay in the tenant houses that were just across the yard. Sometimes there were ten to twelve people in a house. I remember that we would give them some bacon, bread, and molasses from our pantry. Usually they stayed just long enough to help us get a crop in, and then Daddy would take them back to South Carolina.

"Paul and Lonnie Dennis lived there longer than anybody else. They were young and spry, and Daddy was happy for them to stay even though they didn't pay any rent. They kept to themselves and made themselves useful around the farm by helping out with the hog killings and during the planting season. They had a little garden of their own on the farm, and they grew their own vegetables.

"I remember that Paul always wore these raggedy overalls. His shoulder blades were bony, and the gallowses of his overalls were tied in the back and hooked over one shoulder—to take up some room. I wore overalls, too, but mine were always pressed and they were never ragged.

"Paul's wife, Lonnie, was skinny, too, and her dresses always looked like they were going to swallow her they were so big. Lonnie's dresses were made either from the flour sacks in our pantry or they were my mother's hand-me-down house dresses." He paused, and I used the opening for a question.

"Can you tell me something about the class distinctions between tenant farmers like Paul and Lonnie Dennis and people like your family who owned their own land?"

"They were black as the ace of spades and that put them down the ladder at least a couple of pegs. Blacks in the South at that time were only a generation removed from slavery. You might not be a slave, but you were still a Negro. Even if a black person owned land, or practiced a trade or profession, there was a distinction made on the basis of race. Negroes were still below the white tenant farmers and the people who were sometimes referred to as 'white trash.'"

He looked at me to see how I was going to react. I thought it best to let him keep unraveling that ball of string, so I said nothing. He continued.

"We weren't so high and mighty ourselves, but at least we were white." White doctors, lawyers, and maybe preachers got the most respect. Merchants, especially if they were wealthy and white, were somewhere in between. In the 1920s and 30s, we all knew our places.

"Daddy and the other white men in the area wanted to make sure the blacks remembered theirs. They did not want blacks to take over anything, especially any political office. Grandpa Johnson was very prejudiced, very anti-black.

"Although there was never any discussion about it in my family, we were all aware of the private secret meetings that Daddy attended. He took me with him once. I overheard threats of hangings being discussed with some of his friends, but I never questioned him, or asked him about the cross that lit up the dark that night or the sheets the men were wearing.

"I'm not sure to this day exactly why he took me or what conclusions he wanted me to draw. It was a topic that was strictly off limits to us as children. We kept it very secret in the family and didn't talk about it, even among ourselves. If these men had gotten ready to hang a black man, I don't know whether or not Daddy would have participated."

I tried not to look shocked. Sometimes when you mine another person's memory, especially someone in your family, you dig up rocks along with the gems. He went on with his explanation.

"My father was a member of the Democratic Party, and I have reason to believe because of what I saw and heard that he was also a member of the Ku Klux Klan. The two went hand in hand. If you were black, you were a Republican. Any white person who joined the Republican Party was looked down upon. I remember that Mr. Duncan, the postmaster in Clayton, was a Republican, and that people shunned him. He owned the finest grocery store in town, and they still treated him like a second-class citizen. Some people wouldn't even do business with him, and I'm sure that was the Klan's doing.

"Burning crosses were frequently left in the black community when there were disturbances there. A black person in my neck of the woods had to keep his nose clean and watch his back, too. The law enforcement agencies were not as forceful as they needed to be, and Daddy would have wanted to protect his family. He would have seen Klan membership as the way to do it."

I remained perfectly still. *From personal experience, I knew the Knights of the Ku Klux Klan had been active in Johnston County as late as the mid-seventies. Every morning on my way to work in Smithfield, I had driven past a billboard located just past the Neuse River on highway 70, that read, 'Welcome to Klan Country.' That sign was not taken down until 1977, although it was no longer socially acceptable to belong to the Klan.* Uncle Legs interrupted my reverie.

"If I had been his age at that time, I would have been a member, too." There was no defense in my uncle's voice.

"But you weren't?"

"No. When I went off to Oak Ridge Military Institute, I went back to visit my family, of course, but I was never part of that environment again."

If you had stayed on the farm? I wondered to myself. I thought for a minute and then asked, "But what about when you were a company commander? Did you have black soldiers in your company and was this a problem?"

There was no hesitation. "It wasn't a problem at all. They were all men whose lives had been entrusted to me. Discrimination on the basis of race or religion would have had a demoralizing effect on my troops. I did not practice discrimination, nor would I have tolerated it if I had seen it. I would have busted some britches in short order. Actually, I think being in service helps people get past their prejudices. We all needed each other to survive. Lee Holstein, my mortarman, was Jewish, but he was very well respected among the men for his ability to take out his target when there was fire falling all around us."

He paused as though this thought had just occurred to him. "The Klan is almost as prejudiced against Jews as against blacks. You couldn't be a Jew and be a member of the Klan.

"Under the conditions of war, there just wasn't room for that kind of tension. It was always, 'Fine shooting, Lee!' and we patted him on the back each time he was successful. No one concerned themselves with his religion. Lee and I remain close friends."

I stood up and stretched. "I probably should be going now." The story about how he came to be known as "Legs" would have to wait until next time.

It was four o'clock. The sun was still high in the winter sky, but the shadows playing off the woods hinted at evening. I was looking forward to the drive home and some time to process this revelation in my family history.

I remembered that Sam Robertson, my uncle's childhood friend, had told me he thought it was funny that these grown men dressed up in sheets and marched in the Christmas parade. He and my uncle had stood on main street in Clayton and watched that parade. My grandfather had most likely been part of the procession.

"You knew exactly who they were," Sam had said, "because you knew how tall each man was and how he walked." It was hard to reconcile the man I knew as my grandfather, with active membership in the KKK.

I also wondered if Uncle Legs' sisters, Aunt Sulou and my mother, had been aware of their father's affiliation. I could not wait to ask my mother what she knew.

My uncle did not get up. "Mary Susan, I know what it feels like to be treated like a second-class citizen. My parents tried very hard to better themselves. Daddy hated farming, and he worked very hard to get away from the farm. But then there was the fire that nearly burned up Clayton and what you know as the Great Depression that sent us right back there. Those circumstances became a challenge for me. That's what I want to tell you about next time, and that's why I always try to see a person for who and what he is."

"So there was class in Clayton?" I asked.

"There was," he said, "and I was not high class." The pain of rejection passed like a shadow across his face, and I wondered if he, too, was seeing the little boy in overalls that I had just glimpsed.

I bent over to hug him goodbye. "Love you," I said.

He smiled. "Love you, too." I let myself out.

Falling Down and Getting Up as "Legs"

"I never carried an ugly girl to a dance."

—Lieutenant Colonel Lehman H. Johnson, Jr.

March was still cold that year, but the Saturday afternoon sun was warming the den where Uncle Legs and I had reconvened. The gas logs were back on pilot, and his lap robe hung over the back of his chair. Regret was budding in Uncle Legs' voice just as surely as the dogwoods around his house were preparing to flower.

"When it was time for me to go to high school, I fussed a bit because my parents did not make arrangements for me to go to Clayton High School. Mother's parents had made it possible for her to go, and that's where I wanted to go as well. There was a gym at Clayton, and all we had at Wilson's Mills High School was a dirt outdoor court. All I needed was transportation. But there was no money for that.

"I always wondered what kind of ball I could have played if I had gone to high school in Clayton."

Goodness, I thought. *Even you aren't immune from the "what ifs" that sometimes turn up like pebbles on our lives' paths. Even small stones are painful when the traveler walks over them again, remembering. Why haven't you already put regret in the pocket of those overalls your mother found so distasteful, and moved on?*

89

When he didn't continue, I prompted, "You said you were going to tell me how you got your nickname."

"It was winter when we played. Practice started in November, and we didn't finish up until February or March. Our uniforms were skimpy. The game shorts were what you'd call short shorts today, and out jerseys were sleeveless. I could see my breath sometimes. It was so cold before we started playing that I could feel my knees knocking together. I was glad for all kinds of reasons that I didn't sit on that wooden bench very much during the games.

"The court was as even as we could make it, but it was hard and unforgiving. We couldn't run as fast because dribbling the ball on dirt was slower than dribbling on a hardwood floor. The ball didn't return the same way. If it rained, we had to cancel the game sometimes. Depending on how much damage was done to the court, we played anyway. If you fell, chances were that you were going to get hurt.

"It was right there on that outdoor court in Wilson's Mills that I became 'Legs.' I had fallen down and skinned my knee during a game. There was black dirt on my knee and on my hands.

"Instead of asking to be taken out, I wrapped a handkerchief around my leg and kept going. There I was—a skinny thing, six feet, four and a half inches tall, running up and down a dirt court with my 'bandage' flapping around. The blood from my knee kept it stuck on.

"Somebody in the stands called out, 'Get it, Legs!' and the name stuck. We were outside, so he had to holler pretty loud for me to hear. Everybody else heard him, too. His voice was clear as a bell. I've been Legs ever since." He grinned and stretched his legs.

"I was a very big fish in a little pond. If I had gone to Clayton High School, my pond would have been a little bigger. Looking back though, I would have to say that it got bigger soon enough.

"I played center on the basketball team at Wilson's Mills, and it was no coincidence that the school won the state championship three times during my time there."

"Then it wasn't all bad?"

"Oh, no. Life was good. I just didn't know how good it was at the time. I got an athletic scholarship to Oak Ridge Military Institute out of that experience."

"Can you tell me more about your time in high school?"

"I remember my teachers. They were young, only about nineteen or twenty years old, and they had all been to what was known as ECTC —nearby East Carolina Teacher's College. They were all fired up, very idealistic, and ready to teach, although they were just getting used to the idea of being in authority. New shoes have to be broken in."

He chuckled. My uncle was not usually given to figurative language.

"I think my class changed some of these teachers' ways of instruction. Perhaps it was because there was not much difference in our ages. They talked to us like we were adults, and we were certainly not that.

"Teaching was a different profession then. My teachers lived in a teacherage about seventy-five yards from the school building. They lived there and took their meals together dormitory style. Appearances were important. It was expected that they would look and behave professionally and provide good examples of moral living for their students. They were always well-dressed and what we called 'spic and span.' We were expected to be the same.

"We were taught mainly by what you would call seminar now. They would tell us stories just to get us started. Sometimes, they would write a quote on the blackboard with chalk and ask for discussion—something like 'The only thing we have to fear is fear itself' (Franklin D. Roosevelt, 1933). That might be our history lesson for the day. Our opinions were always respected, and there was a good deal of give and take in our classes. We were a very outspoken group."

Imagine that, I thought when he grinned at me.

"I'm sure our female teachers wouldn't have called it dating, but the guys did. My teachers followed our high school basketball team, and we would all go out together after the games and get a Coca Cola, or maybe a milk shake, and rehash the highlights. Goldie Harris was my English teacher, and she once kissed me right on the mouth in front of everybody at an athletic awards assembly. Much later, after I had graduated from Oak Ridge, I walked all the way downtown to see her. By this time, she had married John Hocutt, my math teacher, but I still wanted her to see me in my military uniform."

"So you got out of the overalls?"

"I did. But before that, my social standing in Wilson's Mills improved considerably. Daddy was chairman of the school board, which meant that he could hire and fire teachers. That position got him into the limelight, and he liked that. I liked the fact that his position reflected on me."

The mood in the room had lifted, and a smile played across my uncle's face. The late afternoon sun was meeting the horizon and making peace with the approach of darkness. I waited for the closure that was coming.

"Those were very happy times for me. Everything was going my way, everything that is except my grades. I got along fine in history and civics, but otherwise I was not a good student academically. I could do the math, but I didn't like it. *The Canterbury Tales* was a waste of time." My uncle glanced at me to see how I took his assessment of Chaucer's greatest work. When I did not comment, he continued.

"Fortunately, neither my parents nor my teachers thought grades were the most important thing. Otherwise, I suppose today what we call my 'self-esteem' would have suffered. They weren't the least bit worried about my self-esteem. They were concerned about my conduct.

What mattered was being courteous and respectful to my teachers and how I got along. We call that 'social skills' now. In that area, if it had been graded, I would have gotten an A plus."

I understood. "You mean there was a connection between the way you presented yourself and the way you were. It was a lesson you learned at home and reinforced at school?" He nodded, so I asked, "Can you tell me something about your classmates?"

"There were thirteen people in my graduating class — eight boys and five girls, and my parents allowed me to associate with them all. Mother and Daddy did not involve themselves in my social life or put restrictions on me. I don't recall ever having a curfew. I do remember dating blue-eyed Margie Youngblood. She was my favorite girlfriend."

A shadow passed across his face. "I went to see her when she was in the hospital just before she died. Those blue eyes were still beautiful."

That day his memory was like a pail that had drawn up unintended debris when all he wanted was a cool, fresh drink. The taste of Margie's death was acrid.

He remembered others. "There was Ola Day Uzzle and Nancy Stevenson — both pretty girls in my graduating class. Then there was Francis Johnson. She married and still lives in the area. I dated her quite a bit, too." His eyes twinkled. He paused to see how I was taking the girl talk and looked sideways at me, bashful.

"A big date was going to the movies, attending a church social event, or maybe a dance. The dances were sponsored by the schools, Clayton High School and Wilson's Mills High School."

In today's terms, you would be a player, both on and off the court, I thought.

He leaned back in his chair and sighed with satisfaction. "I never carried an ugly girl to a dance." This time I laughed, and so did he.

"What about the other guys in your class?" I asked. "What do you remember about them?"

"Paul Otto stands out. He was the first child of German immigrants, and he was the smartest person in our class. His parents were farmers. Their farm was right next to ours, so I knew him and his family well. Paul could have gone off to any college on scholarship, but all he ever wanted to be was a farmer. He stayed right there, and the last I heard, he was still there.

"He never went off to war either. Me? I couldn't wait to go. At that time, you could get an exemption for certain types of jobs, and he was the oldest son of a farmer. I believe he applied for and was granted this exemption. The fact that his parents were German may have also played a part in his not being drafted.

"A few years back I was invited to a birthday party for Paul. I asked his daughter, who was giving the party, if her father had been happy. She replied that as far as she knew, her father had been very happy on the family farm, and that he did not regret his choice. Of the thirteen of us in that graduating class, no one dropped out, and five of us went off to continue our education. I don't think any of us felt limited by our circumstances or by finances as to college. Some of us wanted to go, and some of us wanted to stay.

"As for me, I had begun to see the world as a great, big place. My parents were very unselfish. Certainly, their life on the farm would have been easier with me there, but they did not encourage me to stay. In fact, we all left. I applied for and received a scholarship to Oak Ridge Military Institute, and they moved to Kenly."

"So everybody got a fresh start?"

"Everybody got a fresh start." He nodded in agreement. "I found that I was well suited, well prepared for military life, and then, of course, the war came along."

"Sometimes you make your luck. Sometimes you fall into it." He had said this before.

"What was it this time?"

"A happy combination of the two." He said this as if the answer to my question was obvious. Uncle Legs smiled at me tolerantly. "A happy combination of the two."

Before I could ask him to explain, the corners of his mouth tightened and he pressed his lips together. There would be no war stories that day.

Sweet Genevieve

She had been the queen of his spring
when the whole world bloomed just for him.

"I need to tell you about meeting your Aunt Genevieve. Do we have time before we go eat?"

Genevieve Wooten was his first wife and the mother of his four children. She had been the queen of his spring when the whole world bloomed just for him.

"We can go in the back door, as well as the front," I said, "just so we go in. It makes no difference to me. And according to you, I'm on your dime. I'm also on your time."

He smiled. "This is one for the book." His whole body relaxed.

"I was the officer on duty to receive visitors at Oak Ridge Military Institute when Genevieve walked in behind her parents and her brother Seth. They were bringing her brother back to school because he had gone AWOL, which he had done on a number of other occasions. It was a Sunday afternoon.

"I don't remember much about checking Seth Tyson Wooten back in, but I do remember the way Genevieve looked that day. I remember as if it were yesterday. She was wearing the prettiest navy-blue straw hat, a navy-blue lace dress, and black laced-up shoes. She was very fair skinned, with high cheek bones and dark hair. I couldn't take my eyes off of her. She looked like a little doll.

"Genevieve was very off-hand in her conversation with me, and of course her parents were right there giving Seth Tyson Wooten a good talking to. Pretty girls usually like a man in uniform, and I was hoping that would be the case this time. I couldn't tell whether Genevieve was interested in me or not, but somehow I managed to find out that she was a student at Greensboro College. After leaving 'little Seth' at Oak Ridge, her parents were going to take her there.

"That was all the information I needed. I called the school a few days later and found out which dorm she was in. Back then there was a phone for the dorm, not even each floor, and you went through the dorm mother to talk to one of the girls. I was so nervous when I called, but I was more than happy to jump through all the required hoops if Genevieve would see me. When she said she'd like to do that, I was over the moon.

"There was just one little problem. I had to work at Oak Ridge on the weekends and that was the only time Genevieve could have visitors. Even though I was on an athletic scholarship, I was required to wait on tables in the dining room during the weekends. That wasn't just to keep us humble. I had to earn my keep on and off the court. Somehow, I had to get that job covered."

"How did you do that?"

"I approached a friend of mine, whose parents were paying his way through school. When I told Bob Arey about this girl I had met and how much I wanted to see her on the weekends, he was sympathetic. Then I told him, 'We get all the desserts we want when we clean up.' That information closed the deal.

"'Sure!' he said.

Then the only obstacle to getting to see Genevieve was getting there. My uncle slapped his leg and held up his left foot. He put that one down and held up the right one. "Pat and Charlie served me well." Still sitting, he took a couple of steps in place.

"I didn't have a car, so to get to Greensboro from Oak Ridge, I walked some, hitchhiked some, and caught rides with other cadets. Then, of course, I had to get back. Oak Ridge is a few miles northwest of Greensboro. It was complicated, and, of course, I could never tell Genevieve exactly when I would be there. But she was patient and understanding about my situation. Looking back, I think she must have wanted to see me as bad as I wanted to see her—or she would have never waited for me like that.

"To begin with, Genevieve and I met in the parlor at GC, where the girls could entertain their dates. When one of us arrived, we checked in and the house mother would send for the girl, who would be waiting in her room. We all got the once over while we were waiting, and the visits were closely supervised.

"I distinctly remember that I had to leave that building promptly at 10:20. If we weren't gone by 10:30, the house mother reappeared and witnessed our good-byes. So, I left when I was supposed to, but I didn't always make the return trip to Oak Ridge by curfew. Between having to leave GC at a certain time and having to sign back in at Oak Ridge, the timing for our dates did not always work out. I can't tell you how many times I walked the quad for coming in late."

"Did it ever occur to you that maybe this girl wasn't worth it?"

"Never!"

My uncle leaned over and winked at me. "Candy wasn't even a twinkle in my eye then, but Bob's kindness sealed both our fates."

Candy is my first cousin, Uncle Legs' youngest child and his only daughter.

Jane breezed into the room. "Dinner time!" she announced.

"It is that," he said. "We've been to Oak Ridge, and I've worked up an appetite."

"If you don't mind," I said. "I'd like to go there again."

"Consider it done."

* * * * *

But when we had settled ourselves back in the den, we took a side road instead of going back to my uncle's college days.

"Bob and I had no contact during the time our children were growing up. I had not forgotten Bob's kindness. We just didn't get together, so imagine my surprise when Candy called and said that she was going to marry Robert Jackson Arey, Jr. As it turns out, my daughter and Bob's son had been dating for about a year and a half during the time they were both students at Lenoir Rhyne College. We didn't even know they were at the same college, and they were about to announce their engagement.

"Naturally, I went to see Mother in Kenly and share the good news. We sat there on the couch together in her living room and I told her, 'Mother, Candy is going to marry Robert Arey.' I was very proud and expected her to congratulate me. I waited.

"She said nothing. I waited some more. After making chitchat for a while, I got up and left. But it really bothered me that she hadn't commented or responded in any way.

"The next day I decided I would call her. 'Mother,' I said, 'aren't you happy that Candy is getting married?'

"There was dead silence on the other end of the line except for her breathing. Then she said, 'Don't you think he's a little old for her?'

"I busted out laughing. I laughed until my insides hurt. When I could talk, I said, 'Are you still there?'

"'I am.' That was all she said. Mother was always very dignified, very restrained.

"'It's the son, Mother! Candy is marrying the son, Robert Arey III, not Bob. Bob is my age.'

"'I know that. That's why I was concerned. Bob Arey is old enough to be her father. Besides, isn't he married? Why didn't you say it was his son? Why, that's wonderful!'

"Finally, I had gotten the reaction from Mother that I was hoping for." He leaned back and sighed.

"Would it have been difficult for you if Candy had decided to marry someone your Mother didn't like?" I asked.

He nodded emphatically. "Most definitely. Mother remembered Bob and had met him when were both at Oak Ridge. She just didn't think he would make a good husband for her granddaughter because of the difference in their ages."

"I'm guessing she would have made no secret of how she felt about the matter."

"That is correct."

He paused, and I thought we were about to take another detour. That was all right with me. The side trips were as interesting as the main ones.

Instead, my uncle concluded. "When Bob stepped up for me in the dining room, he sealed the future of our families. The son Bob would have, would later marry my daughter."

Launching from Oak Ridge Military Institute

"I do remember that I had to sit out a
semester on account of my grades."

—Lieutenant Colonel Lehman H. Johnson, Jr.

We were seated at the Blue Ribbon for Sunday lunch. The shiny chrome tables and bright blue and white tiles were reminiscent of the 50's. There in that jukebox atmosphere, Uncle Legs, Jane, and I would go still further back in time, back to Oak Ridge Military Institute, 1935, just as I had hoped. The crooning of Bobby Darin was an ever-present counterpoint to a more distant past, and my uncle picked up his story thread there.

"When I got my first semester average from Oak Ridge, I had flunked everything except history. My parents looked over my failing grades at Christmas but didn't say much."

"So, then what happened?"

"After I had been home for a few days, Mother asked, 'What do you think you should do about this?'

"My answer was, 'Change curriculums.' I had already made up my own mind about that."

"Your parents didn't tell you what to do, or make any suggestions?"

"They did not. It was up to me to solve my own problems. I do remember that I had to sit out a semester on account of my grades."

"Do you remember anything about your professors at Oak Ridge?"

"I do. The faculty members there at Oak Ridge were, for the most part, military men who had been given honorary commissions to teach. They may not have been the most qualified in their fields, but they knew how to get young men to do as they were told. There was definitely no talking in class while they were teaching. You spoke only to them, if you spoke at all.

"They were all good, solid people, but a few stand out in my mind. I remember Captain Stough, my history teacher, for the remark he made in class about Hitler. All of my professors had strong political opinions and voiced them, but Captain Stough was exceptional in that way. 'That man Hitler is not worth saving. Somebody ought to kill him!' he had said. Hitler had not yet invaded Western Europe—just Poland.

"There was Captain Prince, or Prim and Proper Prince, as we called him. His classroom was the cleanest one in the school. We were required to police his classroom—to straighten up and clean up before we left. If we didn't have a work ethic, we acquired one before we left Oak Ridge.

"The school president, Col E. (Earle) P. Holt, was a frugal man who set a good example for us. He ran that school on a shoestring. Not one to delegate, he also measured all incoming cadets for their military uniforms. I still remember Col. Holt stretching that tape measure across my shoulders, down my arms and legs, and making notes of his calculations.

"I wore that uniform day and night, but I didn't mind. After all, it was Leonard's Oak Ridge uniform that had impressed me in the first place and got me interested in Oak Ridge." He stopped eating for a moment, and his eyes took on that dreamy, faraway quality that signaled that we were about to take a side road.

"Leonard always had his uniform on when he stepped off the train in Clayton. I wonder now if that was for effect, or if he wore it because he didn't have any other traveling clothes. He had work clothes for the hardware store, just like me, when he waited on customers. I didn't think about that then. Anyway, I was proud to wear the same uniform as my dad's younger brother." The haze in Uncle Legs' eyes suddenly cleared, and we were on the main road again. He cleared his throat and took a long, deliberate drink from the sweet ice tea that had just been refreshed by our waiter.

There was a click behind us and the record changed. Our background music became Glenn Miller's "Chattanooga Choo Choo" because someone had fed another quarter into the juke box. Uncle Legs paused at the sound and then thumped the table for emphasis. "Besides being president and attending to his administrative duties, Col. Holt did double duty as the school's baseball coach.

"'Your Uncle Leonard was one of my best baseball players,' Col Holt told me, when he tightened that tape measure around my waist."

Patting his ironing board flat stomach, Uncle Legs said to Jane and me, "That measurement is larger now than it was then." She smiled.

"I didn't know it at the time, but I was storing up another lesson about motivation, about leadership. I was already motivated but, of course, then I was on fire. If Leonard had been one of Col. Holt's best baseball players, then I would be among his best basketball players.

"My basketball uniform was another uniform at Oak Ridge that I was pleased to wear. I made All-State Center, and Lee Boddie, a teammate, made All-State Guard. It's fair to say that because of the two of us, we won the Junior College Championship two years in a row. I was so proud I thought I would bust my buttons."

"Is there anybody else in particular that stands out in your mind from your time at Oak Ridge?"

"Yes, there is. Mrs. Royster was the dietician there, and I worked under her and her kitchen staff as a server, dishwasher, and anything else they wanted me to do. Besides all that, I carried a full load of classes. Being on an athletic scholarship at Oak Ridge didn't mean I got a free ride.

"It seemed like everyone there who was playing a sport was on this same kind of scholarship, and nobody thought anything about it. The kitchen staff was all black, and like me, the ten or twelve boys who took orders from them were white."

"Did you have a problem with that?" I studied his face for any sign of a mismatch between the words and his thoughts. He answered without hesitation.

"No, I did not. We were expected to work. I understood that.

"Major R. P. Larkins, Commandant of the Cadets, was another important person in my life at the time. He was in charge of discipline. Trials were held every Monday morning, and he presided over these. I was present on more than one occasion.

"'How do you plead?' Major Larkin would always ask. 'Guilty or Not Guilty?'

"Sometimes a cadet, myself included, would answer, 'Not Guilty, Sir!'

"He would reply, 'I am the commandant, and I say you are guilty. That is my privilege.' One time he restricted me to campus for six weeks for coming back late too often from seeing Genevieve."

"Did that change anything between you and Aunt Genevieve?"

"It did not. I just got a little more cautious about how I got back into the barracks. The fact that I had no money for dates and that her parents did not approve didn't stop us from seeing each other either. Her parents wanted Genevieve to finish college, and I think they would have liked for her to marry someone who would have been more likely to settle close to their home. As a parent, I understand that now, but I didn't like it at the time."

"Is there anything else that you'd like to say about this period in your life?"

"Just that life was good. Basketball was good. Grades were not, and it seemed that grades were more important in college than they had been in high school. But I also learned that they were not the most important thing. I learned how to conduct myself at Oak Ridge, how to take orders, how to give them." He laughed.

"I did graduate though," he added, bending over the check to calculate a tip, "so I suppose that made me a little more acceptable." He straightened and squared his shoulders, hooking his cane over an arm. "I graduated from Oak Ridge in 1939 as a Second Lieutenant in the Reserves."

At the door, he grinned and issued an order. "Home, Jane!" She went out before him to get the car.

"And then what?" I asked.

He caught my eye and winked, but ignored the question.

Memory is selective and colored by the pages one chooses to turn. Some chapters in a person's life are significant. Others are not. My mother, his baby sister, remembered a semester when her brother had been sent home as an upperclassman for hazing. She recalled that their parents sent him up north to live with relatives and to work during the semester that he was expelled. This incident was not mentioned during our interviews.

Things happen and a person makes a conscious choice not to be influenced by them. Some events are repressed and simply forgotten. I did not know which applied here, so I left it alone with the dog-eared page of memory folded to mark the spot.

Courtship and Marriage

"Since we were both of age, we could make our own decision."

—Lieutenant Colonel Lehman H. Johnson, Jr.

"With Genevieve, I think I might have either broken a tradition or started one," Uncle Legs began, glancing toward the bedroom where Jane had taken his sport coat. She was out of earshot. We were home and had taken up our posts. He squinted and shaded his eyes from the glare of the lingering winter sun that crept in between the blinds, like a guest as reluctant to leave as myself.

"Jane is an ordained lay speaker for the Methodist Church, and she teaches the couples' class every Sunday. That's why she spends so much time down there preparing and studying." There was admiration in his voice, and affection in his glance for the woman who now shared his life.

Jane drew the blinds, and then left us to our work.

Uncle Legs and Jane had played on golf courses all over the world. A picture of the two of them on a golf course in Hilo, one of the Hawaiian Islands, hung beside the door to the kitchen. They were a handsome couple, Jane, slim and dark haired, twelve years my uncle's junior, and Uncle Legs, trim and fit, with the ease of a natural athlete, even in his early 70s, as he took his swing. There had been many exotic vacations. By the time we began our interviews, he and Jane had been to Hawaii eight times. But there was still something that pricked at his pride and left it wrinkled and deflated even now because he had not been able to afford dates with Genevieve. He did not want Jane to see that.

My uncle shifted uncomfortably in his chair and looked out somewhere beyond me, so he could say it. "I remember when Genevieve said she wanted to go to the premiere of *Gone with the Wind* at the Carolina Theatre in Greensboro. It was a once-in-a-lifetime experience, and everybody she knew was going. Tickets were seventy-five cents apiece. I didn't get much of an allowance."

He sighed. "Actually, I didn't get any allowance. I had no money, and it hurt me to have to tell her that." The fragility of the moment was a thin, crystal bubble. One tap and it would have burst, its shards piercing and painful. I let it float between us.

Uncle Legs swallowed hard and looked directly at me. "I can still remember how she looked at me." He spoke when he was ready, or when he could. "She said that was all right, that she had some money. Her parents were well-off, and they sent Genevieve spending money on a regular basis.

"I told her, 'I don't much like the idea of my date paying my way, but I'll go with you to see it.' We went on a Saturday night, and I can tell you now that I was country come to town. That theater was the most beautiful building I'd ever seen. It was all green and gold and red on the inside and when you looked up, you could see clouds projected on the ceiling. It looked like some kind of Greek temple, and I was there with a goddess.

"I think we broke ground as far as the way things were done back then." He laughed, and the lines around his mouth relaxed. A smile played across his lips, and his eyes took on that dreamy quality they always had when he talked about Genevieve.

"In spite of my limited financial resources, mine and Genevieve's relationship continued throughout the rest of my time at Oak Ridge. I graduated and went to work at Hanes Hosiery in Winston Salem, along with my basketball buddy, Lee Boddie. We worked on the line together making socks and played Industrial League basketball for the company. We weren't just 'lint heads.' We were stars on the Hanes Hosiery Basketball Team.

"It was good competition, and I was making $75 a week—the equivalent of $150 to $200 a week today. One week of that went for my room and board. The rest went for clothes and incidentals, like dating. Lee and I bought a car together to get back and forth to work and for just getting around. It was nice not to have to thumb to see Genevieve.

"The world was a great big place to me back then, and I felt good about taking on the responsibilities of being dependent on myself. I was happy and enjoying life. Dad's perspective was more 'down the road.' What he said to me about my situation was, 'Don't let that be the only place you work.' It wasn't.

"I had already begun to see that there were no opportunities for advancement with Hanes Hosiery. Given the opportunities that presented themselves in the military, it seemed logical to look at the armed services as a possible career path. Having graduated from Oak Ridge, I had an Army reserve commission, which meant that I could be called up for deployment at any time. Things were heating up in Europe, so with Genevieve's blessing, I applied for active duty status. It was all downhill after that." He smiled his satisfaction and continued.

"My transition to active service was a fast turnaround. Because there was a need, a bill was pushed through Congress that allowed reserve officers who were accepted to come on active duty as second lieutenants for one year. Those who survived would be reevaluated. It was my intention to get that chance.

"I got in, along with Lloyd Hanes, whose family owned Hanes

Hosiery. He and I were the only two from the area who got accepted with two years of college. The rest who made it had four-year degrees.

"Once I received my active duty status, the Army promptly sent me to Fort Benning, Georgia for training, making our courtship a little more difficult. By this time, Genevieve was in summer school at Wake Forest University in Winston Salem to pick up some extra credits and, of course, to be close to me.

"But that all changed with my new status. We saw each other as often as we could. When I had leave, I would sign out to go to Winston Salem, and she would sign out of the dormitory for the weekend. She would always tell one of her classmates where she was going, but not her parents because they might have interfered. By this time, Lee had purchased my half of our car, and I could afford my own." He shifted slightly in his chair and crossed and uncrossed his legs.

"You see, Mary Susan, Mr. and Mrs. Wooten were very concerned about our relationship, and they gave me the impression that they did not approve of me. It wasn't that they didn't like me personally; they weren't so sure about their daughter marrying a military man.

"Mr. Wooten had been wounded in World War I, and he knew that many of the men who came back were changed mentally as well as physically by the experience. Shell shocked was what he called it. They were the walking wounded. Others were missing arms or legs. Many did not come back. It was the waiting and the uncertainty of what might happen that they did not want for Genevieve.

"Her parents might have had reservations, but not Genevieve." He shook his head. "She was not afraid to join me in the military, even knowing that her life would be very different. We both knew we were going to get married. We just didn't know when or how. We hadn't figured that out just yet. In the meantime, we met at Mom and Pop (Kite) Russell's house in Winston Salem on the weekends every chance we got. Lee Boddie and I had lived with them when we were playing basketball for Hanes Hosiery, and they were very accommodating. Genevieve slept upstairs, and I was downstairs on the couch.

"The Russells understood about young people in love. For much of the day they would go out and leave us alone in the house. We courted on that same couch. It was a wonderful time, but both of us knew it couldn't last."

My uncle paused and pulled the afghan from the back of his chair. He took a long time arranging it and getting comfortable beneath it.

You are wrapping yourself up in her memory, I thought. He stretched his legs and kicked his feet out from under the cover.

Then he continued, "There was an intensity about life and love that I experienced immediately before World War II, during the actual combat, and after the war was over. Those of us who were part of the armed services knew we were going into combat sooner or later, and we wanted to get married and have children, in case we didn't make it back. We felt like we needed to grab on to life and hold on to it while we could. Those men who were not married before they left were very eager to get married when they came home. There was an urgency to have someone you could count on, who would be there for you, what-ever changed in the outside world.

"Genevieve and I were married on June 8, 1940. My family, as well as hers, did not want us to get married before I got out of the military. Had we actually done that, we would have had a long wait." The sun shone from the sky of his eyes, and he gazed at me with amusement.

"I'm guessing that delay would have meant that I would be short four cousins," I said.

"Yes." The cloudy expression that played across my uncle's face was half smile, half frown. "Her parents and mine assumed I would do a tour of duty and then get out, maybe go back to the farm. They ex-pressed their views on separate occasions to us both." He shook his head. "In fact, I didn't get out of the military until 1962, when I retired with 22 years of service.

"I don't believe either Genevieve or myself could have waited that long." His eyes twinkled. "For my part, I needed to know that she would be there for me when I got back from the war. Marriage was a solemn promise. I could lead men and fight for my country because I knew I would be protecting mine and Genevieve's family and our home.

"We knew how both our families felt about the situation, but we also knew how we felt. It wasn't a question of if I would be deployed. It was when. We didn't want to be separated before we got married. Since we were both of age, we could make our own decision.

"I thought it would be best if we crossed the state line since the marriage would be registered in the state where it took place. We didn't want any commotion. Clarksville, Virginia was a good-sized city, and not too far away from Genevieve. I knew of other men who had gone there to marry their sweethearts.

"We got to the courthouse after hours. The door to the office of the justice of the peace was locked. I knocked but no one came. When another couple came out, we went in. I asked the man if he would be willing to do one more that night. He said that he would be happy to marry us. His wife volunteered to be our only witness, the same as she had been for the couple before us.

"The only other thing I remember about our wedding is that I wore my uniform. I don't remember what Genevieve wore. She had already packed her clothes for the trip, so there was no need to go back to Winston Salem. Our honeymoon was on the road.

"The next day we drove to Cusseta, Georgia, a little town close to Fort Benning, where I had no trouble renting an apartment. I hadn't done that before I left, but people in the community were more than happy to rent to servicemen, especially if they were married. It was considered a very patriotic thing to do. People who had extra space in

their homes or who owned property listed it on post. Rents were stan-
dardized by the Army based on the square footage of the apartment.
For $25 a month, at military rate, Genevieve and I had all the space
we needed.

"I suppose we were cramped with just a bedroom and a kitchen,
but we certainly didn't know it." My uncle settled back in his chair and
sighed deeply, his chin propped in his hand as he retreated into the
memory of what had been safe harbor in a sea of uncertainty.

"How long did you get to be newlyweds?" I asked, drawing him
back in.

His focus was immediate and intense. "Not long. Not long at all,"
he said. "On July 5, 1940, I was commissioned a member of the 22nd
Infantry, 1st Battalion, 4th Division. I began training immediately
there at Fort Benning. The plan was to graduate seventy-five lieutenants from every class. Heavy losses were anticipated because these men,
and I was one of them, would be the first to have contact with the
enemy. Life got serious pretty quick."

"So at what point did Genevieve tell her parents about the fact that
she was married and no longer attending summer school?" I asked.

Uncle Legs ran a hand through his hair, everything about him bris-
tling. He paused before answering. "You know I don't really remember
too much about all that. I had too many other things to worry about. I
just remember that Genevieve didn't want to worry them any more than
necessary and that she did tell Mr. and Mrs. Wooten we were married.
She spared me their reaction, so I don't know what they said to her.

"At their insistence, however, we did go back to North Carolina
that same summer. While we were there, her parents saw to it that we
had a proper wedding ceremony at their home in Stantonsburg. It was
quite a gala affair, with all of our families and as many neighbors and
friends as the Wootens could assemble. Genevieve wore a beautiful
white dress, and I wore a white suit.

"We were married in the living room where Genevieve could make an entrance. There were candelabras and flower arrangements done by a local florist, and we were married by the Wooten's minister. Her father gave her away, and never even hinted that this ceremony was a repeat. If my parents suspected, they didn't say anything. I don't believe any of the guests, the minister, or my sister Mary, who played for the wedding, were aware of the fact that we were already married.

"This time Mr. Wooten gave me the impression that he was proud to have a son-in-law who was a second lieutenant in the U.S. Army." Uncle Legs sighed with satisfaction. "I could tell by the way he introduced me."

"How did that make you feel?" I asked. It was time for me to leave, but I wanted to know if the memory that had washed over us both today had rinsed away any lingering sense of inferiority or wounded pride.

My uncle took a deep breath and then exhaled. He frowned, considering my question, and then squared his shoulders. His hands were open and outstretched between us. "I had yet to prove myself, but I was committed to a cause that everybody believed in — the defense of democracy and the United States of America. There was a tremendous outpouring of national and community support for anyone in uniform, and it felt really good to be a part of that.

"I was out of overalls, but I never forgot that I had been in them. There were certain things I had learned during that period in my life that I would need to remember." He stood up and drew himself up to his full height, his crew cut so sharp it looked like it might cut your fingers if you touched it. He was every inch the military man. I did not touch him at all in that moment, nor did he reach out to me. The tide of Genevieve's memory had pulled him out from the present shore.

All had been told that would be told that day. Outside it was as though a shade had been drawn across the horizon. It was dark, and I could not see the moon from inside the den.

"Next time we talk about the war?" I rose to go and leaned over to brush his cheek. He stiffened and then relaxed. I was as eager to hear those stories as the little boy who had demanded one at Mebane United Methodist Church.

"Maybe."

I left him in his chair staring straight ahead. My uncle was not ready for the war stories.

The Bombing of Pearl Harbor

"I got the news just like everybody else."

—Lieutenant Colonel Lehman H. Johnson, Jr.

My uncle raised his hand in greeting but did not get up when I entered the den.

He began speaking before I could sit down.

"Do you remember where you were when John F. Kennedy was shot?"

I nodded.

"What about when Martin Luther King was assassinated?"

"Yes."

"Then I know you remember where you were when the World Trade Center was hit by terrorists."

"Definitely."

"It was the same for me when Pearl Harbor was bombed. I can remember exactly what I was doing and where I was when I heard the news. The memory is just as fresh as if it had happened yesterday." Uncle Legs inhaled deeply as if he were out of breath. He was looking at me intently.

We had skipped the family preliminaries this first Saturday in April and launched right into the event that preceded all his other war stories.

"I got the news like everybody else. On that day, December 7, 1941, Genevieve and I were having lunch in Greenville, Alabama, with Dad's brother, Leonard, his wife Emily, and Mother. Mother had come for a visit with me and Genevieve. We had driven over from Cusseta, Georgia, to spend the weekend with them and catch up on the news back home.

"We had missed that closeness since our marriage. Our family support came from the twenty-five or thirty military couples who rented apartments and rooms in that little community just southeast of Fort Benning, Georgia. On this occasion, it was very good to spend time with relatives.

"We were all seated at a table with a red-checkered tablecloth. The diner wasn't crowed so we could easily hear a radio playing big band music in the background. We had finished our meal and because it was a special occasion, we had ordered desserts. Our waitress had just brought them out. There we were, talking among ourselves about the most trivial things back home when the music suddenly stopped. An announcer blasted out, 'We're interrupting this program to tell you that Pearl Harbor is being bombed!'

"I will never forget the gravelly sound of that man's voice. I had a fork in my hand, and I remember laying it on the table. We all stopped eating, and I stood up. Genevieve also got up from her chair and moved to stand beside me. She knew what this meant. I don't remember how Emily and Leonard looked, but I can see my mother's face and remember how all the color drained out of it. She was as shocked as if someone had thrown a glass of cold water at her.

"Looking down at them, I said, 'Folks, sorry I can't stay for dessert. I need to report back to my unit.' Funny how certain details stand out in your mind, even if what you are remembering is way back in the past. I was eating a piece of lemon meringue pie. That pie, as well as the other desserts, was left on the table."

You prepared your whole life for this moment, I thought. *There had been the fire in Clayton that taught you how single events can change everything in just a moment. Your resilience had risen from the ashes. It would rise again and soar.*

"Just before we left the restaurant, I do recall politely saying, 'It's been nice visiting with y'all, but we'll have to go. I have to get my bag packed. We'll be moving out in seventy-two hours.' Mother rode with us this time. Now looking back, I think she didn't want to be separated from me although she was in the back seat. There was very little conversation on the way back to Leonard and Emily's house.

"Genevieve cried a little, but she did it privately, when we went back into the bedroom where we had slept the night before. Mother did not cry. She just sat there in Emily and Leonard's den, but I remember being very aware of her feelings.

"It's odd how memories layer themselves, but at the time this happened I could see my mother crying when our tobacco barn at Powhatan burned down. Someone, either me or Daddy, had forgotten to turn the heat down, and the barn had caught fire." Uncle Legs glanced over at me. "She had put her apron over her face, so we couldn't see, and cried like a baby. Like we didn't know. Her shoulders were heaving, and we could hear her sobbing. This was after we had done everything we could to save the barn. Maybe it was the expression on her face, a river of lines without tears that triggered that memory. I knew she would cry later.

"On this occasion, both the women in my life composed themselves, at least outwardly. I was grateful. They knew I had all I could handle, so they did their best not to add anything to the burden I was carrying. Genevieve came back into the den and said, 'We've got to go and get Legs packed.' Already she was too much of an Army wife to let the shock of my impending deployment, and our separation, carry over into her family." He tilted his chin out proudly. My uncle was a young second lieutenant again with bright blue eyes that were suddenly lit with excitement.

Events don't diminish in importance until people stop telling the stories they associate with them. Uncle Legs and I would talk about the bombing of Pearl Harbor for the last time on January 21, 2006, shortly after his 90th birthday. But today this recollection needed to be nailed down, not left flapping around like a loose shingle, dislodging others that were adjacent to it.

"Do you remember what you were thinking at the time?" I asked.

The fire behind his eyes dimmed, but he answered easily and without hesitation. "My thoughts centered on my family, more so than on what I would be facing. How soon would I have to leave and go into combat? Where was Genevieve going to live while I was gone? I was anxious to get some answers, but there weren't any. There wouldn't be any explanations for some time."

Uncle Legs narrowed his eyes and then looked my way. He did that when I got too close to the flame of memory and asked questions that singed. This time he did me the kindness of answering my question about how he felt before I asked it. "The stress level for all of us was very high, but as for myself, I have never had that same feeling before or since, thank goodness. I left many times after that. But to leave your family for the first time—that was something."

He breathed deeply, closed his eyes, and exhaled slowly through pursed lips. His shoulders sagged beneath the afghan which had been pulled up to his chin. I waited to see if he wanted to say more. He didn't.

Like any story, this one was a living thing each time it was told, and I expected that parts of it would be painful. I had heard it before. He and his family were eating lemon pie in one version, when they heard the announcement that Pearl Harbor had been bombed, pecan in another. The essential truth of the event, however, never changed.

"Are you tired?" I asked. His eyes flew open.

"Yes, and hungry."

"It's 1700," I observed.

He smiled his appreciation that I was remembering we marked our pace in military time. "Supper time!"

"It is that," I replied. "I'm ready when you are."

"I'm always on alert for meals. I think I shall have pie tonight, if they have it at Huey's."

"Lemon or pecan this time?"

He smiled broadly. "Pecan, I think." He stood up from the chair too quickly and then steadied himself with the cane. "Where's Jane? Let's go."

Preparations and Delays

"They were training while they were sleeping."

—Lieutenant Colonel Lehman H. Johnson, Jr.

"The word *War* was out there, like an explosion." Uncle Legs picked up the story even before he picked up his fork at Huey's.

Our waitress smiled knowingly and left menus at our booth—always the same seat if possible—last one on the right at the back, so that my uncle faced the wall with Jane and me on the other side, looking out over the whole restaurant.

"After the announcement that Pearl Harbor was being bombed, I dropped Mama and Genevieve off at our apartment in Cusseta and reported to my unit at Fort Benning. The men of Company B were preparing themselves to go overseas, and I got in line with the rest. The first thing we had to do was get our shots. The nurses were moving down the line on both sides, vaccinating us in the most efficient way possible. We got shots in both arms at the same time.

"I remember that while I was waiting, the man in front of me, Lieutenant Hawkins, fainted and fell flat on his face when he got popped. He was a very large man, and I can still hear the smack of his head hitting the floor. He wasn't the only one to faint, and no one made a move to catch him. To this day I don't know why. The medics came and

125

put him on a stretcher. I don't know what happened to him either." My uncle shook his head.

"My unit followed Standard Operating Procedures for our preparations. 'Men, get your rifle clean if you need to and be ready with your bag and baggage,' our commanders told us. We were to be ready to deploy in twenty-four hours. Within that time frame, there were three inspections done to make sure each man had what he needed: a rifle, a bayonet, and a GI pack, which included a change of clothes, toiletries, and an extra pair of boots."

"What happened to Granny Johnson and Aunt Genevieve?" I asked.

"When Genevieve's parents got the news that I was deploying, they insisted that she come home to Stantonsburg while I was gone. As soon as Genevieve could pack, she and Mama were going back to North Carolina."

"How did you feel about that?"

"Of course, it was not a good feeling to suddenly be separated from Genevieve, but I was grateful. We had two families to love and support us. They understood I would have to go where the Army sent me. I didn't have to worry about Genevieve and our unborn child. I could concentrate on preparing for combat." He paused when the waitress brought our food.

"Washington, D.C. was in such an uproar. Orders were written, rewritten, and then cancelled because of the way things were developing over in Europe. In three days' time, both Germany and Italy, as Japan's allies, declared war against the United States. Our military was reeling, and we were all fouled up in Washington.

"As fast as possible, we loaded ten men and their equipment onto each truck for the ride to Savannah, Georgia. It felt good to be moving, and I was ready for whatever came next. Within the next four days, we should have cleared Fort Benning. In three more days, the entire

Fourth Division would have been on the ships." He leaned back in his chair and sighed.

"We thought we were going to Aruba, an island in the West Indies to protect the French fleet that was in the harbor there. That was the plan. At least that's what we were told."

My uncle shook his head. The knife in his hand clattered against the plate. "Abruptly, we were told that our orders were cancelled. I called Genevieve and Mama at the apartment, and they came and brought me back there.

"The first unit had already gotten to Savannah, but there were no troop ships there to transport the men. Apparently, the word had passed more efficiently through the Navy than it did through the Army, so they didn't send any ships. We weren't going to Aruba.

"Anyway, the group that had left came back, and the rest of us never got on the trucks or the ships. We just sat there and went back to our training duties at Fort Benning in preparation for going overseas."

"How did you react to what happened?"

"It wasn't so much what happened, as what didn't happen. We knew we were going to go somewhere because we were one of the top ten units trained to go into combat. We were expecting to be one of the first infantry divisions to enter the war, so we were frustrated. Waiting for new orders was hard. The 12th Regiment, Washington's finest, had been sent down to join the rest of the division at Fort Benning. That meant there were more of us waiting—and we didn't know what we were waiting for. My men were demoralized by the change in plans. Like myself, they were anxious to prove themselves."

He signaled to our waitress. "Check, please." His face flushed, and his eyes blazed with passion. Then he smiled at me.

"Personally, I was very annoyed at the delay. I was more than ready to go. As a young Army officer, I was feeling all those good things that a soldier experiences who has been trained for combat. I wanted to see what I could do and how I would fight." My uncle bent his head to sign the check.

At that moment, he reminded me of a racehorse being held at the starting gate, even as he stood unsteadily to balance himself against the booth. *A thoroughbred*, I thought.

In the car he was silent. I could see only that he was staring straight ahead, as though he were wearing blinders. We turned onto Cook's Mill Road, in front of the garage with the sign out front, 'Closed On Sundays'—as though that fact was somehow unusual in Mebane. Everything, except restaurants, grocery stores, and churches, was closed on Sundays.

In the den my uncle leaned back in his chair and sighed. He took a sip from the glass of red wine that Jane had left on the tray beside him.

"I should have been gone. I was ready to go. Instead, I was given the job of training others. The order to set up a cadre finally came down about the 9th or 10th of December. Orders always come down." He smiled and pointed to the floor with his right thumb.

"It had been approximately three days since the bombing of Pearl Harbor, and I had been sitting on go. It was a relief to know what I would be doing, at least for a while. We, that is the cadre, were to receive orientation at Fort Benning and then go on to Fort Meade, Maryland, where I would assume my first command. In May of 1942, I left for Fort Meade, where I would serve as Commander of Company L, 417th Infantry Regiment, 76th Division."

"What about Aunt Genevieve?" I asked.

"She stayed with me until I left. Then she went home to her family in Stantonsburg until I could find a place where we could live together close to the post. That place turned out to be Glenn Burnie, a little town just outside of Fort Mead.

"We were not alone. Almost overnight Glenn Burnie became a boom town from the sudden influx of men and their families. The family-owned grocery stores and businesses like Law Bros. Hardware welcomed the sudden growth in population. If you wanted to go to the Ritchie Drive-in Movie Theatre, you needed to get there early.

"Genevieve joined me just in time to celebrate my promotion from first lieutenant to captain at a big party that was held at the Emerson Hotel in Baltimore, Maryland." He chuckled and glanced sideways at me. "I think we need to save that one for after church tomorrow."

"I'll look forward to it. The training," I prompted. "You said you were training men to go off to war."

"Yes. I had the best job in the Army, being a company commander." My uncle sat up straight and squared his shoulders. The greatest reward that any career officer ever has is the privilege of training his men to go into combat and then seeing them be successful. It's an awesome responsibility—but an honor to have that responsibility."

"How old were you and how old were the men you trained?"

"I was twenty-six years old at the time and most of the men that I trained were nineteen and a half to twenty years old. I got them before they had really spread their wings. Many of them had not left home yet. Some of them had never left their home state, and now they were in the Army preparing to fight a war.

"I made it clear and simple. We would do things a certain way in order to survive. I also made sure they were aware that even if they did these things, they might still be killed. Those are very sobering thoughts when you are that young."

"Did you lose many?"

He paused and I waited. Death. Always death on the doorstep, waiting to come in uninvited without knocking. I remembered one of the questions my uncle had raised earlier. 'Why am I still here?' I thought now I knew the answer. You need to tell this story while you can still remember it, and I need to hear it. He did not invite death in to have a seat between us. Not yet. My question remained unanswered.

"One of my areas of responsibility was called Basic Infantry Training, which is the discipline and marching of soldiers. I also taught them to take care of their equipment and to have it ready with an hour's notice.

"Col. Jake Zellars, my commanding officer, told us that we were a mobile unit and advised us to prepare accordingly. 'Mobility,' he said, 'is my middle name. If the bugle blows at one o'clock in the morning, you be ready to go by two. If it blows at two, your men should be prepared to go by three.'

"We were what you call a full-field pack, so that when we were alerted, our packs were already rolled and ready to go. All we really had to do was throw them on our backs, sling our rifles over our shoulders, and move out. Col. Zellars knew what he was talking about because we were awakened by that bugle more than once in the middle of the night."

"How long was the training before the men you were training shipped out?"

"Approximately three months elapsed between the time of enlistment and when their boots were on the ground."

I stared. "I want to be sure I understand. Do you mean that these men had only twelve weeks of training before they were fighting a war?"

"Not necessarily. The men I trained received six to eight weeks of intensive combat training. At that point, they were considered to be combat ready." He grinned.

"Actually, we finished up within five to six weeks because seriously, they were training while they were sleeping." Then he yawned and stretched.

"Speaking of sleeping, I'm ready." My uncle stood up and swayed back and forth like one of the loblolly pines in the woods surrounding his home, its root system weakened by age and disease, in danger of falling although there was no storm. The wind caught up pieces of debris from the yard outside our view and threw them against the window.

Uncle Legs looked down at me and regained his balance by resting his right hand on the arm of his chair. "How about if we turn in, and continue tomorrow after lunch?" He was already shuffling off down the hall toward his bedroom.

Had he stayed, I might have asked him, "How on earth can you train while you are sleeping?" But that possibility was closed to me as surely as the door to inquiry had been slammed shut when we approached the casualties among his men.

For now, Uncle Legs closed his bedroom door firmly behind him. He needed to dream the dreams of old men, dreams of contentment and accomplishment. There would be a time to awaken the nightmares of his losses, but it was not then.

A Warm Welcome to Mebane
United Methodist Church

"Everybody doesn't get that kind of introduction.
I think I was the first, and I know I was the last.

—Lieutenant Colonel Lehman H. Johnson, Jr.

"Do you mind driving today?" Uncle Legs asked me the next morning when I came downstairs. My uncle was seated at the table already drinking coffee, and fully dressed for church. Jane had gone on to choir practice.

"Of course," I answered, joining him at the table. "We'll take my car."

"Oh, no," he replied, casually buttering a piece of toast. "I want you to drive the Jag."

I set my own coffee cup down hard. The Jaguar was sitting in the garage shining like a new penny in some loafers. It was a 2003 XJB, a standard four door sedan.

"Jane's son Warren even washes the engine," he confided, as we finished breakfast. "I pay him, of course, but he does such a good job. He washes that car every two weeks whether it needs it or not. Warren and I have a special relationship."

Once in the garage, Uncle Legs lowered himself in on the passenger's side. He was alert as I drove, scanning the road as it came up before us. We were on our way to Mebane United Methodist Church on 4th Street, the church where he and Jane were members.

The drive gave me pause to think. I knew my Uncle Legs had been a Methodist long before he and Jane met. In fact, he and my Aunt Genevieve had been founding members of Benson Memorial Methodist Church in Raleigh. My cousin Candy had been married in Benson Memorial, and my Aunt Genevieve's funeral had been preached in that church. I remembered her death on April 29, 1982—lung cancer the family said. My uncle had been miserable in the year following Genevieve's death. When he visited, I heard talk about the "casserole ladies," who were paying regular calls. But he wasn't interested.

It was this church connection that provided the introduction to Jane Hook. At the time of their meeting, Jane was an active member of Mebane United Methodist Church and NC President of the United Methodist Women. She had been married to a prominent dentist in Mebane and had been a widow for about five years. Jane's pastor, the Reverend Willie Teague, had once been Legs' pastor at Benson Memorial. They had remained close. He knew Jane well and thought she and Uncle Legs would enjoy each other's company, so he "introduced" Jane to Legs by giving her a book about the history of Benson Memorial Church. Uncle Legs' name was mentioned in that book.

Their first meeting took place at a United Methodist Conference in 1983, at Methodist College in Fayetteville. The Reverend Teague had told Uncle Legs that besides being a devoted Methodist lay person, Jane was also an avid golfer.

According to Uncle Legs' account, "I looked her up and asked her to play golf with me the next day. She didn't let me win. In fact, she beat me! I thought I was a pretty good golfer and then she went and beat me on our first date. I remember thinking at the time that she could have gone a little easy on me." It would always be that way between them.

I was turning into the church parking lot. "What do you do while you are waiting for choir practice to end and Sunday School to begin?"

"I sit in the hall outside my class and talk to anybody who comes by." He turned his head toward me and smiled. "This morning I get to talk to you."

"Did I ever tell you about the welcome I got when I joined Mebane United Methodist Church?"

"You have not."

"I had a room at Willie Teague's house during our weekend visits. I would come in and Willie T. would say, 'Your room is ready, Legs.' I would go to church with Jane on those Sundays."

* * * * * *

I remembered Jane's account of Uncle Legs' proposal. On one of the rare occasions when she and I were alone, she had told me how it happened.

"Legs was going to the Philippines in October of 1984, for the anniversary celebration of the invasion of Leyte."

From my research, I knew that the Battle of Leyte began on Oct. 20, 1944, when 100, 000 American soldiers landed on the island. My Uncle Legs had been among them. It had been the bloodiest battle of the war, but it had also been the beginning of the end for the Japanese. That much the history books could tell me. But I didn't know his story, and I certainly didn't know the details of his proposal to Jane.

"The grandson of General George Pearson, Legs' commanding officer, had a grant to do a documentary on the Battle of Leyte. The grandson had told General Pearson that he could invite a guest. That one guest was Legs.

"They were to retrace the tour that General Pearson and Legs had taken there during WWII. Legs was coming back through Hawaii and wanted to stay and play some golf. Before he left, he asked me to meet him there, at the Fort DeRussy Hotel, an Army installation where soldiers were sometimes sent for Rest and Relaxation.

"At first, I told him that I wouldn't come.

"'Why not?' he asked.

"I remember I said, 'Because I'm from Prospect Hill! That's not the way we do things in my neck of the woods.' I just didn't think it would be right.

"But when I talked Legs' invitation over with my pastor, Willie T, he said, 'Jane, you are a fool. You need to go.' I presented the proposed trip to my children, and they agreed with Willie T.—that it was okay.

"Before I left, I was up late watching the news. I saw a bulletin flash across the screen that said there had been a fire at the hotel in Manila, where Legs and General Pearson were staying. Two Americans were dead, and five more were missing.

"I went for about 24 hours not knowing whether he was alive or dead. The phone lines were jammed, and people didn't have cell phones like they do now. I just sat beside the phone and grabbed it every time it rang. I can't tell you how many times I was disappointed. I was so afraid that I had lost him.

"When Legs did finally get through, he explained that both he and General Pearson had safely evacuated the hotel. 'Thank God, you're alive' was all I could say.

"After I joined him, Legs and I traveled all over the islands playing golf, although he actually proposed in Maui. Legs had had my diamond shipped to the hotel where we were staying so that it would be there when we were. It was around Christmas time, and he gave me that diamond ring and a fur coat.

"I was flabbergasted. 'I can't accept until I talk to my children,' I said. I did just that when we got home. Once again, they gave us their blessing.

"Legs isn't the only one who has been lucky twice," Jane had said.

* * * * *

I had found a parking place right in front of the fellowship hall convenient to the entrance closest to Uncle Legs' Sunday School class. We both relaxed in the soft early morning light coming through the windshield.

"When did the two of you get married?"

"I married Jane Hook in this very church on October 19, 1985. Willie Teague married us. Since I was used to moving and Jane was not, we would live in her home in Mebane. Three of her four children were close by.

"Mebane United Methodist Church would become my church home, and these people would be my church family." He raised his right hand and gestured toward the building.

"Shortly after we were married, I requested membership by transfer from Benson Memorial. I was voted in at the end of the service. Then, as is customary in the Methodist Church, I was invited to the front of the church by the lay leader to be presented to the congregation.

"Jane happened to be the lay leader at the time. She made a little speech about me, like she would have for any new member. She told something about my background and the areas where I had previously served in the Methodist Church.

"Anyway, when she finished with the preliminaries, Jane said, "I have the privilege and honor of presenting the newest member of Mebane United Methodist Church—my husband, Lt. Col. L. H. Johnson, Jr. But you can call him Legs.'

"Then she turned to me. 'I want to be the very first to welcome him.' She kissed me, and it wasn't just a little peck. Jane planted a big juicy one on me, right there in front of God and everybody."

"You mean she kissed you on the mouth?"

"You could say that. Yes."

Sitting beside him, I could see that my uncle was grinning from ear to ear. *My grandmother, your mother, would have said, 'you are grinning like a possum right now,'* I thought.

We got out of the car and walked toward the church together. Even though he was hitting the sidewalk every other step with the end of his cane, there was a spring in his step. I had to work at keeping up with him. Tugging at his sleeve, I said, "That seems to have happened to you more than once."

"Ah," he said, obviously pleased that I had remembered. "You are good at connections."

"I'm getting better, and I'm learning from the master." I noticed a web shining in the shrubbery that bordered the church. When we got closer, I could see the spider. *Memory is never an isolated incident,* I thought. *It busies itself spinning and connecting until it makes enough threads to span the space between the beginning and the end.*

"I'm guessing everybody who joins this church doesn't get welcomed like that?" I said.

"No." He smiled and held the side door of the church for me to go in ahead of him. "Everybody doesn't get that kind of introduction. I think I was the first, and I know I was the last."

That you are, I thought and looked up at him. "As your own mother would have said, 'God broke the mold when He made you.'"

He smiled his appreciation. If it is possible for a man walking with a cane to swagger, my uncle swaggered down the hall. We entered his Sunday School classroom and prepared ourselves for the morning lesson.

It was on pride.

Kicking Ass and Saving Face

"We were not supposed to hit enlisted men."

—Lieutenant Colonel Lehman H. Johnson, Jr.

"Pride goeth before a fall." The man who had taken Uncle Legs' place as Sunday School teacher of the men's class opened his lesson by asking if we were familiar with this reference.

Uncle Legs and I sat on the back row in straight back chairs facing the front of the men's classroom. Jane referred to this class as the older men's class. The median age was probably 75, and in his early 90s, Uncle Legs was no doubt the senior member. If not, he was the senior member still able to come.

"Pride goes before destruction, a haughty spirit before a fall," the teacher intoned. "That's the translation from the Life Application Study Bible (Proverbs 16:18). Can anyone in here give an example from your own life or from someone else's that illustrates this verse?" The silence in the room hung like an unrung bell in a church steeple.

"I can." My uncle's voice rang out. "But I suppose I helped this young man along with his fall. I don't think that's exactly what Solomon had in mind, but I'll tell you the story anyway, if you like."

My uncle looked around and sized up his audience. The other men turned around to be sure to hear. "We were not supposed to hit enlisted men. You see, I was an officer, a newly promoted officer at that, and it would have been most inappropriate for me to be fighting with a man who might serve under me. Why I could have lost my promotion right then and there.

"Here's what happened. But before I get started, I need to say that I was not sorry for my part in this, and I am not sorry today.

"It was August 11, 1942, and Col. Jake Zellars had just pinned on our silver captain's bars at Fort Meade, Maryland—we referred to them as railroad tracks. Col. Zellars was one of the finest commanders I have ever known in my life, anywhere, any way. When we stood before him, he had spoken to each one of us individually when he presented us with our bars. It cemented our relationship and was an example I was to follow many times when I promoted my own men.

"After the ceremony, we, that is all the newly christened captains, had been invited, along with our wives and girlfriends, to a big party over at the Emerson Hotel in Baltimore.

"The party was quite a gala affair, and the Emerson Hotel provided us with a very grand setting. The ballroom was two floors and was divided by a staircase that looked like a fly landing on the wood banister would have slid all the way down. The food and various beverages were upstairs, so even though people were milling around below, most everybody was eating and drinking up there.

"My friend and fellow officer, Dave Franson and his wife Doris were with me and Genevieve. Anyway, we all had been enjoying the drinks that were available at the open bar, so at some point in the evening, it became necessary for us to go downstairs. There was no bathroom on the second floor.

"Dave and I were on our way down, and these enlisted men were on their way up. They had also been enjoying the drink and were probably on their way to enjoy some more. They could hardly make it up the stairs.

"As they passed us, one of them asked, 'Where did you pick those girls up?'

"Another one leaned into me. 'Are there any more like them?'

"By this time Genevieve and Doris were looking down at us over the railing, and we had attracted an audience both upstairs and down. It's useless to reason with a drunk, but I couldn't help myself. 'Those "girls" are our wives,' I said, lowering my voice. I took him by the collar.

"He responded, 'Are you really married to them?'

"I did not hesitate. I spun him around, so that he was facing the crowd that had gathered below us. Then I planted my size fourteen shoe right in his butt and kicked him all the way down the steps. Dave was right behind me with the other one.

"I suppose, looking back on the situation, that our conduct was unbecoming as officers and gentlemen. Ordinarily I would never have done such a thing. But when they carried their disrespect into our families, I couldn't help myself. The alcohol that both Dave and I had consumed had nothing to do with our reaction. Neither he nor I could take that kind of talk, especially around the wives in the company. Most of us were married."

Uncle Legs glanced sideways at me to see how I was taking his story. "There was no real harm done. Those enlisted men got their feelings hurt, but other than that, nobody got hurt. We were not tried or charged in any way.

"The rest of the night was uneventful. Those guys did not come up the steps any-more, and Dave and I were able to go to the bathroom without being interrupted. Maybe they had learned their lesson, or maybe they were afraid of us. Dave was about 6'2" and weighed 210 lbs. I was 6 feet, four and a half inches tall and 190 lbs.

"Our wives were quite disturbed about the incident, but the other guys from our regiment didn't feel that way. Fortunately, they had not joined us in the ruckus, but they did stand off to the side and applaud just a little bit, so as not to attract too much attention to themselves. After it was all over, they slapped us on our backs and congratulated us on a job well done. They were very proud that we had saved face and upheld the reputation of our ladies."

The buzzer that ended Sunday school sounded in the hall. The men in the class applauded and stood to shake my uncle's hand. He sat straight up in his chair and grinned.

"We've certainly had our lesson on pride, and a fall to boot." Our teacher beamed. "Thank you, Legs."

Uncle Legs and I left last. "Did I mention that Genevieve was pregnant at the time?"

I took his arm. "No, you did not. I hadn't made that connection."

"She was very pregnant, if there is such a thing. Lee was born less than a week after that party."

"Did that make a difference in the way you felt about the situation?"

My uncle was still thinking about that one when we took our seats on his usual pew, third row, an aisle seat for him, on the right-hand side. He never answered. Instead, he leaned over and said, quietly, "Col. Zellars was nowhere around when this little incident occurred. If he was still there, he did not make his presence known. That was something else I learned from him. Just because you see and hear something doesn't mean you have to call attention to it."

Memory tied that knot and picked up a needle with a different colored thread to work the incident into the pattern of his thoughts. Jane opened the service by playing the prelude, and the congregation became silent. For the Doxology, I stood with them while Uncle Legs remained seated. "Praise God from whom all blessings flow," we sang.

My uncle pulled my sleeve. I leaned down to hear him. I was close enough to smell his Old Spice aftershave. He whispered, "Remind me to tell you about Lee being born. Definitely a blessing, but it was without a doubt the most traumatic experience of my entire life."

I stared down at him. I hadn't heard any of the real war stories yet, the ones that people usually asked about, those he didn't talk about—like the story little Bobby had wanted to hear on another Sunday, the one about executing Nazi war criminals. But childbirth, the most traumatic experience of his life?

"I will certainly remind you." I patted his shoulder. It felt thin and sharp underneath his sport coat.

Delegating Authority

"Lee was born that night, and his birth was, without a doubt, the most traumatic event of my life."

—Lieutenant Colonel Lehman H. Johnson, Jr.

Over lunch, my uncle sawed away at his chicken and then finally put down his fork and knife. "Fingers were made before forks," he said, using an expression I had heard often from my grandfather, but not my grandmother. From her I had learned which fork to use when, as I imagine my uncle had also. Between bites on his fried chicken leg, Uncle Legs told me why he no longer taught his Sunday school class. Jane already knew.

He looked directly at me. "One Sunday I had gotten dressed and eaten the breakfast Jane always leaves me. I sat down in my chair to read the paper. It wasn't quite time to go, so I was just killing time. Instead of leaving like I was supposed to, somehow I nodded off. I slept all the way through Sunday school! That was when I decided I needed to step down." He shook his head. "I could imagine those men just sitting there waiting for me the whole time. They didn't want me to resign, but I felt like it was time. I still go to the class though."

Jane nodded. "The class I teach is a couples' class, and Legs always takes part when we do projects and go on trips. But he wanted to stay in his same Sunday school class. I understand that, of course."

I understood that as well. My uncle was a man's man, and he felt comfortable expressing his convictions among men. Jane was a strong spiritual leader in her own right. While there were some differences of opinion between them, I never heard either of them express any resentment about those differences.

The story of what Uncle Legs referred to as the most traumatic event of his life was saved until Uncle Legs and I were alone in the den. We never spoke of it, his privacy about Genevieve, but those stories were always reserved for the time I had alone with my uncle. Jane had disappeared into her basement office to catch up on some correspondence.

"I keep a picture of Genevieve in my desk back there," he began. He got up abruptly and disappeared down the hall to his bedroom. He returned at a trot, as though energized by the thought of her. "Genevieve gave this to me shortly after we met." He eased himself back down in the chair and studied the wallet-size photo of his first wife for a moment before he passed it to me.

"She was beautiful, and Candy looks a lot like her," I said as I handed the photo back.

My uncle crossed his feet at the ankles and stretched his legs out to reach the footstool that was always in front of his chair. "I remember the births of each one of my children, but Lee being born was, without a doubt, the most traumatic event of my entire life." He waved a hand toward the wall behind the couch, where there were pictures of each of his four children when they were young.

"I remember Lee's birth like it was yesterday," he began. "I had taken Genevieve home to Stantonsburg right after that promotion party I told you about. The hospital on post wasn't accepting births, and Genevieve didn't want to go to the local hospital where she didn't know anybody. She was in Stantonsburg, waiting, nine months pregnant, with her parents. I went back to my post.

"The baby was due that next weekend, and I had a three-day pass. The Atlantic Coast Line came right into Wilson, so I caught a train out of Fort Meade, Maryland, on Friday night. Genevieve and Mr. and Mrs. Wooten met me at the station.

"After dinner, I was tired from the training and the travel. We had trained especially hard during the week. Genevieve and I went to bed early. That was the last I knew of anything until the next morning when Mr. Wooten came into the room. 'I think we had better go to the hospital,' he said loudly. He had switched on the light. I cracked my eyes open and turned over. My father-in-law was standing over me.

"My arm went where Genevieve should have been. I realized that she was not beside me. I was fully awake now, and I jumped out of bed. 'Where's Genevieve?' I asked.

"'She started having some pains during the night, and when she got up, her water broke,' Mr. Wooten said. 'Nancy and I took her to the hospital. We decided to let you sleep. Nancy is with her now.' He was very matter of fact in telling me this.

"At the time, I wondered exactly who made that decision, and I was very grumbly about the whole situation on the way to the hospital. It wasn't very pleasant—to have them take my wife off to the hospital to have a baby and leave me lying in bed." My uncle cleared his throat and uncrossed and crossed his legs.

Watching him, I thought, *A rankle is still a rankle. Even when the thorn of resentment has long been removed, and the wound healed over, it can fester. Whatever sliver of emotion might be left is refreshed by the rain of recollection.*

"Anyway, we found the room and Genevieve, with her mother. Genevieve was in the early stages of labor. The room was very white and Genevieve, looking very pale herself, was lying back on her pillow.

Everything was quiet and peaceful. I pulled up a chair, sat down beside her, and took her hand. Then Genevieve had her first really sharp labor pain, and I remember how hard she squeezed my hand. Then more contractions followed, and she started screaming. I had to leave the room.

"On my way out, I said to Nancy, 'You'll have to take care of this.' I was some kind of upset, and there was nothing whatsoever I could do about what was happening.

"I remember hearing my mother-in-law say, 'I will take care of my daughter!' as the door swung shut behind me. Those screams followed me down the hall and into the waiting room, where there were other, equally miserable men." He exhaled as though he was exhausted.

I smiled at his agitation. *That lasts a long time, too,* I said to myself. "Why do you think you were so—what's the word—unhinged?" I asked when he paused.

"That's an easy one." His eyes met mine. "I like to be the person in charge. I was not in control there, and there was nothing I could do about the pain Genevieve was going through." His mouth curled up in a half smile, and then he cleared his throat, the sound like the noise a cat makes when you rub its fur the wrong way.

"There are different ways to be in charge. I had already learned that in the military. Sometimes you have to delegate authority, and it was very clear to me that was the only thing I could do here.

"Lee was born that night, August 16, 1942, and his birth was, without a doubt, the most traumatic event of my entire life. I was so afraid that I would lose Genevieve and I knew I was going to have to leave her—I just didn't know when."

The mid-afternoon sun streaming through the blinds created a pattern of lattices that did not connect on the rug. If you looked just right through the angle of the slats, you got a panoramic view of the wooded landscape that surrounded the house. He stood and adjusted the blinds, so that only a little light from the mid-afternoon sun filtered in.

Turning back to me, he said, "Do you mind if we take a break right now? I want to say more about this, but I need to rest for a few minutes."

"Of course," I replied.

He went to the kitchen and I heard the squeak of the cabinet door. When he returned, my uncle had poured himself a goblet of red wine. For a moment he hesitated. Then instead of sitting down like I expected, he returned to the window. With his free hand, Uncle Legs shut out the outside light of the dying sun. His movement was slow and deliberate as he pulled the cord that would finish closing the blinds.

My uncle would never speak of some of these things again. I had wanted the night to steal in on us together as he closed the door on the first time he realized he could not always protect those he loved. But that was not to be. Some occurrences, childbirth being one, are solitary. He was alone even now in his thoughts, as he had been then.

"Do you want something?" Uncle Legs asked as he eased himself back into the chair. He had forgotten to ask me while he was up.

"I'll get it," I replied. He covered himself with the afghan on the back of his chair and sipped from his glass with satisfaction.

When I returned with my diet Coke, his eyes were closed, and the glass he had drained was resting on the metal table beside him.

I already knew that birthing babies was something that women did in his generation. For a husband to have been in the hospital room when his child was born would have been the exception. My uncle was prepared to fight a war and to die, if necessary, but he was not prepared to stand by while the woman who was the centerpiece of his life experienced discomfort of any sort, much less the extreme physical pain of childbirth.

While he napped, I remembered Uncle Legs had told me that each time he returned to Stantonsburg to collect his family, his in-laws rolled out the red carpet. Each homecoming had been celebrated with a "tipsy cake," a dessert his mother-in-law knew was a favorite. But on this occasion, the birth of his first born, my uncle felt that his in-laws had gone "a bit overboard" to exclude him when they left him sleeping and took Genevieve to the hospital themselves. Perhaps since they knew that their son-in-law was going off to war, they were already stepping up to fill that place in their daughter's life. But I knew my uncle didn't see things that way.

Suddenly, his eyelids fluttered, and he began speaking as though he had not slept. "When we slept out in the open, I always rested on my left side because I'm right-handed, and I needed for that hand to be free." He held up his right hand. "Even an instant can make a difference in whether you live or die."

Then he looked over my head at the baby pictures. "Lee's birth convinced me that the mother has the right to name that child anything she wants. I was, of course, gratified that she chose to name our first child after me."

Uncle Legs massaged his left shoulder. "Of course, I didn't want to leave Genevieve and our son. I had no idea when or if I would ever see them again, but I was fortunate in that I was able to be there for Lee's birth. I had what was called VOCO—leave by Verbal Order of the Commanding Officer. That was how I was able to be in Stantonsburg for the weekend. When Genevieve had the baby, I just called up the adjutant officer from my regiment and asked for more time. He put me on special leave for a week.

"Two days after Lee's birth, I got a telegram from Sgt. Anderson, my first sergeant back at Camp Mackall. The telegram was copied from the morning report.

"It read, 'One additional soldier added to our roster, and he brings our number to 189. We welcome Private Johnson and put him on the rolls of Company L, the 423 Regiment.'" My uncle raised his chin and smiled. "At the time, I was the Company Commander for Company L.

I felt quite proud that my Sergeant had thought to do this, and I was pleased that he had sent a copy of the report to my family. Adding the new baby's name to the company roster is an old Army custom. It's like a birth announcement.

"This was a very special time for all of us. Mother and Daddy knew that I was about to go off to war. I was the oldest Johnson child, their only son, and Lee was the first grandchild for both the Wooten and Johnson families. He could carry on the family name in the event that no more sons were born.

"Because of Lee's birth, I also learned something new about how the Army functions and how close-knit the units were to members of the various companies. I returned to my company at the end of the week.

"Genevieve stayed down in Wilson until she was able to travel. Then Mr. and Mrs. Wooten brought her and the baby up to join me. I knew they wanted to find out what kind of housing conditions I was providing for their daughter and their first grandchild.

"They needn't have worried. The new apartment I had rented was in a two-story house. We had the upstairs, which consisted of a larger bedroom than in our first apartment and a bath. We also had the use of the kitchen facilities. The lady who owned the house wasn't there much, so privacy wasn't an issue. I think I paid $35 a month, $10 more than for the apartment we had as newlyweds, but it was worth it for the extra space.

"Anyway, when Mama and Papa Wooten brought Genevieve and the baby up, they were very pleased with our accommodations. Genevieve and I settled in although we didn't know how long our being together would last. One thing we did know though. When I was away, Genevieve would always go home to her parents in Stantonsburg. Anything else would have been unthinkable."

There was no shadow now on the carpet, and it was dark outside.

It was considerably later than my usual departure time. I stood before him and over him. "It's time for me to go," I said and lightly brushed his forehead with a kiss.

"Yes."

"Are we going to war next time?"

"We are."

"Thank you for letting me go there."

"Thank you for coming." He reached up to give me a hug.

I leaned down to accept it. His arms around my shoulders were firm. There were none of the tremors of old men. Then he let go.

Jump Training

"That is the most beautiful sight in the world—seeing that white canopy when you have just jumped out of an airplane."

—Lieutenant Colonel Lehman H. Johnson, Jr.

The dogwoods had already bloomed out for spring by the time I returned to my uncle's home in mid-May. The foliage was thick, and the dogwoods were so close together that I could not see the house until I was right in front of it. Getting out of the car, I remembered the dogwood trees in my grandmother's yard. When I was a child, she had explained the symbolism. The dogwood flower is shaped like the cross on which Jesus died as a living sacrifice for our sins. The redbuds with their heart-shaped leaves that stood out in contrast to the dogwood's purity, in brilliant relief against the darkness of the woods, meant something as well. According to legend, Judas hanged himself on a redbud tree, so remorseful was he that he had betrayed his Lord.

There are absolutes in that story. There were absolutes in my uncle's personal sacrifices. I wondered if we would talk about those.

Uncle Legs was waiting for me in the den. He took a deep breath and began without preliminaries: "I think I already told you that we were in New Guinea for approximately five months of training. We landed and made camp there on May 29, 1944."

153

I nodded.

"Our engineers did the best they could to create conditions that would duplicate what we expected to meet in real action. At our parachute training center, they built a pierced plank runway where the planes could take off and allow us to get high enough in the air to jump. The local 'fuzzy wuzzies' assisted in clearing out the coconut trees. The area where we practiced was surrounded by the jungle."

"Did you say *fuzzy wuzzies?*" I asked.

"Yes," he nodded. "We called them that because they took turns picking the lice off of each other's hair." I stared, but he took no notice and went right on with his story.

"Like many other officers, I got my paratrooper training in New Guinea. I was among the many 'volunteers' for the New Guinea branch of the division jump school. General Joseph Swing, who was my commanding officer, wanted to qualify as many men as possible as paratroopers. We got extra pay."

"Can you tell me something about what that was like?"

"Once the plane was in the air, the procedure that we followed was to stand up, hook up, and examine the equipment of the man in front of you. You checked his chute, and someone behind you checked yours. A green light over the door meant that all was clear, and it was your turn to jump. As one man jumped, another one got in position, and the next man got lined up and followed him.

"Most of the men leaned out of the door to the airplane and jumped up, but I had to jump out. The door of a C-47 airplane is 44 inches high, and I was a good 76 inches tall. If I had jumped straight up, my pack would have hit the top of the door, and I would have tumbled out, off balance."

"Did that ever happen?" I pressed.

"No. There was one time when I landed on a rock that was on the runway. It wasn't supposed to be there, but I landed with such force that I split all the leather bootlaces on my left foot. I was laid up for a week, propped up on a blanket—we didn't have pillows—and soaking my foot. Fortunately, Dr. Bob Robinson's tent was right next to mine, and he took care of me. My foot was not broken, just badly bruised.

"The biggest problem from that little incident was that I was now down to one pair of boots. I wore a size 14, so extras for me were not easy to come by."

This afternoon he was wearing bedroom slippers, and he slipped off the left one and flexed his arch. "This foot reminds me of that event, especially when it rains.

"Anyway, I did my five qualifying jumps in just two weeks, along with the other twenty men on my stick. 'A stick' was those who were training and jumping together. I got my parachute badge on August 18, 1944." He sighed with satisfaction and held up a glass shadow box that had been propped up on the other side of his chair. "That's it," he said proudly. He pointed to a silver badge with feathery wings curving inward toward an open parachute.

Handing the box over to me, my uncle continued. "There is no experience like jumping out of an airplane. When you stand at the door, you are 1200 to 1500 feet in the air. It's like being on top of the world because of what you can see below. Then you step out into space, into nothing, and fall at 75 feet per second." His lips curved with obvious delight, and his clear blue eyes were bright with the adrenaline rush. His glance toward me was brief, but intense.

"I can't imagine," I said. He laughed at the effect of his words.

"That's a treasure." I handed the shadow box back to him. "Were there any other incidents?"

When he did not answer, I rephrased my question. "While you were in training, were there any deaths or near-misses?"

He gazed at me thoughtfully. "Yes. One of each. Mine was a near-miss, obviously." He glanced up at a black and white photograph that hung on the wall behind his chair. "That's not me, but it could have been me." The billowing white parachute was the most prominent feature in the picture. The descending soldier was so small as to not be recognizable.

"That is the most beautiful sight in the world—seeing that white canopy when you have just jumped out of an airplane. After you are out and descending, the first thing you do is look up to see if your chute is completely deployed. That's what you hope to see." He gestured toward the picture. "But from another angle, of course.

"Once after I had jumped during training, I looked up and discovered that instead of looking at my open chute and the blue sky above, I was seeing the ground, and it was coming toward me. My feet had somehow gotten tangled in the lines of my parachute, and I was hanging upside down and falling. I remember telling myself, 'Keep your cool, Johnson. Keep your cool.' I knew I had just a few seconds to reach up, untangle my feet, and pull the cord. Obviously, I was successful." The grin that slid across his face was a lightning bolt that struck and was soon gone.

I examined the carpet and did not ask the obvious question about the other instance—the one that didn't end this way. He stared straight ahead. His eyes were like empty buckets, dry as though he had already poured out all the emotion.

"I recall only one fatal accident in all of the training sessions. Private Johnny Youngblood's parachute didn't open. I still remember his name although I do not recall the names of many others. For some reason Johnny's parachute didn't deploy properly. We heard him screaming all the way down. The rest of us were all still in the plane, so I don't recall hearing any sound when he hit the ground, except that the screaming stopped."

"What happened then?" I asked.

"Training was suspended for that day, but nobody turned in his boots. We just sucked it up, tightened our belts, and jumped again.

"I had nothing to fear except how being afraid might cause me to react." Uncle Legs' hands gripped the arms of his chair, and his knuckles were white. "In order to lead my men and accomplish our mission, I had to move past that feeling. That's not to say I was never afraid, because I was."

My uncle had been seventeen in 1933, the year that President Roosevelt had said to our nation, "We have nothing to fear but fear itself." He had lived that charge before it was made, when finances forced his family back to the farm. He lived it as a commander, and he was living it during our interviews. Uncle Legs did not comment further. Instead, he took his handkerchief out of his pocket and passed it across his forehead.

He sat up at attention and squared his shoulders, causing the cane that stood by his chair as though guarding it, to fall clattering to the floor. The handkerchief was balled up and clenched in his right hand.

Memory could be tight fisted, holding the storyteller in her grip until the stories were told and retold, until finally providing a release. My uncle was old, and he knew that he was old. But he was fearless, even now as he faced his own mortality.

It wasn't the first time he and death had met.

Chilling in New Guinea

"Life takes on a certain intensity when you are faced with the prospect of dying."

—Lieutenant Colonel Lehman H. Johnson, Jr.

That night at Huey's, Uncle Legs ordered unsweetened ice tea. He raised his glass in a toast to Jane and me. "Not my drink of choice. But I guess you could say it has chosen me."

My uncle set the glass down carefully on a paper coaster. His hand trembled slightly, enough to cause the tea to slosh over the top. Watching him, I thought, *even you are not indestructible, Uncle Legs. Time has a way of overtaking the most nimble runner, and you're no longer trying to outrun him. That's why you wanted me to come now.*

My uncle sipped his tea and frowned. "We drank beer in New Guinea. At least once a week, we sent a C-47 all the way to Australia to get it. I would say that we trained hard and that we drank hard, but that would be only partly true. We were issued only three cans of beer for every man each week.

"Still the beer was government issued and there was no distinction made according to rank or position. Everybody got the same ration. We got cigarettes, too, but I always gave mine away since I did not smoke. The beer I drank. In fact, I don't remember anyone giving up his share.

159

"The beer parties that we had were the highlight of the week. I don't recall anyone abstaining, and I don't recall anyone getting drunk or trying to take more than his share. Everybody joined in, including Ed Dunn, our Catholic Chaplain, and Jim Mormon, our Baptist chaplain. I didn't know that Baptists drank, but as I've already said, there were no distinctions made or taken after a hard week of training in the jungle.

"Temperatures climbed as high as 107 degrees Fahrenheit, so we had to be really creative to get the beer cold. Our favorite method was to put the beer in a huge marmite can, stick it in a P-51, and have one of the pilots take the can up to 20,000 feet. That particular plane was capable of rapid assents and descents. Ice crystals formed on the marmite can chilling the beer on the way up, and the pilot came down fast enough so that our beer was still cold when he landed.

"The rest of us would, of course, be waiting on the ground. During that time, we shared training stories and simply enjoyed each other's company. Although rank is emphasized in the military, there are certain situations when it doesn't matter. These experiences create bonds between people that have nothing to do with rank, position, creed, or color. Some are very serious and some are not. This one was not.

"More ice, please," my uncle said to the waitress, "and another glass of tea."

No rations here, I thought. Plenty of ice.

* * * * *

Back in the den, my uncle sipped his single glass of red wine, the one he allowed himself every night before bedtime.

"More doctor's orders," he said. This time he smiled over his glass, and his hand was steady. "Do we have time for another story?" he asked.

"I am definitely up for it, if you are."

"Good. I've got this one on my mind, and I want to make sure I give you an accurate version of how I tried to create a sense of commitment and community among my men. The beer parties that we had were not the only way that happened."

I nodded, knowing that the well of his memory was deep here, and that the water would come without priming on my part. My uncle would draw it up.

He set the wine glass down with finality on top of the tray that was always by his chair. Then he laced his fingers together in his lap and stretched his legs out over the ottoman. Relaxed, he crossed his legs at the ankles and began.

"While we were in training in New Guinea and before we saw combat, I had the natives to build us a chapel. I wanted to encourage the spiritual preparation of my men for what I knew they would be facing. On numerous occasions in my life, even before the military, I had been less fearful because I was prepared to meet my maker. I wanted my men, all in my company, to have that same opportunity.

"Our chaplains took care of the chapel's design." He looked sideways at me and smiled; the humor spread slow and smooth across his face. "I've already told you that we had two chaplains and no rabbi. Protestants and Catholics worship differently, but it's amazing how denominationalism disappears under certain conditions. Our seats were made out of bamboo poles, and there was never any complaint about somebody taking somebody else's pew or sitting in somebody else's place. If there was ever any controversy about the design of the chapel, or anything else for that matter, I didn't hear about it, from either Jim or Ed."

"How large was the chapel?" I asked.

"It would easily hold fifty to seventy-five men, depending on how close they sat together. The roof was thatched with jungle grasses that we threw up over some bamboo poles. Otherwise, it was open air."

"Did the chaplains hold joint services?"

"No. They took turns. This opportunity was also preparation for our chaplains, neither of whom had ever served in this capacity on the battlefield. Attendance, of course, was optional, but I remember that the chapel was always filled by Protestants and Catholics alike during our services. Lee Holstein, who was Jewish, attended as well. I don't recall that anybody was particular about who was preaching. Jim and Ed alternated Sundays, but that didn't matter. The sermon topics were always about urgent matters."

"Urgent matters?"

The fingers that had been relaxed were laced together. Then with a brief nod, my uncle brought his hands to his chin in a position of prayer and bowed his head over them although his eyes were still open and watchful. He was silent for a moment. When he looked up, his eyes locked with mine.

"Life and death and how you meet them. How you live with uncertainty. How you live and perhaps prepare to die when you are away from everything that is familiar and everyone you love."

Uncle Legs paused and rested his hands on the arms of his chair. He sighed and relaxed into the leather. "When you are going about your daily business under ordinary circumstances, you have the feeling that you can dismiss death. Of course you can't, but you have that illusion, so, for the most part, you are not afraid. When you are preparing for combat, that illusion explodes in your face like a grenade.

"I wanted my men to know how to protect themselves spiritually, as well as physically. Somebody in our regiment used that chapel every day for prayer and meditation. Life takes on a certain intensity when you are faced with the prospect of dying."

Uncle Legs laced his fingers together behind his head this time and leaned back. He closed his eyes, and I was silent. I was not sure if he was praying or dozing. Our session was over.

You have no illusions, I thought, *and you are neither afraid of death nor resigned to it.* I kissed him lightly on the forehead and went up the stairs to bed. The house was quiet, except for the sound of his deep, even breathing.

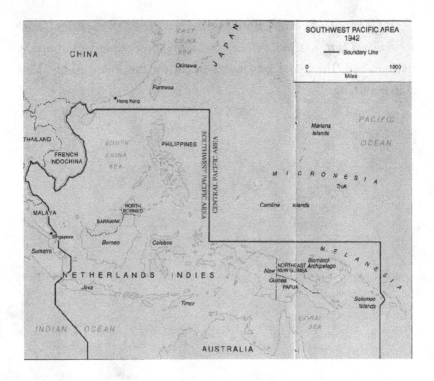

The 187th Regiment was formed at Camp Mackall on November 12, 1942. Later that month, both the 187th and the 188th were designated as glider infantry regiments and assigned to the 11th Airborne Division under the command of Major General Joseph Swing.

They were deployed to Lae, New Guinea, in May of 1944, for a period of intense training in the tropical climate, designed to prepare them for combat in the Philippines. The troops practiced parachute drops in the jungle, as well as around the airfield at Dobodura. Many soldiers, including my uncle, Lehman H. Johnson, Jr., graduated from what he referred to as the Swing School for Paratroopers. The Division was deemed to be combat ready six months later.

(Map Credit: Center of Military History)

Delivered from the Enemy

"Even if you have no religion, you are eligible for baptism."

—Lieutenant Colonel Lehman H. Johnson, Jr.

"I'm a Methodist now." Uncle Legs picked up his story after Sunday lunch and church. We had taken Communion that morning as part of the service, and the pastor had invited all who believed to participate.

"Communion is pretty much the same in the Methodist church as in the Baptist church. The only difference I see is that the Methodists sometimes use real wine, and the Baptists never do," my uncle said.

My uncle leaned forward intently in his chair, one hand on each knee. His elbows were turned out. With one foot he pushed the ottoman out of the way for emphasis. "In the Methodist church, we christen babies. I have no problem with that, but it seems to me that christening is more for the parents than for the child. They're promising to bring that child up in the church and to teach him or her to love and obey God. The baby has no idea what is going on.

"I think a child should be baptized again. You need to be of the age of understanding and accountability to make a decision about your faith." He paused and slapped his knees for emphasis.

"The age of accountability is around twelve or thirteen years old. The youngest men in my company were nineteen. I didn't know how many of them had made a profession of faith or anything about their spiritual backgrounds, but I did know that my first priority as company commander was those men and their lives. Those who had already dedicated themselves to God would most likely welcome the opportunity for recommitment.

"By the time I was having these thoughts, we were on the island of Leyte, and we all knew that, more than likely, we would be in combat within the week. I did not feel that I had adequately prepared them to fight unless they were also prepared to die with the assurance of salvation. The second man in each line — every other person — would either be dead or wounded before we got to Tokyo. I wanted every man who was willing to be baptized."

My uncle paused and stared out over the lawn where the afternoon sun was casting shadows. He was about to bring out the key players, and as an audience of one, I did not interrupt. He was there, center stage on the island of Leyte, 1944.

"I talked to my first sergeant, Art Leveque, and to the two chaplains about my idea for a baptismal service. Art thought it would improve morale, and the chaplains shared my concern for the men's spiritual well-being. There was no quibbling about how the baptism would be done, and I preferred immersion because of my Baptist upbringing. Both agreed they would 'dunk 'em.' Besides, we had Leyte Gulf right there next to Bito Beach, where we were camped, so it was a logical decision.

"That evening I assembled my men. In presenting baptism to them, I said, 'Now I'm giving you an opportunity, tomorrow morning, if you so desire, to be baptized. For those of you who don't know what baptism is, baptism is when you repent of your sins and publicly state your belief in God, the father, and in the Lord Jesus Christ. That means you are saved and that when you die, your soul goes to heaven.

"'All of you are eligible to be baptized — all Catholics, all Protestants.

I know we have different religions within this company, but I will offer you the opportunity to be baptized before you go into combat. Even if you have no religion, you are eligible for baptism.' The message was short and sweet.

"In dismissing them, I added, 'Go back to your tents and consider what I have said. This is between you and God, and you may want to pray before making your decision. Tomorrow morning, we'll line up and go down to the shore, and everyone who wants to participate will get baptized. I guarantee that you'll feel like a different person when you come out of that water.' I remember that most of them were looking at the ground as they left."

My uncle's eyes took on that dreamy quality that I had come to expect when he retreated from the intensity of a moment, a bubble so fragile that it might burst if I reached out to touch it. His lowered eyelids were a curtain of privacy separating him from me. He was very still, and I remained motionless, waiting for him to come back. I cannot say how much time passed before he took a deep breath and continued, looking directly at me.

"There was no further sermon the next morning. The men simply lined up for baptism and waded in, one at a time. Over each man, our chaplains spoke the words, 'I baptize you in the name of the Father, the Son, and the Holy Spirit.'

"Every man in my company was baptized, including Lee Holstein, my mortarman, who was Jewish. It has been said that there are no atheists in foxholes. The same could be said of my company that day, given the urgency of our situation. We all recognized the need for a source of courage that was outside ourselves.

"Some of the men even went and got prospects from other companies because I know more than 192 men were baptized. To my knowledge, no other companies did this, and we had quite an audience."

"What about yourself?" I asked. "Were you baptized?"

He nodded. "I had been baptized the first time when I was twelve or thirteen in the Baptist Church in Clayton. But I always tried to lead by example. I don't remember if I was the first or the last, but I came up out of there with water in my boots, just like the rest of them."

"Do you remember if anyone said anything about the experience?" He nodded and smiled.

"I wanted to know how they felt about what they were doing, so I asked one young man. 'Do you feel any different now?' I don't remember his name, but I do recall what he said.

"His answer was, 'Yes, I'm satisfied. My mother and dad would be proud of me.'

"'You can thank my dad,' I told him, 'because this is what he would have done if he had been here. I wanted to offer you this part of my upbringing.'"

Then my uncle was silent. The shadows outside the window had gotten longer and joined hands for the evening. He closed his eyes again. The players had made their final bow, and it was time for me to leave.

I stood up, uncertain as to whether I should touch him. I patted the hand that was now resting on the arm of his chair. "I'll see you next month," I said.

He roused.

"I had been brought up to believe that you should be spiritually prepared for things. I would have been remiss in my duty if I had not done this." His voice was clear and strong with conviction.

"Ah," I said, "Did you say 'duty?'" I rose to take my leave of him.

"I did. But that's not the title. Understand?" Still there were no quavers. My uncle's posture was erect, even though his shoulders were rounded slightly in weariness. I knew he would not allow himself to slump until I left.

"Understood."

The curtain was down, and I went out into the night.

Survival

"It's easy to shoot people when they are running toward you and firing rifles at you."

—Lieutenant Colonel Lehman H. Johnson, Jr.

"Old soldiers never die. They just fade away," my uncle said, when I joined him in the den. It was June when I realized that he no longer met me at the door for our monthly sessions. The family preliminaries were shorter as well. I seated myself without invitation.

"Do you know where that quotation comes from?" he asked.

"It's familiar."

"General Douglas MacArthur." Uncle Legs sighed and gazed out across the room at his war books in the bookcases that lined the far wall.

"MacArthur had been relieved of his command by then President Harry S. Truman for disobeying orders. That statement was part of his farewell address to Congress. MacArthur also talked a good bit in that speech about wanting to be remembered and specifically how he wanted to be remembered."

I thought, *we're not just talking about MacArthur.* My uncle and I went to war that weekend.

"Tell me about Leyte," I said. According to his official Army resume, the Battle of Leyte had to have been the first time my uncle saw combat. He had given me a copy of that document.

Uncle Legs did not answer immediately. Instead, he looked down and studied the hands folded in his lap. Then he laced his fingers together reflectively and cupped them behind his head. He leaned back against his open palms and began.

"The instance I am about to tell you about makes me blush in shame for the man who was involved, even today." His eyes blazed with anger and embarrassment. When he spoke, it was with the urgency of a man who needed to find a safe place for his feelings.

"We landed on Bito Beach in mid-November of 1944. The Japanese were waiting for us, and what followed soon after we landed seemed like one long battle that lasted for approximately three months.

"The Japanese were hard fighters, survivors of what we were just learning as jungle warfare. There on the beach, they attacked us on a straight line and stayed there. We fought man to man in hand to hand combat for days at a time, with very little let-up." My uncle exhaled and cleared his throat as though removing any obstruction to what he needed to say. He leaned in toward me, his hands on his knees.

"You see, Mary Susan, unlike the American soldier, who wants to survive, a Japanese soldier does not normally try to find a hole for protection when he is fired upon. It is an honor for him to die in battle." Uncle Legs settled back in his chair again.

"There were kamikaze attacks on our naval force. Our Navy had ships surrounding the island to protect it from enemy attack. We had been there for one day, when I remember seeing a Japanese pilot crash-dive his plane into an American destroyer (November 19, 1944). His fuel tank burst on impact, and the bombs he was carrying exploded.

"Although several of our ships were damaged during the Battle of Leyte, the Japanese lost eight destroyers, three battleships, four carriers, six heavy cruisers, and three light cruisers. We lost only three destroy-ers, two escort carriers, and one light carrier."

I waited for my uncle to let me witness through his words what he himself was seeing, the harsh, unrelenting movies of memory that were playing out in living color across his conscious mind.

After a moment, Uncle Legs crossed his feet at the ankles and added, with no more emotion than if he were making a menu selec-tion, "They made easy targets—the Japanese that is. The day I am going to tell you about, we destroyed them—all of them. But that wasn't the way I wanted it." He glanced toward me and then away, fixing his gaze on a point that I would see only through his eyes. Then he spoke.

"I had captured a Japanese warrant officer, and he was walking towards me, with one hand in the air. With the other hand, he was unbuttoning his shirt. Even as he was coming closer, the man was step-ping out of his pants. He was not carrying a weapon.

"I could see the outline of his entire body, and I can see it now." I nodded, but my uncle did not notice. "As a soldier, he was short, but very muscular. There was nothing hidden. The Japanese men didn't wear boxers like we did. They wore little G-straps." He spoke deliber-ately. In the pause, his lips became a thin line of disapproval, and his jaw hardened. He swallowed hard at the memory, as if something with an overdue expiration date wouldn't quite go down.

"The man was showing me that he did not have any hidden weap-ons, and he was in the process of surrendering. Out of nowhere this young lieutenant came up behind me and shot him in the head with a 45 caliber pistol.

"I couldn't believe it." Uncle Legs shook his head. "I was so aston-ished that for a moment I just looked down at this Japanese soldier who was now sprawled out on the ground. His eyes were frozen in the same cautious expression that had been there when he was alive and moving toward me. He didn't see what was coming and had, in fact, been advancing toward the bullet when he was shot.

"Of course, his head was not literally blown off, but a hole from the shot had opened up between the man's eyes. He still had one leg in his pants, and there was blood on his open shirt. He had fallen straight back. His legs were open toward me.

"Then I looked at my soldier. 'What in the hell are you doing?' I remember yelling at him and grabbing his gun. He did not resist. I outranked him, and what he had just done was grounds for a court-martial.

"When I got the gun, I shook the bullets out, and threw them on the ground. I stomped all around and cussed him in the dust I raised.

"'Damn you,' I said. 'Couldn't you see that he was surrendering?'

"'I just lost four of my men this morning.'

"'We could have interrogated him.'

"By now this young lieutenant had turned away from the dead Japanese soldier and was staring at the ground."

My uncle looked at me over his glasses and shrugged his shoulders, laying aside the man's rationalization as easily as the afghan that had slipped from his chair to the floor. "The lieutenant's emotions got the best of him and he overreacted. He was not directly under my command, so I did nothing. If he had been mine, I would have felt like I had to report the incident to keep the chain of command from breaking down. His commanding officer witnessed the incident but took no action either."

My uncle sighed. His feelings were spent, and there was a delicate balance in the moment as he steadied himself. "I remember the lieutenant's name, but he will be unnamed in this story. His family shouldn't have to think of him that way.

"I've asked about him at conventions and reunions that I've been to over the years, but he's never shown up at any of them. No one seems to know anything about him, so I don't know if he even made it back after the war.

"I've never told this story to anyone."

"Why is that?"

"It's easy to shoot people when they are running toward you and firing rifles at you. At that point your reaction has nothing to do with bravery or heroism—or even revenge. It's just survival. It's them or you.

"But when a man has been faced with a situation like I just told you, sometimes he goes berserk and shoots anything and everything, whether or not he himself is threatened at the time. His emotions are raw, and he's still in overdrive. Unless you've been there, you can't possibly understand that."

"In war, you mean?"

He nodded. "It isn't fair to judge unless you've been in those boots."

* * * * *

We were back in the den after having had a break for dinner.

My uncle's eyes narrowed to the point where his field of vision was as focused as a sniper's scope. In spite of the wine, his breathing became more rapid and shallower. He set his night cap down on the table beside him. That hand was shaking.

"The story I told you earlier today took place in Leyte. This one happened on the island of Luzon, later in the war, but they are related in my mind because they involve similar reactions."

I nodded again and waited. I was learning not to pass judgment and when to comment. He continued.

"We had discovered an underground Japanese hospital, including some patients who had been left behind there at Nichols field. The orders were that they were to be turned over to our medics and processed as prisoners of war.

"I was in a different area of the underground tunnel from where the worst incident occurred, but what happened in front of me was bad enough. I noticed there were some pints of beer that had been left out in the patient wards. My men thought the Japanese had gotten in such a hurry that they had left their beer behind, although I had previously warned them about eating or drinking anything under such conditions.

"In fact, the Japanese had deliberately poisoned the beer and left it out, hoping the American soldiers would drink it. The patients in the beds were, of course, aware of the danger, but said nothing. I called out to warn them, but it was too late. One of my men died almost instantly after chugging down the beer. Another man who bent down to taste it was turning black when I kicked the bottle out of his hand.

"A second warning was unnecessary. The rest of the men had just witnessed the consequences. I'm not sure whether the incident that followed was related to this trick on the part of the Japanese or if something else caused the man to snap."

Turning to me and draining his glass, my uncle said, "This one may keep you awake. Do you want to hear it tonight or save this one until tomorrow?"

"Now is good." *I don't want to dam up the flow,* I thought. *Being caught in this current is fine sailing, even if the water is getting choppy.*

"It hadn't been long after we had discovered the poisoned beer the hard way that my platoon sergeant stood before me.

"'Sir,' he said. 'I regret to inform you that I have relieved one of the men of his weapon due to his shooting unarmed patients on the hospital ward. I stopped him as soon as I found out about it. He is unarmed.'

"'Where is he now?'

"'Between two other men,' was the answer. No further action was required on my part, and I chose not to take any. His commanding officer, my platoon sergeant, had dealt with the situation and put a stop to any chain reaction that might have followed."

My uncle's eyes bored without apology into mine. "If what he had done had been reported higher up, the kid could have been shot or imprisoned for life." Then Uncle Legs looked away.

"The patients who survived this incident were turned over to our medics and processed as POWs."

His breathing became slow and regular. His eyes widened, and he looked somewhere in the distance outside of our immediate surroundings.

My uncle had chosen at least two times not to report moral and military lapses. To this day, he did not regret those decisions. He picked up the empty wine glass again and studied it. This time the hand was steady.

On November 11, 1944, the troops were conveyed by Navy transports to the island of Leyte, arriving on November 18. They were engaged in combat within the week, but as an infantry division, not as airborne.

In January 1945, the 11th Airborne Division landed at Nasugbu Bay on the island of Luzon, to prepare for the liberation of Manila. My uncle remembered the hospitality of the mayor of Nasugbu to the men of Company B before they set out on the road to Manila.

(Map Credit: Center of Military History)

Grace

*"Fear is a soldier's worst enemy and his best friend. Courage is just
the other side of the coin."*

—Lieutenant Colonel Lehman H. Johnson, Jr.

"Why did I make those decisions?" My uncle picked up his story in
the den as though there had been no break in our conversation. In fact,
we had slept, been to Sunday School and church at Mebane United
Methodist Church, and out for lunch at the Blue Ribbon. The lesson
that morning had been on the grace that Paul had received on the road
to Damascus.

I knew what grace was, but Uncle Legs told me anyway. "It's un-
merited favor. It's being given a second chance — like Paul. He even
got a new name. Before that he was known as Saul, and as a Roman
citizen, he slaughtered Christians and watched while the apostle Stephen was stoned." My uncle leaned toward me intently. His knees were
relaxed, and his hands were clasped between them.

I watched his hands as he clenched and unclenched them. Then I
met his unflinching gaze. "Do you know anything about the Vietnam
War?" he asked.

I nodded. "That's the war that took many of my high school classmates. They were drafted in 1969."

"I was supposed to go. That would have been my next assignment, except that I retired. I knew there was a bullet out there somewhere with my name on it, and I had a feeling it would find me in Vietnam." My uncle was no longer seeing me. There was a pause during which time he did not blink.

"If you know about Vietnam, then you know about My Lai." His voice was flat and without emotion. I inhaled sharply and waited.

"My Lai was the infamous attack by the Army on an unarmed village. Even the elderly, women, and children had all been victims. The Army had covered up the incident and prosecuted no one until a soldier leaked the story to the press. Only one man, William Laws Calley, Jr., was convicted and court-martialed although at least twenty-six U.S. soldiers participated, and many more had knowledge of the attack.

"It's easy to sit behind a desk in an office, or in your living room, and say what you would or would not have done in similar circumstances. Until you've marched in those boots, you don't know. Except for the grace of God, that could have been me—or any other soldier." His eyes were as bright with intensity as the first star of the evening now visible through the blinds. He took a deep breath and plunged into the darkness of his story.

"I was there on Nichols Field, which was located on the island of Luzon. We, that is the 187th Regiment, were charged with clearing the airstrip of Japanese and occupying it. We were the offense and we had overcome heavy resistance. It was critical that we maintain our position.

"I was standing on one side of the field when I observed a group of about 10 or 12 people approaching us. It was late evening, about this time of day, but even from a distance I could see they were not in uniform, and that they were wearing civilian clothes. It looked like a group of families with children. They were all carrying backpacks—which could have contained anything, including grenades. The Japanese would kill you any way they could, and it didn't matter how many of them died in the process.

"I knew all this and yet I let them come closer. I ordered my men to hold their fire, but I cocked my own rifle. I had not yet identified their nationality. From a distance, you can't tell who is an Oriental and who is not. Up close, you can identify the Japanese by the shape of their bodies, the color of their skin, the slant of their eyes, and their little Buddha heads."

I winced at that, but if he noticed, Uncle Legs made no comment.

"I watched as they came closer. If anybody did any shooting, I wanted it to be me. As they approached, I watched for any sudden movement on anyone's part, including the children. When they stood almost in front of me, I could see that they were Filipino, and although I did not understand what they were saying, I recognized the language.

"Apparently, they were trying to go north to Luzon, perhaps to some of their kin, where they thought they would be safer. I did not observe any weapons, and I did not think they were prepared to even defend themselves. They were just trying to take the shortest route across the airport to get to their destination.

"I nodded in the direction that they pointed. I ordered my men to put their weapons on safety and stand at ease while they went through. I took my finger off the trigger of my own rifle."

His left hand had been coiled around an invisible rifle. He flexed those fingers now and rested that hand on the arm of his chair.

"Mary Susan, if I had shot them when they were coming toward me, it would have been like shooting someone on our side. The Filipino people almost worshiped us because they had been treated so badly by the Japanese during their time of occupation. As a people, they assisted us in our operations."

Uncle Legs leaned back in his chair and exhaled. "I can't tell you how close I came several times to just blowing them all away.

"I was afraid. I was afraid that one of them was carrying a grenade and would wipe us out while we were playing a waiting game. While I watched them, we passed the point of no return—when that fear could have easily become a reality—I feared that one of my men would break down and shoot them anyway. I was afraid that we would lose the ground we had fought so hard to gain and I feared for the loss of my men.

"Even though they were obviously families, the question utmost in my mind was 'Are they the enemy?' I had to make that decision over and over again while they came toward us.

"Usually, a soldier has only a split second to make that call. Sometimes he calls it correctly. Sometimes he doesn't. In this instance, fortunately, I guessed correctly, and I was able to exercise restraint.

"It was not the same for everybody. We were all under a tremendous amount of pressure, and some things were done in the peak of emotion. I'm not sure I could have told you this story if things had ended differently.

"Fear is a soldier's worst enemy and his best friend. Courage is just the other side of the coin."

That I wrote down and rose to gather my things. But there was more.

"My friends, people at church, send their sons, and occasionally a daughter, to see me if they are planning to enlist in the military. I guess the parents feel that I can tell them what it's really like. I can't do that because they'll have their own story.

"Instead I ask them, 'Do you want to be behind a desk, where it's safe, shuffling papers, or do you want to be where the action is? You need to be very honest with yourself before you make that decision.' I tell them, 'I always wanted to be where the action was.' Their parents are probably disappointed."

He grinned and accepted my embrace.

Photographs

Early Famly Life

Pictured are Lehman H. Johnson, Jr., Lehman H. Johnson, his father, and Mabel Johnson, his mother. Lehman, Jr. was born January 12, 1916, and his sister, Sulou, was born two years later, on December 5, 1918. Since she is not included, it may be surmised that the year of this portrait was perhaps 1917, and that Lehman Jr. was approximately one year old.

Lehman H. Johnson, Jr. stands protectively beside his little sister, Mary, at the house in Clayton. Mary was born in Clayton on June 7, 1923. There was seven and a half years' difference between their ages. In this picture, Mary looks to be about one or two years old. Lehman Jr. would then be about nine or ten.

Stairsteps: The three Johnson children pose in their Sunday best. From Left to Right, Mary Allene (birthdate June 7, 1923), Sulou Virginia (birthdate December 5, 1918), Lehman Holson Johnson, Jr. (birthdate January 12, 1916). Uncle Legs' middle name, Holson, was made by combining the last names of his grandparents, Holland and Johnson.

Young Adult Life

Lehman H. Johnson and Mabel Allene Johnson as they were in 1935, when they moved to Kenly, North Carolina. Their daughter Mary was in the ninth grade. The older children left for college that same year—Lehman, Jr., for Oak Ridge Military Institute and Sulou for East Carolina Teacher's College.

Lehman H. Johnson, Jr. (far right) poses in front of the family home at Powhatan in Clayton, on the day of his high school graduation (Summer of 1935). Other family members are (from left to right) his sister, Mary; father, Lehman; mother, Mabel; sister, Sulou.

Lehman H. Johnson, Jr. stands at attention, even though he is home on leave from Oak Ridge Military Institute (about 1936-1937). To his right are his mother, Mabel; his sister Sulou; and his sister, Mary.

Even though there was no reason to hunt for food, after the move to Kenly, North Carolina, Lehman H. Johnson, Jr. (left) and his father, Lehman H. Johnson still enjoyed the sport. The same rules applied though. The Johnson family always ate what they killed, usually quail or dove, by that point.

Oak Ridge Military Institute: Lehman H. Johnson, Jr. poses in his full-dress uniform in front of a cannon on the campus of his alma mater. He graduated in 1939 with an Army Reserve Commission. His signature can be seen in the lower right corner and the inscription, "Always Yours" to his future wife, Genevieve Wooten.

Courtship and Early Marriage

Genevieve Wooten Johnson and Lehman H. Johnson, Jr. pose for an official wedding photograph, in the living room of the Wooten homeplace in June of 1941. The Johnsons were already married, having eloped on June 8, 1940, but her parents insisted on a proper wedding ceremony at their home in Stantonsburg, North Carolina. The Johnsons were legally married by a justice of the peace in Clarksville, Virginia.

More than likely this portrait of Genevieve Wooten Johnson and Lehman H. Johnson, Jr. was taken when they came home to Stantonsburg during the summer of 1941, for the wedding ceremony her parents wanted for them. There are no captain's bars yet on his uniform. Lehman, Jr. was promoted to captain in August of 1942 and their first son, Lehman H. Johnson, III, was born that same month.

Genevieve and "Legs" Johnson are home to visit his family in Kenly, North Carolina, most likely during their first year of marriage and following their formal wedding ceremony.

"Legs" Johnson admires his first-born son and namesake, Lehman H. Johnson, III. Wife and new mother, Genevieve Johnson holds on to the happiness of having her family together. Baby Lee was born August 16, 1942.

Deployed: New Guinea and the Philippines — WWII

Captain Lehman H. Johnson, Jr. (right) with one of the natives who assisted Company B with the construction of both the parachute training center and the chapel, built during training in New Guinea, prior to their entrance into combat in the Pacific Theater of World War II.

Captain Lehman H. Johnson, Jr., Commander of Company B, 187th Regiment, is standing in front of the chapel that was constructed for worship services and private meditation on site in New Guinea. Their period of jungle training lasted from May 29, 1944, until they deployed for Leyte on November 18 of that same year.

Captain Lehman H. Johnson, Jr., is taking a break in front of his tent in New Guinea, during training prior to his WWII combat. He sent this picture home to his wife. Genevieve Johnson. On the back is stamped, "Passed by Base 2452 Army Examiner."

As stated in his own handwriting on the back of the picture, Captain Lehman H. Johnson, Jr., is, "five miles west of Tanauan in Southern Batangas, just east of Lake Taal." He writes, "Sorry of short haircut. Not such a good picture." This photograph was sent home to his wife, Genevieve Johnson, to whom he says in closing, "I love you darling."

Captain Lehman H. Johnson poses in front of his tent in New Guinea. New Guinea's climate and terrain provided the U.S. Army with the environment to train for the jungle warfare they would encounter in the Philippines during WWII.

"The chapel in New Guinea would easily hold fifty to seventy-five soldiers, depending on how close they sat together for services," said Captain Lehman H. Johnson, Jr. (pictured.) "Some used it every day for silent prayer or meditation."

Downtown Manila as it was in January 1945.

Major Lehman H. Johnson, Jr., circa 20 May 1945—5 January 1946, after his promotion while serving as provost marshal in the 11th Airborne Division, but prior to being sent to Japan and later Germany for occupation duty.

Most likely this picture of Major Lehman H. Johnson, Jr. (left) was taken during the time he served as provost marshal, since he lays claim to the leather seat and calls attention to the fact that he has a driver. On the back of this picture, he has written, "Neither turned out so well. They're true Army men—my driver next to the jeep, McBride and Driosick. I love you the same, darling. How do you like my nice soft leather seat?"

Germany (August 1946–1948)

Major Lehman H. Johnson, Jr. enjoys a respite from his duties as the officer in charge of executions at Landsberg Prison in Germany. He and his two sons, (left) Julian Wooten Johnson (Jule) and (right) Lehman H. Johnson, III (Lee) play horse, in the front yard of their first home in Germany.

Lee (left) and Jule (right) enjoy the sunshine from their window-sill perch. Lee would have been four to six years old and Jule would have been two to four years old. Jule was born Feb. 9, 1944, while his father, Lehman H. Johnson, Jr., was deployed to the Philippines.

Bill, the Johnson family's German Shepherd, is pictured in the foreground of their first home in Germany. Always on guard, Bill keeps a watchful eye on Lee and Jule, who are playing next to the fence.

Genevieve Wooten Johnson and Lehman H. Johnson, Jr. are shown in a train car during his tour of duty in Germany. Their location allowed for travel to other European countries. One known trip was to Paris, France.

This glamour shot of Genevieve Johnson was taken during a trip that the couple took to Paris, France, during the time that Major Lehman H. Johnson, Jr. was stationed in Germany.

The Minister of Defense in Luxembourg presents the Order of Adolphe of Nassau, Luxembourg Commander's Cross, to Major Lehman H. Johnson, Jr., in 1948. The purpose of the medal is to honor those who have provided service of special merit to society, as well as to the Grand Duke and his family. (As told to Col. Johnson's granddaughter) . . . "the royal family had a castle in Germany, and when war broke out, his daughter, the Princess, was at the castle. She died, and the King wanted her body brought back to Luxembourg for a proper burial. Colonel Johnson received a medal for taking her body to Luxembourg." (Nicole Johnson, US History Report, 1994).

Back in the States

Family portrait from the Johnson family's Christmas card, 1949: Baby Steve (Stephen Hal) was born September 24, 1949. His mother, Genevieve Johnson, is holding him. Other family members are (from left to right) brother, Lee; father, Lehman H. Johnson, Jr., and brother, Julian.

Co. B ROTC Camp, 1950, at Fort Benning, Georgia: Major Lehman H. Johnson, Jr. commands the troops.

Korea: November 1951-March 1952

This official Army portrait of Lieutenant Colonel Lehman H. Johnson, Jr. was most likely made at Gulfport, Mississippi, just prior to his deployment to Korea in 1951. The intensity of the expression speaks to his perspective on the assignment as advisor to the Commanding General of the Korean Army—KMAG—Korean Military Advisory Group—but what he, and many others, called "Kiss My Ass Goodbye in Korea."

From left to right, Major General Clovis E. Byers, Commanding General, X Corps; Lieutenant Colonel Lehman H. Johnson, Jr., Senior KMAG Advisor; and General Lee Chung Il (hands on hips), Commanding General, 7th ROK Division, meet the officers of the 3rd Regiment on November 4, 1951.

Dated November 4, 1951, from left to right, Lieutenant Colonel Lehman H. Johnson, Jr., Senior Advisor, 7th ROK Division; Major General Clovis E. Byers, Commanding General, X Corps; Commanding General Lee Chung Il ; and officers of the ROK Army watch a field problem run through in the vicinity of Sooin-Ni, North Korea. (Photo by PFC Paul E. Curan)

December 5, 1951, Lieutenant Colonel Lehman H. Johnson, Jr., Senior Advisor, 7th ROK Division, briefs General Willis B. Palmer, X Corps Commander, (far left). General Lee Chung Il, Commanding General, 7th ROK Division, stands beside him and listens intently to the exchange. They are surrounded by other officers, both American and Korean, who are associated with the 7th Division.

Christmas 1951: General Lee Chung Il, Commanding General, 7th ROK Division, stands to welcome his guests on December 25, 1951. Seated from right to left are Lieutenant Colonel Lehman H. Johnson, Jr., Senior Advisor to General Lee; Major Macadam, Senior Advisor, 8th Regiment; and Major Barker, Assistant Advisor, 8th Regiment.

Major General Willis B. Palmer congratulates Lieutenant Colonel Lehman H. Johnson, Jr. for being awarded the Bronze Star Medal, (Oak Leaf Cluster) in Korea, December 28, 1951. General Lee Chung Il, Commander of the 7th ROK (Republic of Korea) Division is smiling his appreciation. In referencing this award, his official record states that Lieutenant Colonel Johnson's "fine professional knowledge and clear thinking were of great value in supervising the intensive training and increasing the overall efficiency of this division."

Dated January 27, 1952, Lieutenant Colonel Lehman H. Johnson, Jr., (far right) Senior Advisor, 7th ROK Division, discusses strategy with Commanding General Lee Chung Il, (center), Commander of the 7th ROK Division, and other American and Korean officers.

Commanding General Lee Chung Il leads the way in Korea (date unknown). Lieutenant Colonel Lehman H. Johnson follows close behind. On the back of the picture, Lieutenant Colonel Johnson writes, "I assure you it's a hard climb—General Lee, in front. See how I'm leaning on my knees. Captain Wokeman is to my left, typical terrain."

Hawaii, 1956-60

*Welcome to Hawaii! Lieutenant Colonel Lehman H. Johnson, Jr. (right) leads his wife,
Genevieve, (center) and children off the ship and into their new life with his assignment
as advisor to the National Guard., Hilo, Hawaii. From left to right are sons, Jule and Lee,
followed by daughter, Candy, and youngest son, Steve. Both Candy and Steve appear to be
uncertain about wearing the welcome flower leis and the life before them. In fact, none of the
children wanted to leave Hawaii when they returned in 1960.*

The Johnson family's typical Christmas family portrait made soon after their arrival in Hawaii, in 1957. Candy, 5, is front and center, next to her mother, Genevieve. Behind them, from left to right, are Jule (age 12, seated), Lee (age 15, standing), Lieutenant Colonel Lehman H. Johnson, Jr., and Steve (age 7, seated).

Lieutenant Colonel Lehman H. Johnson, Jr. is shown at his desk at Schofield Barracks, his second assignment in Hawaii, this time as a Deputy Battle Group Commander, 1959-60. In the foreground on his desk can be seen a Japanese mortar round tail that landed in my uncle's foxhole (while he was also in it) during the Philippine Campaign of WWII. For some unknown reason, it did not explode. Now, with the fuze removed, he kept it on his desk as a reminder that he had been spared.

Lieutenant Colonel Lehman H. Johnson, Jr. toasts his return to the mainland States from Hawaii in the summer of 1960, by ship. He and his wife Genevieve end their journey there as they began — with the traditional farewell of the flower leis.

Lieutenant Colonel Lehman H. Johnson, Jr. as he was in 1961, at Fort Campbell, Kentucky,

his last duty assignment. Lieutenant Colonel Johnson retired effective February 28, 1962,

because as he said, "There's a bullet somewhere out there with my name on it"—in Vietnam.

THE FOLLOWING LIST REFLECTS LEGS' OFFICIAL ARMY RECORDS
SHOWN IN THE FRAMED PHOTOGRAPH OF HIS MEDALS:

Combat Infantryman's Badge—2nd Award (top center)
Army Airborne Glider Badge (top left)
Senior Airborne Wings (top right)

(Remaining awards are second row left to bottom row right)

Silver Star
Bronze Star with one oak leaf cluster
Army Commendation Medal
American Defense Medal
American Campaign Medal
Asiatic Pacific Campaign Medal with 3 bronze stars
World War II Victory Medal
Army Occupation Medal—Germany
National Defense Service Medal
Korean Service Medal with 2 bronze stars
Philippine Liberation Medal (not in display but earned)
Philippine Independence Medal (not in display but earned)
Order of Adolphe of Nassau , LUXEMBOURG Commander's Cross
Chungmu District Military Service Medal with Gold Star
United Nations Korean Service Medal
Republic of Korea Presidential Unit Citation with Army Frame
Army Presidential Unit Citation with 1 oak leaf cluster

Post Retirement

Lieutenant Colonel Lehman H. Johnson, Jr. (Ret.) (far left) stands with his adult children, from left to right: Stephen Hal (Steve), Nancy Candace (Candy), Julian Wooten (Jule), and Lehman H., III (Lee.) Most likely, this picture was taken during the 1970's.

Jane Hook and Lieutenant Colonel Lehman H. Johnson, Jr. (Ret.) were married on October 19, 1985. Of his second wife, my uncle was fond of saying, "I don't know how one man could be so lucky twice."

Jane and my Uncle Legs pause for a picture during one of their favorite activities—golf.

From left to right, Jane Johnson, Lieutenant Colonel Lehman H. Johnson, Jr., (Ret.) and his sister, Mary Allene Johnson Simmons, celebrate the wedding of his grandson, Michael Vickers Johnson, to Hannah Poteat, on October 26, 1996.

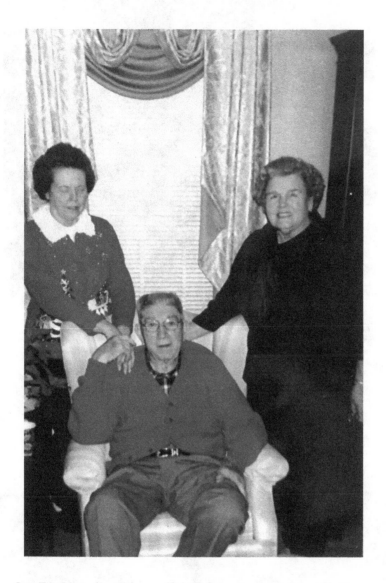

Betty Toler Johnson (far right), my uncle's double first cousin, grew up on a neighboring farm at Powhatan. Here she is visiting her cousin, Lehman, Jr. and his wife, Jane, in January of 2005, at their home in Mebane, North Carolina. He was 89 years old on January 12, 2005.

Lehman H. (Legs) Johnson, Jr. shares a moment with his youngest sister, Mary. He was always protective of her, perhaps due to the difference in their ages (seven and a half years). He was deceased on May 1, 2009, at age 93. Mary celebrated her 97th birthday on June 7, 2020.

Lieutenant Colonel Lehman H. Johnson, Jr. (Ret.), is shown as he was during our interviews, always in his favorite brown leather chair, with the afghan behind him. This picture was taken when he was in his late eighties/early nineties.

Lieutenant Colonel Lehman H. Johnson, Jr. (Ret.) pauses in the light of his reflections, during one of our last interview sessions. He had gone back to the military high and tight haircut from his early military days by this point.

The Death of Joe Rangel in Leyte

"Duty. He had given all he had to give to his country and that was his life."

—Lieutenant Col. Lehman H. Johnson, Jr.

The heat at the end of summer had drained the vitality from the bed of irises visible from the patio door in Uncle Legs' den. The blooms, a deep purple, dark as death and languid in their repose, were a memory. My uncle was stretched out in his chair, bedroom slippers aimed at the ceiling, his legs ramrod straight across the footstool. He had not gotten up to greet me when Jane called out, "Legs, Mary Susan is here!"

Standing beside me, she interjected smoothly. "Legs has a heart murmur. His cardiologist found it since the last time you came."

My uncle shook his head in disbelief. "He said I could drop dead of a heart attack any moment.

"I just casually mentioned driving to his office, and the doctor shot back, 'What!!! You drove here? You could kill somebody!' I surrendered my license last week."

"I'll drive you to church tomorrow," I offered.

"Then it's agreed," Jane said. At that, she picked up her pocketbook and left us.

"How much time do we have?" my uncle asked abruptly.

"I don't know." His question caught me off guard.

Uncle Legs unhooked his cane from the arm of his chair and stabbed the rug with it. "What do you mean you don't know? We always go to dinner at 1700 hours."

"It's two o'clock. We have time."

"Good. I'll ask you about your family over dinner this time. The story I'm about to tell you is not good conversation for eating. His voice, rough and raw with exposed emotion, cut the space between us.

"One of my platoon sergeants stood before me on the island of Leyte in December of 1944. We were in a rice paddy. 'Sir, I think you should see this,' he said and motioned for me to follow.

"When he and I came up on this foxhole, he pointed at two dead soldiers lying beside it. A Japanese soldier and my soldier were locked together with their faces almost touching one another.

"The Japanese soldier's right arm had been almost blown off. My soldier's right hand was in the back of the Japanese soldier still holding the bayonet he had used to stab his enemy. Their blood had mixed together and soaked into the ground, discoloring the dirt around their bodies.

"It was not a pretty sight, but we could see clearly what action had taken place. The Japanese soldier had slipped up on my soldier during the night and jumped into his foxhole, where he had perhaps been sleeping. My man reacted by stabbing the enemy with his bayonet.

"Before he died, the Japanese soldier released his grenade, blowing them both up and out of the foxhole.

"The exact date that this occurred was December 6, 1944, and the American soldier's name was Joe Rangel (Company B, 187th Infantry Regiment). Joe died the night the Japanese jumped on my men at the 5th Air Force Headquarters, located at Buri Air Strip. I can see that picture right now, and I need not to see it for a while after I tell you.

"Every Dec. 6, I remember Joe. He was only eighteen years old. I lost a good soldier that day. But I also had a feeling of accomplishment that he had done his duty. I was proud of him."

"Duty?"

"Duty. He had given all that he had to give to his country, and that was his life." The lines of my uncle's face were trench-like, deeper than earlier today, and his eyelids drooped. His chin dropped to his chest, and he breathed deeply. "If you don't mind, I need to rest after all that's been said before we go out." In a few minutes he was snoring.

I was curled up on the couch when Jane flung open the kitchen door and put the groceries on the table. "Gracious," she said, "You all must have been working hard. Wake up, Legs! We need to take Mary Susan to dinner."

Uncle Legs opened his eyes, and I sat up. "Give me just a minute," he said as he stood unsteadily on his feet and then shuffled off toward the bedroom before our departure.

At Huey's, my uncle checked his steak for rareness and promptly sent it back. "It's overdone," he declared, replacing his knife on the table with unnecessary force. It clattered when he dropped it. Heads turned.

"Legs!" exclaimed Jane. Then because she knew him, she asked, "What were you two talking about while I was out this afternoon?"

At first my uncle did not answer. "I lost someone in the war, and I was remembering the circumstances of his death," he said finally.

There was another pause. Then with exquisite delicacy, Jane asked, "How many men did you lose?"

"Probably twenty-five to thirty and I never got used to it. I'm not used to it now." The hand that had held the knife trembled, and it was not from weakness. "I lost some in New Guinea in training and some more in Leyte, like this young man. I also lost some on Tagaytay Ridge, on the island of Luzon.

"I was fortunate, based on the training of my men and the missions that I was given to have lost no more than that. Some companies had as many as fifty to sixty casualties."

He picked up his spoon and stirred his tea. The spoon and the ice clinked against the glass with the ringing clarity of a bell choir. Jane covered his hand with hers. The ensuing silence was deafening.

When Uncle Legs did speak, it was not about the losses and certainly not about his duty. His service did not fit the word as he defined it. Instead, he spoke of action, and he spoke of it slowly and with deliberation.

"A soldier's death meant I had another letter to write home. I always wrote them myself, and in writing them I tried to put myself in the family's place, as if I were receiving them.

"I tried to answer the question that I thought they would most likely want to know: How did he die? I would explain this in detail to each family and talk about my relationship with that soldier. I wrote those letters because I wanted to and because it helped me deal with my own grief. Otherwise, all they would get was a telegram. I knew they would want to know more than what would be sent that way. They also needed to know that their soldier's life meant something to somebody who had been with him when he died.

"I got back some of the finest letters you've ever seen from some of the dependents and their families. Unfortunately, I do not still have any of these."

Twenty minutes had passed, and our waitress appeared at our table with another steak. It was lightly seared, the juices running blood red in the single plate she held out to him.

"Try this, Colonel Legs," she said with easy familiarity. "Be careful though. The plate's hot."

As if he had not heard her, my uncle used both hands to adjust a dish as large as a platter, so that it was centered directly in front of him. Then he picked up his knife and fork and hacked away at what must have been a 16 oz. steak, even though the original order was for an 8oz. He cut off a piece that could easily have 'choked a horse,' in Jane's words. He held the dripping hunk of meat between his thumb and forefinger and took a huge bite. He chewed thoughtfully for what felt like several minutes and then swallowed. Our waitress hovered beside our booth.

"Perfect," Uncle Legs announced loudly. A hush fell over this friendly family restaurant followed by a collective sigh. Our fellow diners had become our audience.

There had been redemption in that day and a kind of catharsis. Although my uncle told and retold many of the stories that he wanted to make sure I included in his book, he did not ever tell me that one again.

Expediency in the Field

"The air was smoky and the noise was steady, like Mama's Singer sewing machine with the pedal stuck."

—Lieutenant Colonel Lehman H. Johnson, Jr.

The next morning, my uncle shuffled to the breakfast table in his purple silk bathrobe. His hair was sticking up in stiff grey peaks like a porcupine, and he was unshaven. "I've been fighting the Japs all night," he said wearily as he collapsed into the chair that was his customary place at the head of the table.

"I hardly ever even think about it, but last night I dreamed that I was on the island of Leyte again, and that the Japanese jumped on my men." Hunched over the table with his chin on his chest, his nose looked like the beak of an eagle as he peered out from the collar of the robe he had drawn up around his ears.

"When was this?" I poured his coffee.

"Cream please, and sugar this morning, I think." Without resistance, I handed him the sugar bowl. Had she been there, Jane would have urged restraint, but she was already at church, and I was no match for him. "It was the winter of 1944," Uncle Legs said, as he put three heaping teaspoonfuls of sugar into his steaming mug and added milk.

"Do you often have these dreams?" I joined him at the table with a cup for myself.

"Not so much now, but when I remember during the day, like I did yesterday, sometimes I can't let it go. Talking about Joe's death made me remember other things about that time, and my subconscious mind takes over when I go to sleep."

He nodded, sloshing coffee into his saucer as he stirred vigorously with his spoon. "Leyte was just a lot of little coastal villages with a mill close by to process the sugar cane that was their major crop. Our mission was to secure the villages and then cross the mountains to support our units that were being attacked on the west coast of the island.

"We marched by day in mud that covered our boots and slowed our progress. Much worse than that discomfort was the fact that the jump boots issued to us were not designed for our present weather conditions. It rained constantly in the jungles of Leyte, so our feet were always wet, and our boots never had a chance to dry out. This was probably the first use of jungle warfare by U.S. troops, and the powers that be had not considered the effect of this constant soaking on our shoes.

"When the soles began to rot and come off, we attempted to tie or tape them to the boots' uppers. Only a few men were lucky enough to get replacements. For my part, with my size 14 feet, there was hardly ever a replacement pair available, anywhere, any time—and certainly not then. We did the best we could with what was available, and we marched on.

"When we arrived at the 5th Air Force Headquarters, located at Buri Airstrip, the sight that met our eyes was anything but reassuring. A number of the men had been executed while they were sleeping. They were still lying in their hammocks, having been run through with a bayonet or shot. The survivors were in shock, but they were, needless to say, very glad to see us.

"My men experienced the aftershock. I remember one young man, his face white as fresh cream, who kept saying, 'He never woke up. He never woke up,' as he pointed to each new discovery. One soldier had suffered a bayonet wound to his cheek but had somehow turned before he died, so that the wound was not visible. When we turned him over, we could see the hole in the side of his face and the blood on his hammock. My soldier excused himself and was sick in the grass.

"Our medics did their best to patch up the survivors, and Graves Registration took care of the rest. They identified the deceased and prepared the necessary paperwork for notification of the next of kin. Cemeteries were created on the spot and the dead were buried without ceremony."

My uncle glanced in my direction and leaned toward me over the table. "Just so you know, Mary Susan, these bodies would later be moved to a large permanent cemetery on Luzon, not far from Manila. Families would have the option of having their soldier's body exhumed and sent home in 1948, at U.S. expense."

I nodded, grateful for the explanation, and my uncle picked up the stitch he had dropped and continued knitting his story together. "Having disposed of these matters and having literally cleaned up the mess, we settled in to secure the 5th Air Force Headquarters and defend the airstrip. Within the week, we would experience a different kind of attack by the enemy, and this time their arrival stole up on us while we were fully awake. In spite of what we had just witnessed, we had been lulled into a false sense of security. We hadn't seen any Japanese, but the air strip we were defending was critical to our defense in the Philippines, so, of course, they returned.

"It was about 5:00 p.m., at dusk on December 6, 1944. Our cooks had prepared a meal out in the open for us, and I was standing there in the chow line, holding my plate, when I happened to look up. What I saw should have alarmed me, but it didn't. Flying toward us were these planes that looked like our C-47s. I remember wondering why they were here. We weren't expecting any supplies or reinforcements, so instead of filling my plate, I continued to watch.

"They came closer and flew lower, and I saw the crest of the rising sun on the side of one of the planes. At once I understood what was happening, but by this time, they were overhead. The kamikaze pilots were flying directly toward us and their paratroopers were descending.

"I dropped the empty plate I was holding and ran to my tent to get my weapons. On the way, I shouted for my men to do likewise. Those that were already eating pitched their dinners and grabbed what was most available. We fought back with a combination of M-1 rifles, machine guns, carbines, and Browning automatic rifles. The smell of our uneaten dinner mingled with the scent of gun powder. The air was smoky and the noise was steady, like Mama's Singer sewing machine with the pedal stuck. The Browning held a magazine of 21 bullets, and that was the sound I was most conscious of.

"Our machine guns and anti-aircraft guns shot one plane down. As it fell from the sky, the men inside jumped out. Beneath their parachutes I could recognize them as Japanese, Nips we called them, by the shape of their heads, and as they came closer, by their slanted eyes. Others followed. There were about 250 of them, and all I could think of was that the Japanese had jumped on my men. The attack was very personal to me, and since most of the Japs got to the ground, the next 72 hours of fighting was definitely up close. We made good use of our bayonets and our grenades under those circumstances." My uncle's breath came in short and shallow, even though he had not moved.

"Is this when Joe Rangel was killed?" I asked.

He sighed. "Yes. Normally when night falls in battle, the fighting ceases. But as I've already said, this was a different kind of war and we were fighting a different breed of enemy.

"Joe was one of the five casualties we experienced in three days of fighting. I remember the names of two others from Company B, who were also killed. They were Burnett and Flanders. But for our part, we were successful in following Col. George Pearson's orders to leave none of the enemy living. We leveled the playing field. They either retreated or were killed. I didn't count bodies, but it didn't look like many of them ran away."

With this pronouncement, Uncle Legs picked up the pitcher of milk on the table and poured it over his cereal. "It is amazing to see the expediency of the American soldier when he is in the field and trying to survive. I am privileged to have been a witness and to recall those events."

"I think we missed Sunday School," I observed, watching him as he thoughtfully ate his shredded wheat.

A few spoonfuls later, he stopped and added sugar. "What time is it?"

"10 o'clock." I remembered then that I had not eaten, but I was no longer hungry.

My uncle glanced at his Rolex, the one with the fluorescent face that he said could never have been worn on the battlefield. At night it would have given his position away to the enemy, so he especially enjoyed wearing it now. "Can you get dressed in thirty minutes? If so, we can make it to church."

"I can." We took my car.

Genevieve sent Legs this Heart Shield Bible in which she wrote in the margins the letter printed later in this book. These Bibles were sized to fit into the chest pocket of a soldier's uniform and meant to stop a bullet from reaching his heart.

Planning for Survival and One Who Did Not

*"We lost one of our best combat officers because he couldn't talk
without gesturing for emphasis."*

—Lieutenant Colonel Lehman H. Johnson, Jr.

"My theory of combat, if you want to call it a theory, is finding, fixing, and finishing the enemy. In order to do that, you have to protect
yourself," Uncle Legs said reflectively. We were back in the den after
church.

"For my part, I always covered my eyes when I was running for cover." My uncle shaded his eyes from the afternoon sun that warmed us
through bare windows. "I could have easily been blinded by a grenade.
Then how could I be the commander of 192 men?"

"Why do you do certain things?" He shrugged his shoulders. "If
you don't take precautions, you are going to be killed. Even if you do,
you might be killed anyway. You want to stack the odds in your favor.
I told my men. 'Hide behind a tree before you shoot. If your butt is
hanging out, you're an easy target.'

"We learned that Japanese snipers were trained on a site with
weapons that had bolt action—delivering a single lethal shot from a
distance. They didn't follow a target, like I'm doing now." He aimed an
imaginary rifle at a bird outside the window and followed its flight, his

left hand supporting the barrel and the second finger on his right hand firing the trigger.

"Anybody who walked into an area targeted by a Japanese sniper was at the mercy of his aim, so we put eight to ten paces between each soldier when we were marching. That way if one person got shot, the next man didn't follow him. He turned out to avoid getting hit."

My uncle had stopped shooting at the bird, but his eyes were alert with interest in its movement. It was a black cinder flung out from the evening sun's dying fire. The bird, a crow, flew off into the woods, and Uncle Legs turned back toward me.

"Shooting has never been a sport for me, even at Powhatan. These skills I don't need any more. I don't particularly enjoy talking about the conditions under which I made use of them, and I don't need to kill anything to eat. I talk about them now only because I want others to know and remember." He was studying me intently.

I recalled his swath of boyhood memories of shooting squirrels and the rabbits he had skinned. His mother had cooked them for supper. I would have never known except that he told me.

Then he plunged me back into the mountains of Luzon. "I trained my soldiers to be very aware of their surroundings because that was the way I was trained.

"I would tell my men, 'Be sure to watch to your right and to your left.' Before we went out, I would always say, 'Be alert.' Col. Jake Zellars had said the same to me as a newly promoted captain, and it was good advice to pass on. 'If you see a dark area around the vines, shoot then and there—don't wait until you actually see something.'

"When we moved out, I would divide my men into two columns, a column on each side of the road. We could move faster by observing on either side. I would stand aside and let them pass so I could view each man personally, not as a mass. I could see if this one was missing his canteen or if another one still had his ammo.

"One thing that I always looked for was an extra pair of socks that had been washed the night before, drying across every man's backpack. If I didn't see the socks, that probably meant I needed to make sure that soldier got another pair. Even a simple thing like clean, dry socks was important for survival. Not changing your socks meant that you were more likely to get 'jungle rot,' and various other kinds of infections of the feet.

"Other little things were also critical. We learned that you don't use your hands when you talk. The Japanese could pick out the leaders because they would give directions and wave their arms and hands about. That's the reason we lost so many second lieutenants. They would be in front of their platoons, talking and giving orders.

"Paul Bashore had to use his hands. When he gave orders, he used them to punctuate his sentences. He was shot by a Japanese sniper on April 8, 1945. We lost one of our best combat officers because he couldn't talk without gesturing for emphasis and because he made a second critical mistake—using the same trail twice.

"We had been ordered to take Mount Macolod. The enemy was entrenched all over the mountain and they stood between us and Manila. The day's events went something like this. Companies A, B, and C (1st Battalion, 187th Infantry Regiment) were slowly making their way to the summit of Mount Macolod. A Company was going up by way of Brownie Ridge. C Company was making their way to the top by way of Cuenca Ravine on the north side. B Company was advancing to the right of C Company. For the most part, things had been pretty calm that day. Captain Bashore, commander of Company B, had gone ahead of his company to check on the situation.

"I had been moved from company commander to battalion executive officer on March 7, 1945—second in command to the battalion commander. It was also on that date that Paul had assumed his command, so perhaps he had not had long enough to learn that lesson.

"His body language had already clearly conveyed his leadership to the camouflaged Japanese. When Paul attempted to return to his men by way of the same path that he had just climbed, he walked right into the sight of a Japanese sniper.

"Much commotion followed Paul's death. As he fell, we were immediately assaulted by mortars and machine gun fire, and by the snipers who were hidden all along Mount Macolod. Others who were killed that day included Private Pelfrey and Staff Sergeant Hawkins. Because he was our commander, we named the place where Paul was shot Bashore's Ridge.

"I had a similar experience earlier in the war when we were on the island of Leyte. I, too, returned by the same path, primarily because I didn't know any other way. I was reporting to battalion headquarters to get my orders to move out. The only thing that made my destination 'headquarters' was the fact that the battalion commander was located at a specific set of coordinates in the jungle.

"Anyway, I was making my way through a coconut grove, always watching to my right and to my left, very aware of any dark spots that might signal the presence of a 'little Buddha.' The leaves around me were perfectly still when the first shot cracked through them. When the next bullet zinged past my head, clearly my only choice was to run like hell. I didn't look back and I didn't shoot back.

"I reacted instinctively and ran in a zigzag fashion all the way to headquarters. I would run so many steps this way and so many steps another way." In the space between us, my uncle used his hands, palms together, to trace his path through the jungle. "One, two, three, four, this way. One, two, three, four, that way. Then I would change up the numbers to confuse them. Sometimes, two steps. Sometimes, six. I was conscious of counting the whole time I was running. Fortunately for me, the Japanese were not very good shots that day.

"It was a long ten minutes getting there, but finally I staggered into headquarters. I stood at attention and saluted my commanding officer." Still seated in his chair, my uncle saluted the air and then laughed. "When I was advised that I could be at ease, I became conscious of the fact that my right pants leg was wet. But when I reached down to check my wound, I found that it was my canteen that had been hit.

"I had survived, and I was there for a purpose. Focusing on what was said to me was of utmost importance because orders were not written down. That was to prevent them from falling into the hands of the Japanese, in the event that the person carrying them was captured. I returned to camp the same way I had come with my orders, but for whatever reason, no one shot at me.

"Nothing changed for me after this incident. I went where I was supposed to go and did what I was supposed to do. Our troops were there to liberate the islands, as General MacArthur had promised, and I was doing my part to fulfill my country's commitment. I was luckier than Paul.

"I survived. If you were killed or wounded, someone else had to do your job, so protecting yourself protected the next man as well. I could not let fear take over my mind. If it ever waltzed through my conscious thoughts, I didn't dance with it. My behavior was the same, whatever I felt.

"I never thought of disobeying the orders my commanding officer gave me. For one thing, I would have been court-martialed had I done so." My uncle paused reflectively.

After some time when he did not continue, I asked, "What are you thinking about?" Turning toward me, he clasped his hands between his knees and leaned forward.

"I had the privilege of taking Paul's Silver Star to his wife Nancy when I got back to the States," he said earnestly. "Otherwise, she would have received it years later by way of the mail, if I had not personally delivered it. I knew this was what Paul would have wanted. It was a moment I have never forgotten.

"Genevieve went with me. As we were getting ready to go see Nancy, I said, 'You could have been receiving this.' It shook her up so bad, I was sorry I had said anything. Anyway, we drove up from Stantonsburg, where we were staying with Genevieve's parents, to somewhere in southern Pennsylvania and had a meal with Nancy Bashore.

"We presented her with Paul's Silver Star at that time. She was most grateful and very emotional. Their son was maybe four or five years old. He had questions, too. He wanted to know if this was for his daddy. I was so emotional myself that I had to stop several times and get cranked up to start again. There was no other way to do it.

"Paul's body was never brought back to the States. He was buried in Manila in the Punchbowl National Cemetery. The wife (or the family, if the soldier was not married) got to choose the burial site. When asked if she would like her husband's body to be returned to the States, Nancy said, 'No, leave him with his men.'

"Nancy has come to quite a few of the Company B reunions. She was living in San Antonio, Texas, and doing well the last time I knew." My uncle sat motionless in his chair and was silent.

It was the time of day when the sun and moon occupied the sky at the same time, and I could see both from where I was sitting. This time I did not ask Uncle Legs about his thoughts.

Giving Orders like Papa and Loving like Mama

*"I remember seeing one man cleaning a wound by running
a piece of gauze in one side and out the other side of
the hole that was in his leg."*

—Lieutenant Colonel Lehman H. Johnson, Jr.

An Indian summer held the promise of summer's return when I came again to Uncle Legs' house. He was sitting at the kitchen table waiting for me when I arrived on a Saturday afternoon early in September. He waved toward the kitchen window that was covered by neither blinds nor curtains.

"There were three deer grazing in my backyard when I was having my coffee this morning," he said. "It was about daybreak, and I just sat here and watched them. The smaller one, I think, is the fawn I saw in the spring. It's half grown now."

"Do you think they'll come out again?" I asked.

"Probably not until the evening, and then there's no guarantee. Let's go into the den." Using the table for leverage, my uncle steadied himself before gesturing in that direction. I was to go first.

Once seated in our usual places, he asked abruptly, "When was the last time you went to see Sulou?" This was in place of his usual question,

254 | MARY SUSAN HEATH

"How's your family?" Sulou Johnson Wagstaff was the middle child, the sister between himself and my mother Mary.

I had to think. "I took Mother to see her last summer around her birthday—Mother's birthday. Aunt Sulou doesn't remember her own birthday, or anyone else's for that matter."

"I know. That's why I don't go see her anymore. If you live, aging is inevitable, but the loss of memory is the cruelest death. Jane and I went to see her a few months ago and she called Jane 'Mother' and me 'Daddy.' She thought she was at Powhatan and that she was a little girl again." He leaned back and rested his head in the place that had been hollowed out over the years to hold it. The leather exhaled.

"Living on a farm, I learned many things that I have been able to apply to the rest of my life. Have you heard of that book *All I Need to Know I Learned in Kindergarten* by Robert Fulghum? Well, I learned just about everything I needed to know at Powhatan."

"Like what?"

"Sometimes, having been told to do so by my father, I would spend all day chopping corn or cotton to keep the weeds out of the rows. There was none of this spraying for weeds, like farmers do now. We were practicing organic farming before organic farming was invented. Besides the fact that weeds between the plants would keep the plants from growing, it was considered a sign of laziness if your crops were overgrown with weeds. So for one thing, I learned not to be lazy or to be thought of that way by our neighbors.

"At age fourteen, I was doing a man's work on the farm, and my shoe size matched my age already. In that respect, I was treated like a man, but when I came in for the evening, my mother treated me like the child I still was. My feet were always tired at the end of the day and sometimes blistered.

"She would put the kettle on the wood stove in the kitchen and heat some water that I was to pour into a pan. 'Be sure to put some salt in that water,' she said each time, like I might not remember. Then when the water cooled down sufficiently, she would take off my shoes and socks and wash my feet. That was the most soothing and loving thing she could have done for me.

"I learned then that when my feet hurt, I hurt all over, so that kind of pain was nothing new to me as an infantry soldier. As a commander, I took such things very seriously. The wounds to his feet and legs are of special concern to an infantry man because he knows that's how he's going to get by—with his feet and legs. Do you know the song about *'dogfaced soldiers who march'?"*

I shook my head.

"It's the official song of the infantry's Third Division, but it applies to any foot soldier. You can look up the whole song, but the part that I remember best goes like this:

> *I'm the walking pride of Uncle Sam.*
> *On all the posters that I read*
> *It says 'Be all that you can.'*
> *So they're tearing me down*
> *To build me up again.*

"Do you remember any more of it?"

"I'll never forget it." He continued, tapping out the rhythm on his knee.

> *I'm just a dogface soldier*
> *With a rifle on my shoulder*
> *And I eat raw meat for breakfast every day.*
> *So feed me ammunition,*
> *Keep me in the Third Division.*
> *Your dogface soldier boys okay.*

"I don't get it," I said. "What's the connection between dogs and infantry soldiers?"

"We sleep in pup tents and take cover in foxholes. When we march, which is how we move from one place to another, we get that hangdog look." My uncle's expression hardened, and he turned his face away from me although I could see the chiseled outline of his jaw.

"I remember seeing one man cleaning a wound by running a piece of gauze in one side and out the other side of the hole that was in his leg. It's a thing like that that makes a man feel like he's worth nothing—less than a dog even—especially an infantry man. Those that couldn't walk, and it was a matter of pride to do so, were carried on G.I. litters. Six walking soldiers, two in front, two in the middle, and two in the back manned these. If you could possibly walk, you stumbled along."

A muscle in Uncle's cheek twitched, and he took out his handkerchief and wiped his eyes. Then he turned toward me and smiled, his expression like the sun returning to the horizon from behind a cloud after a shower of rain. "In Leyte, my destination was Lubi, which was about halfway to the west coast of that province. Our mission was to support or relieve the U.S. troops that were there. But when we arrived at the coordinates specified in our orders, we found that the area had already been secured, so we turned around and marched back to the east coast of Leyte. It was about 155 miles round trip, and the entire march took about five days. Communication in the field was not what it is today."

"I guess not," I said.

"I remembered the sweet relief I had gotten from those foot baths my mother gave me, and while I couldn't wash each man's feet, I did the next best thing. I made sure they had clean socks and some of Doc Robinson's Jensen Violet powder to put in them. I believe the medical name for what we were using was gentian violet.

"Captain (Doctor) Robinson was our physician. 'Be sure to check your men's feet every day,' he said, and I followed his advice. At the end of a day's march, I had my soldiers take their shoes and socks off and wring out the blood, sweat, and mud from their socks. Those who were most in need got new socks if we had them. Otherwise, we washed them out with the water we were carrying or, better yet, in the cool mountain streams of Leyte. There's something about having someone attend to your physical needs that makes you feel better all over, inside and out. In that respect, I was their mama and their papa.

"In spite of our best efforts, many of the men got rashes or what we called 'jungle rot' on various parts of the body. You can get it from walking in contaminated water in the jungle and it isn't necessarily confined to the feet. I took their word for it when men complained of jock itch. Adding insult to injury, leeches from the mud hooked onto our pants' legs and sometimes got our legs.

"At Powhatan I had learned to improvise and make use of what was in front of me. On this march, I had the men wade out into the streams barefooted although otherwise, they were fully clothed. The water was cold and refreshing, and the leeches would turn loose. Clothes got washed and wounds were cleaned. The longer they could stay in, the more benefit they received.

"The best bath we got though was in Leyte Gulf. 'Go on in,' I said to my men, knowing full well from my own experience what their immediate sensation was going to be, given the fact that Leyte Gulf was saltwater from the Pacific Ocean. The salt Mother recommended was there all right.

"The first time in, the men hopped around, yelling and complaining about the burning and stinging of any place where the flesh was raw. With all that whooping and hollering, it was quite a war dance. The next day, the order to wade in was unnecessary. They were amazed at the medicinal effect of saltwater on aching muscles and insect bites.

When their wounds began to heal, they would go in several times a day up to their necks, some fully clothed, others nearly naked, their boots, socks, and weapons left along the shore. We were able to remain there for several days.

"The men were most grateful. I told them, 'That's the reason I thought of it. So that it would do y'all good.' Living on a farm, I knew these things, and now my men knew them. I was happy to pass along the information."

Uncle Legs glanced at his watch and out the window at the dying sun and the sky resplendent with swaths of autumn's gold and orange. The deer had not reappeared, or if they had, we had missed them. Guessing at his thoughts, I said, "I don't think they're coming, and besides, it's about time for dinner. I want to ask you some questions about what you ate as you were marching. I imagine it wasn't quite what you were used to."

My uncle grinned. "Not exactly. Makes for good dinner conversation though."

"Jane!" he called, loudly, and she appeared.

Food in the Field and on the Farm

"Spam was a staple. To this day, I cannot eat Spam."

—Lieutenant Col. Lehman H. Johnson, Jr.

"We had mostly pork at Powhatan, and I've got a taste for it tonight. I've told you, cows on the farm were for milking." Uncle Legs spoke to me over his shoulder when we were on our way to Smithfield Chicken and Barbecue. "I'm also going to get some banana pudding. Not the same as Mother's, but it does remind me. At least the name is the same." He smiled.

We all ordered barbecue plates, although the portions varied. Uncle Legs ordered a large. Food was important to my uncle. As we ate, he explained to me that while food was a necessity, it wasn't treated that way when he was growing up.

Uncle Legs took the last bite of his barbecue and used his spoon to scrape out the rest of the Brunswick stew. When he had finished, he raised his hand and signaled to our waitress.

"Could we have three banana puddings, please, ma'am?"

I wondered if he would eat it this time. When she returned with our desserts, I noticed that someone had removed the lids from the individual containers in which it was served, and that a topping had been added. Those that could be seen behind the counter had only a few graham cracker crumbs on top for garnish. My uncle stabbed his with his spoon. "Just as I expected. Cool Whip!" he said disdainfully.

My uncle's spoon made a scratching noise against the inside of the plastic dish that held his banana pudding. "I still don't like to waste food," he added and polished it off.

"Can we talk about the food you ate in the field?" I asked.

"At home," Uncle Legs said, and then loudly, "Check please." Our waitress was busy at another table and did not turn around. Louder still, my uncle announced, "I need my check."

"Hold your horses. I'll be right there," she said, disappearing into the kitchen. Her face flushed, our waitress returned a full five minutes later and slapped the check on the table as she brushed by us.

Jane and I stared at each other, waiting for the other shoe to drop as Uncle Legs pulled out his bank card. I could tell by the ripple in his jaw that he was clenching and unclenching his teeth.

"Legs, we still need to leave a tip," Jane said firmly. She knew him, and I was getting to know parts of my uncle that I had not known before.

It was a quiet drive back to their home, and it was only after he had settled himself in the den with a glass of wine that I dared ask, "Can you remember what you ate on that march to Lubi and back to Bito Beach?"

"How could I forget? All we had to eat were C-rations. We built fires when it was not too wet or too unsafe. Boiling water was heated in our helmets for coffee, for Nescafe powder, or perhaps for hot bullion. Otherwise, we drank our beverages cold.

"Spam was a staple. To this day, I cannot eat Spam. Some lady brought a Spam casserole to a church supper and asked me to try it. I told her I did not eat Spam." My uncle shook his head in disgust. "We also had canned chopped pork with egg yolk mixed in. A little can of processed cheese might also be part of a particular meal. The food came in small O.D. cans, so named because they were olive drab in color. Each can was about the size of a can of tuna—one serving." He swallowed hard as though tasting it now.

"We even had dessert! There were two standard dessert bars, one of which was usually part of the meal. Our fruit bar was made of dried raisins and apricots pressed together. Then there was the Hershey Tropical Chocolate 'D' Bar that could also be melted in boiling water for a cup of weak hot chocolate. Sometimes there was a pack of lemonade or grape powder, made by Miles Laboratories, to be mixed with water to wash it down."

"Did you have a favorite and was there a choice?"

He smiled in amusement. "I can't say that I did. Neither was very good, and we never had choices. We ate what we were given. That much at least was like home. My mother never asked us what we wanted to eat.

"Our 'after-dinner mints' were six small candy wafers that were hard as rocks. Three were pure sugar and the other three were chocolate. We concluded our dining with a stick of Wrigley's gum that came wrapped in that olive drab paper and a government-issued cigarette, if you smoked. Packaged in a little box of four, your after-dinner smoke was either a Camel or a Lucky Strike. I didn't smoke, and I always gave my cigarettes to my runner, Johnny D., who also dug my foxhole.

"Anyway, we arrived in time at Bito Beach to have our turkey and all the trimmings our cooks could prepare for Christmas. It was December 25, 1944. I ordered the cooks to make desserts, cakes and pies, all the men could eat. We had chocolate pies, and I don't think they were made with those government-issued chocolate bars. They were too good or maybe it was because we hadn't had anything like that in a long time. We had sweet potato pies although I'm sure the sweet potatoes were canned. There was a tipsy cake and a pound cake as well. I'm sure our cooks used up most of our sugar and flour rations for that one meal.

"It wasn't a mother's love or a mother's cooking, but growing up, I remembered how food that had been prepared just for me had made me feel. It was the best I could do for them—my men." He closed his eyes and breathed deeply. Although he did not say, I supposed he was seated at the table at Powhatan with his parents and sisters in the fellowship of a meal, in itself a prayer of blessing.

When he did not speak, I asked, "What are you seeing now?"

"When I was growing up, the presents that I got for Christmas were mostly handmade, usually a new piece of clothing that my mother had made, and maybe an orange. Oranges were special. Persimmons, pears, figs, and apples grew on the farm, but not oranges. You had to buy those, and we didn't have them any other time. We always had a tree. I chopped it down from the woods on the farm, a holly tree or maybe a pine and we made our own decorations." My uncle paused, and I could see the kaleidoscope of time shifting and aligning itself in his mind. He continued.

"We didn't have a tree that Christmas on Bito Beach. We had seen enough trees in the jungle and we definitely didn't want to send anybody out to find one. It was too dangerous. We didn't have any fresh fruit to give the men that Christmas, but the new fatigues, boots, socks, and underwear that we were able to issue them were presents enough.

"I did it myself," he added.

"What?"

"Handed out their new clothes."

"Then you played Santa Clause," I said.

"I suppose I did, and I was jolly. Good night, Mary Susan." My uncle rocked three times forward in the chair and then got to his feet. He steadied himself with his cane and then stepped lightly down the hall toward his bedroom, where Jane was already sleeping.

"Good night, Uncle Legs," I called to his retreating form.

"Ho, ho, ho," floated back toward me from the other end of hall.

Letters from Home

"You can't go home unless there is a death in your immediate family. This is your job until the war is over."

—Lieutenant Colonel Lehman H. Johnson, Jr.

My uncle was in a somber mood after church. "In January, Jane and I are going to the Methodist Conference Center, near Ashville, at Lake Junaluska for a session on death and dying," he said. "It's called the Festival of Wisdom and Grace. The title of the featured presentation is 'That Place We Call Heaven.'" He had exchanged his Sunday sport coat and tie for a sweater and the blanket that was normally draped across the back of his chair. When he pulled the wrap closer to his chin, I saw that he had taken his shoes off.

"I want to find out more about where I'm going," said Uncle Legs quietly. "The Bible says there are streets of gold in heaven and mansions with many rooms. I think it's described that way so we can wrap our finite minds around understanding an infinite place. I'm looking forward to the conference." Without asking, Jane left the room and returned with another blanket, which she spread over his feet.

"I want to come back before then," I said. What I did not say was that I wanted to finish hearing what my uncle had to say before he left on the glory train. He was carrying baggage, and he had designated this time in his life for unpacking. I wanted to be there while he was doing the sorting.

"Come as often as you can," Jane said and left us alone in the den. My uncle nodded his assent and then lowered his eyelids.

"We were in Leyte," I prompted.

"Yes." My uncle sat forward in his chair and took his wallet out of his back pants pocket. "I want to show you something," he said and retrieved a much-creased piece of paper from his brown leather trifold.

When Uncle Legs handed the sheet to me, I saw that it was a copy of a Biblical passage. Across the top was written *Psalm 91*, in his handwriting. "I had just come out of the mountains of Leyte and we were halfway through that march I told you about. Each morning that we were camped we had mail call. The mail was delivered from headquarters, and for most of us, it was the highlight of the day. Headquarters moved as our commanding officers moved, but the mail always seemed to find us.

"This particular morning, I received a small New Testament Bible, King James version, from Genevieve and a little note about fear. She wrote that she and the boys were doing well and told me about what she was doing to raise our children in my absence. She reminded me that they needed their father and to be careful of my own life. I hadn't even seen Jule yet. He was born after I deployed.

"She also wrote that she wanted me to read Psalm 91. I did so immediately." I handed the paper back to my uncle and he began to read:

(1) He that dwelleth in the secret place of the Most High shall abide under the shadow of the Almighty. (2) I will say of the Lord, He is my refuge and my fortress: my God; in him will I trust. (3) Surely he shall deliver thee from the snare of the fowler, and from the noisome pestilence. (4) He shall cover thee with his feathers, and

under his wings shalt thou trust; his truth shall be thy shield and buckler. (5) Thou shalt not be afraid for the terror by night; nor for the arrow that flieth by day; (6) Nor for the pestilence that walketh in darkness; nor for the destruction that wasteth at noon-day. (7) A thousand shall fall at thy side, and ten thousand at thy right hand; but it shall not come nigh thee.

"In that Psalm, David is reassured by God. I felt protected in that moment."

(8) Only with thine eyes shalt thou behold and see the reward of the wicked. (9) Because thou hast made the Lord, which is my refuge, even the Most High, thy habitation; (10) There shall no evil befall thee, neither shall any plague come nigh thy dwelling. (11) For he shall give his angels charge over thee, to keep thee in all thy ways. (12) They shall bear thee up in their hands, lest thou dash thy foot against a stone. (13) Thou shalt tread upon the lion and adder: the young lion and the dragon shalt thou trample under feet. (14) Because he hath set his love upon me, therefore will I deliver him: I will set him on high, because he hath known my name.

"Mary Susan, those words spoke to me. They have come to me many times when I was trying to find a foxhole, and I have been 'delivered' on more than one occasion." My uncle smoothed the creases in the paper and continued reading.

(15) He shall call upon me, and I will answer him: I will be with him in trouble; I will deliver him and honor him. (16) With long life will I satisfy him and show him my salvation.

My uncle leaned forward in his chair, his face intent. He lifted his chin and the eyes, now grey as granite, bore through the distance between us and closed it. One of the blankets fell to the floor, and he left it there.

"The long life promised in this psalm has been mine, and I have faith that the Lord will show me His salvation—in His time."

My uncle's eyes were alert, watchful as a fox in a hen house, and I imagined he was seeing a shadow box of collected escapes. "Since that time, I have carried a copy of that psalm in my wallet. I have used it in speaking many times, most recently from the pulpit of Mebane United Methodist Church."

As Uncle Legs gazed at me, it seemed that the grey irises of his eyes were transformed into a tranquil ocean blue as we waded out deeper into the pools of his memory, isolated, and separated until the tide of time would come and join them. He glanced reflectively at the portraits on the wall of his children.

"The letters I got from Genevieve were always encouraging. One morning I got a letter saying that she was going to enroll at Atlantic Christian College in Wilson to finish her degree. Her parents were going to look after the children while she was in class.

"The very next day I got a letter asking me to please disregard the one from the day before. Genevieve wrote, 'My responsibility is to raise these children in your absence.'

"I hadn't had time to write back, nor would I have tried to tell her what to do. But I was glad she made that decision. I didn't feel that it was her parents' responsibility to look after our children.

"Genevieve always understood that my first responsibility was to defend this country. I thought about my family, but I didn't worry about them. Genevieve was giving me the freedom to focus on what we both knew I had to do. So many men didn't have that kind of support or respect."

The smile that caused the corners of my uncle's mouth to turn up lifted his whole face and then disappeared. He stretched and tossed the remaining cover aside as he turned toward me. "The story I'm going to finish with is not a happy one, but it has a happy ending." Uncle Legs shook his head.

"By the time we got to Manila, we had been put in reserve by our regimental commander. That meant we had been taken out of combat, to rest, re-supply, and be available if the enemy acted up in another area.

"We were doing just that when one morning one of my platoon sergeants came up to me and said, 'I want you to read this letter.' He was hanging his head, but I could see that he was using the back of his hand to wipe his eyes.

"I read the letter and then I read it again, slowly. What his wife had written infuriated the hell out of me. She told him that when he returned home, not to expect to live with her because she was living with someone else.

"Can you believe that?" My uncle's eyes looked like flint that had been struck with a hammer so that sparks flew indiscriminately. "Her husband was fighting for his country and for his life, for her, and she had betrayed him in the worst possible way. I was so angry I almost choked on it. I remember struggling to find words that wouldn't make him feel worse and spitting them out. Was I successful? I don't know. I don't remember what I said at first.

"My sergeant was, of course, understandably upset that his wife was going to leave him and that she was sleeping with another man. He wanted to go home.

"When I could talk with some sense, I put my hand on his shoulder and said firmly, 'You are assigned to this unit, and we need you to stay here and fight this war.' To make sure he understood, I also said, 'You can't go home unless there is a death in your immediate family. This is your job until the war is over.' Then I added, 'I'm sorry about your wife.'

"When I said that, he looked up at me and said he understood.

"'Find someone back home you can trust to tell you the truth about what's going on,' I advised him. It was the same advice that unfortunately I had to give to many men. If every man with an unfaithful wife had gone home, we would have had a serious reduction in the ranks."

The set of my uncle's jaw hardened like quick dry cement, but his voice softened. "Military separations are hard on families, especially the wife," he said quietly. "Everyone was not as fortunate to have the kind of relationship Genevieve and I had." Then he sighed, releasing his anger like a hot air balloon that soared off into the sky until it couldn't be seen from the ground.

"I will say that to his credit my sergeant did not let the news of his wife's desertion affect his performance. He was able to do his duty like a good soldier, and I had no complaints about his performance. I was able to recommend him for a promotion to warrant officer, and he got it. I'm guessing he coped with his loss like most men in his position. Rather than grieve alone, he found a friend to pour his heart and soul out to, maybe someone who had gone through the same experience. I imagine he took my advice and got the straight of what was going on from someone besides his wife. He survived."

"Is that the happy ending?" I asked.

Uncle Legs laughed. "No. Years later I ran into him at one of our annual Methodist conferences. I couldn't help myself. The first thing I said to him as I was shaking his hand was, 'Did things work out between you and your wife?' He was by himself at the time.

"I'll never forget the look on his face. It was almost like he had to stop and think. 'No!' he said. 'But I've got me a good wife now, and we have children.' The man was positively ecstatic.

"It's been said that suffering has no memory," I said, "especially when the pleasure of the moment has all but erased past pain."

"I disagree," my uncle said. "Letters like the one my sergeant received made my job harder, his job harder. I have not forgotten, and I remember how a letter like that affected the morale of an entire company."

As though to prove it, he added, "His name was Bill Cupit, and he was from Texas. After the war, he became a Methodist minister, and he retired in eastern North Carolina. He had a good life, and he finally got a good wife. He was one of my very best noncommissioned officers."

Jane was coming up the basement steps. "As for me, I can't believe one man could be so fortunate twice."

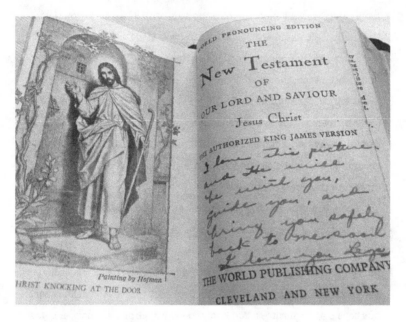

Hand written in the Bible that Uncle Legs' wife, Genevieve, sent to him while he was on duty in the Pacific was her personal love letter to him. For easier reading, it is typed on the two pages that follow.

January 26, 1945

My Darling,

If there were any words to describe the loveliness of our life togeth-er—believe me, I'd use them now. You've given me everything in the world a girl could ever want and I'll never cease being grateful to God for it. Somewhere in this wonderful plan of human life He made you and me for each other. We were quite young when we realized it and thereby have gained so very much. I know the moment I looked into your eyes that for me—it would always be you and you alone.

From the time we met and especially since we've been married, you've been kind, thoughtful, and considerate always. We've had fun, we've known sorrow, and thru Him we've been completely happy.

Ah, my darling I owe you so much that I'll never be able to repay. But I'll do my best—don't forget that. I miss you terribly and at times become so blue and discouraged but always there comes that inward strength and courage from God.

Since you've been away your pictures and letters, and love, have kept me going. I'll be just as true to you as night is to day. I love you Legs more than anyone else in all this world and always will. I am yours—completely and will be waiting for you with open arms until you're in them to stay. I love you, my darling. No, I can't forget the part our boys play in our lives. You know so very little of them now, and yet they're very much like you, both of them. Lee is just large enough to try to comfort the best he can. Sometimes I don't think I could bear it with-out him. He says, "Mommy, don't cry; Daddy'll be back." He's adorable and means the world to me.

Julian is small enough to demand my time and constant attention and sweet enough and near enough like you to make me love it.

Between the two I stay busy and am tired enough at night to sleep soundly.

I love you my precious, never forget how much and please hurry back. I love you. My precious, you have my solemn promise that I will love you with all my heart forever. I will do my best to rear our children into fine Christian men until you can join me.

Wherever you are — whatever you're going thru — don't forget our love and you've got to come back to me. I couldn't live without you. You have —

All my love — All my life -

"Snooks"

The Protection of Rank

"There is no rank in death."

— Lieutenant Colonel Lehman H. Johnson, Jr.

I arrived on my uncle's doorstep on a cold Saturday morning in October. A few daffodils beside the carport nodded their brown tissue-like heads in greeting while the wind swirled around me and them. Some people deadhead their daffodils, pinch off the faded blossoms, but not Jane Johnson. She knew they would be more likely to return in the spring if left alone.

They aren't pretty, I thought, but they're holding their own, stubborn, resistant as my uncle to the changing seasons of his life. The understanding that I had with Jane was that I was to "go on in, so Legs wouldn't have to get up." She would be out shopping and getting her hair done, errands she made up to leave us alone.

I walked in straight through the kitchen and into the den, calling loudly, "I'm here, Uncle Legs."

"I hear you, and I'm still here. And I'm not deaf, you know." My uncle was seated, fully dressed, with socks that matched one of the shades of blue in his plaid sweater. His cane was across his knees and his loafers were within easy reach.

"Yes," I said, bending over to embrace him. He allowed it but did

273

not respond. I seated myself on the edge of the couch and waited. I was about fifteen minutes late.

"Traffic," I murmured.

Before he spoke, I came to understand that excuses were a violation of our relationship. I imagined my uncle stabbing the carpet with his cane, as he had waited impatiently for me. He gave it another good poke before dropping the cane to the floor with slightly more force than was needed.

"Sometimes an officer wears his rank on his shoulder." He tapped his left shoulder. "By that, I mean that some officers take advantage of their authority and abuse the privilege of rank. The story I'm going to tell you, however, is about an officer who should have observed the privileges, as well as the limits, of his rank."

"How so?"

"If I tell you that now, you won't appreciate the story."

I asked no more questions and he began. "Toward the end of the war we were on the road to Manila, otherwise known as Highway 17, when I observed 'marching fire.' Marching fire is fire that gets progressively closer to a unit. We had come to a high ridge and a long sloping hill. We could see enemy fire tearing up the leaves of the foliage beside the road before us, and it was coming toward us. Of course, we did not continue marching toward it. Instead I ordered my men to evacuate to the side of the road.

"We were all scrambling to find a hole to get into as the artillery shells fell around us. I was among them and I couldn't find a hole. We didn't shoot back because we couldn't see where the fire was coming from. I saw men falling to my right and to my left and heard some of them screaming. I covered my eyes and lay flat on the ground. But I could still hear.

"Under these conditions, it's hard to tell how much time passes. Five minutes maybe. Suddenly there were no more high notes. It was quieter and the screaming had deteriorated into the muffled moans of the wounded. I checked myself for wounds and when I determined that I had none, I got up and looked around for those who did.

"The first thing I saw was a body lying motionless on the ground about fifteen feet in front of me. There were no visible wounds, but even before I touched him, I thought the man was dead. He was too still to be alive.

"Because I was not worried about injuring him, I turned him over to check for identification. What I saw was startling. The man looked very peaceful, like he was asleep, except for the shrapnel wound and a little blood trickling down just above his right temple. He was obviously dead, but that was not what gave me a turn. The eagle on his shirt collar identified the man as a full colonel, and his nametag indicated that he was Col. Cole, a member of General Eichelberger's staff.

"After the artillery passed, I called some of my men to get the body up and bring it back down to the road. It didn't seem appropriate to leave him lying out there in the rice field, where we had taken cover. Col. Cole had been no more or less protected than anybody else despite his status. But what was he doing there?

"When the men laid him down, I covered him with a poncho out of respect. Just as I did so, a jeep with three stars on it drove up and stopped in front of us. In it was General Eichelberger.

"I reported to him and asked, 'Sir, do you know a Col. Cole, Sir?'

"'Col. Cole is one of my staff officers,' he replied.

"'He's dead, Sir,' I said, and pointed to the body. 'My men and I have just brought him off the field.'

"'What in the hell was he doing up here?' General Eichelberger exploded.

"That, of course, I could not answer since, before his death, I had in no way been aware of his presence. The commander of the entire 8th U.S. Army was furious. He had more to say in my presence to his officers who were supposedly responsible for Col. Cole being out of place. The whole thing, including the general's remarks, happened in a matter of fifteen minutes.

"I do not know when Gen. Eichelberger sent back for the body, or if Graves Registration handled Col. Cole in the same manner as the enlisted men who also died that day. Col. Cole was just as dead as they were. There is no rank in death."

My uncle stared straight ahead without blinking and then turned his unflinching gaze on me. I was the one who flinched. He took a long, restorative breath and then spoke. "I do remember why Col. Cole was in our general vicinity. General Eichelberger had joined us because he wanted to see the 511th Infantry Regiment jump. We had performed for him and were now making our way to Manila.

"My commanding officer had told me to guard the general and his staff while he remained with us, and I had assigned that task to my first sergeant, Art Leveque. Apparently, Col. Cole was along for the ride, so to speak. Art was in no way responsible for the colonel's death. He would not have been in a position to tell someone who clearly outranked him where to go and where not to go. Although I never asked him, I'm quite sure Col. Cole did not inform Art Leveque of his whereabouts.

"The memory of this incident is one of the most vivid in my mind. I still don't know why he was there. Maybe this was just his date with death, but it still seems to me that he was the one who paid a call on death, not the other way around. As a member of the general's staff, he should have been behind the infantry, not in a position where he would be among the first to encounter enemy fire.

"Maybe Col. Cole wanted to go back home and tell his sons that he had been with a front-line company in combat and that he was a front-line colonel. He didn't make it home to tell his story, so we'll never know for sure. But what we do know is that even colonels aren't immune to pride and there's certainly nothing about rank that protects a man from death if he dares it.

"There were over two hundred men running across the field that day, trying to find cover. Did Col. Cole run like the rest of us? Did he even try to take cover? I'll never know. His death has caused me to ask myself many times, 'How did I get back here and why am I still alive?' Psalm 91 says, 'A thousand may fall at your side, ten thousand at your right hand, but it will not come near you.'

"Was I somehow chosen? I don't know. It is just as much a mystery to me today as it was then as to why Col. Cole died at that particular place and time, and I survived. There is no answer—no rhyme or reason—as to why I am here today and so many others are not."

Being Careful Not to Rankle Rank

"Expressions of feeling had no place in the Army that I knew, at least in connection with those officers above me."

— Lieutenant Colonel Lehman H. Johnson, Jr.

That evening Jane, Uncle Legs, and I were seated in Huey's, enjoying dinner and the celebrity status my uncle's presence afforded us there. Our booth, where we always sat if we could, was the last one on the right from the entrance. Even though she had farther to go to get to us than to any of her other customers, Darla, our waitress, was at his side immediately and took our drink orders.

Uncle Legs waited until she was out of earshot before he leaned across the table toward me. "Some officers give orders and make demands in such a way that the men serving under them feel that their lives are of no consequence to their leaders.

"I tried not to do that then and I try not to do it now with other people who serve me, like Darla there, and anyone else who waits on me — clerks in a store, the man who cuts my hair or mows my grass."

Darla was back with her pen poised to take our order. "What'll you have, honey?" Her attention was directed first to my uncle. He deferred to Jane and me.

279

"Let them go first." The smile that my uncle bestowed on Darla would have warmed ice-cold coffee.

When Darla had disappeared into the kitchen, my uncle continued. "It's a mark against his character when a man in a position of power uses his status to make someone else feel subservient. I know what that feels like. I make it a point not to act like that.

"My parents never talked down to me even when I was a child. I was treated with respect. I didn't have to be told to respect my elders or anyone else who was in authority."

He sighed. "The interaction I had with General Eichelberger at Col. Cole's death was not my last communication with him.

"We were on the island of Luzon, but not yet to Manila. I mentioned to the General that I would like to show him something very picturesque and beautiful. He agreed to go and allowed me to lead him to a viewing point at Lake Taal. I held back the branches that were growing into the path and stepped back so he could go in front of me.

"Lake Taal is a fresh-water lake that was formed by volcanic eruptions thousands of years ago. Volcano Island is in the middle of the lake, where there is an active volcano. Because of the sulfuric content of the water, it's yellow. I had never seen anything like this in Johnston County. I didn't think there was anything like it in the United States, so I was very impressed with my discovery.

"General Eichelberger looked back over his shoulder at me and said, 'Yes, it hasn't changed much since 1918.'" Uncle Legs slumped in his seat.

At that moment, Darla returned to our booth and carefully set our plates in front of us. She stood quietly before him and waited until he spoke to her. "Thank you," he said. "I believe we have everything."

"Call me if you don't," she replied and retreated to the window behind the cash register.

Uncle Legs said grace and then stared at his food. "I was deflated, and I don't remember saying anything other than, 'Yes, Sir.' You see, as a young lieutenant fresh out of West Point, General Eichelberger had been on the island of Luzon in 1918. He had been there with General Douglas McArthur. I had forgotten that.

"That was the last time I offered any of my personal impressions to a senior officer. Expressions of feeling had no place in the Army that I knew, at least in connection with those officers above me. There were lines that were not to be crossed, and I did not cross them again after that conversation with General Eichelberger."

The rest of our meal was eaten in silence. Neither Jane nor I could come up with anything to remove the sting of Legs Johnson being reminded of where he came from. My uncle's gaze across the crowded dining room was a stormy grey.

"Check, please." My uncle did not raise the tone of his voice even as he raised his hand to signal Darla. She was at our table instantly with the bill in hand.

Uncle Legs took out his pen and did a little math on the side to figure the tip. "Here. You can take this," my uncle said, "and thank you for your service."

On the way home, in the passenger seat beside Jane, he was quiet. He fixed his eyes on the road leaping up in front of us and moved his head slowly from side to side as though scanning it. "The farm boy in me is watching for deer," my uncle said finally, as if he could read my mind.

I looked in the same direction to see if I could see any deer poised beside the road. All I could see was the woods and the trees blurring behind us.

Once we were settled back in the den, Uncle Legs resumed his thoughts. "Maybe it's because the people at the corps level can sometimes be four to eight miles behind the front line that causes them to feel so removed. There was give and take between myself and my parents because we lived and worked so closely together on the farm. It was the same between myself and my men. We depended on each other for survival, and we knew it. That truth bonds a commander to his men. When Lee Holstein, who was my mortarman, hit his target, I didn't think about the fact that he was an enlisted man, and I was an officer. What I said was, 'Fine shooting, Lee!' We've been friends ever since.

"You're all in the same position. You're shooting at the enemy, and they're shooting at you. How well the man beside you does his job affects your survival. These types of relationships cement the company together, and that includes their commanding officer. That bond did not exist between me and the men who were my own commanders."

My uncle glanced over at me to see if I understood. I nodded.

"I did learn something from these experiences."

"What did you learn?"

"To use whatever advantage I had and to overcome any disadvantage that might present itself. Just so you don't think that I kept putting my foot in my mouth, I'll tell you this. During the occupation of Germany, General Clovis Byers, the 10th Corps Commander of the United Nations Forces, said to me, 'We know what you're talking about, Johnson. You speak our language.' It was not an off-hand remark, but the very highest compliment coming from him.

"I had once seen General Byers break a full colonel down in one of his staff meetings because the man had used some Southern expression. The general didn't want any Southern slang in any of our verbal reports. After witnessing this unhappy event, I was careful to eliminate any such colloquialisms from my speech.

"But I still had my Southern accent. Maybe it was because I was taller than him that I was spared—seventy-six inches can come in handy. To reprimand me, he would have had to look up, and that would have been a difficult thing for a man in his position to do."

At that pronouncement my uncle drew himself up unsteadily to his full height and stretched. He reached for the cane beside his chair and balanced himself with it. The evening was early, but he was tired.

Without saying good night, Uncle Legs started down the hall. I was sorry he had felt defeated. My grandmother would have said it was tiresome, meaning that it was irritating to be reminded of that unpleasantness.

"Sweet dreams," I called after him.

"Sweet dreams, yourself," he said softly.

Of Morals and Manners

"'Be sure that you don't let your men get so drunk that they can't walk away,' I told my lieutenants."

—Lieutenant Colonel Lehman H. Johnson, Jr.

"I didn't mean to make it sound like my men were saints the last time you were here," Uncle Legs said flatly. "They weren't. My runner was always shacked up with some little Filipino girl, and one time he lost all his weapons, heaven knows where. I had to look after this soldier, but I depended on him to deliver messages to other companies and to bring word back to me. It was dangerous work."

He was stretched out in his chair with the stated intention of tackling a topic that followed naturally on the heels of a story from the time before, during the weekend we had together in October, the one about an unfaithful wife and the demoralizing effect of her letter to her husband. My uncle shook his head in disgust.

The lesson that morning in the older men's Sunday school class had been about Sampson and Delilah. The participants had discussed how Sampson had slept with his head in Delilah's lap and lost his focus because of her charms. My uncle had added that Sampson put himself in a place to be taken advantage of by the enemy. Sampson forgot that Delilah was the enemy, and she cut his hair when he was in that compromising position. His hair had been the sign of God's favor to Sampson and the symbol of his strength. Then the Philistines blinded him.

"Never put yourself or others in a compromising position because of your ego," my uncle had advised.

From the den, I could see Jane's poinsettias on the far end of the kitchen table. I had learned during the announcements in church that for Christmas, you could purchase one in honor or in memory of a member. The pastor had told us that the red poinsettias symbolized the sacrifice of Jesus' blood and the white stood for purity. The poinsettias in the house had been in the church last year. Jane had kept them. Only recently had she brought the plants out of the total darkness required for their regeneration.

The contrast between the colors was striking. I stared at the plants and waited for my uncle to begin. "Sampson was his own worst enemy," I said.

"He was, but when he got himself together, you remember he brought the house down on the Philistines. My story is related.

"There was a competition of sorts to see which company would get to Manila first and liberate the city. Companies A, B, and C all took different routes to confuse the Japanese and make sure somebody got through. I was the commander of Company B.

"As Nathan Bedford Forrest, the famous Confederate general, said on a number of occasions, I wanted to get there 'firstest with the mostest.' I did. Company B got to Manila first with the most men left standing. As part of the 187th Infantry Regiment, we liberated the city from the Japanese and received a Presidential Unit Citation, which we are allowed to wear as a permanent award."

'Proud as a peacock,' my grandmother would have said, if she had heard her son spreading his feathers, though he did so without any self-conscious vanity. Uncle Legs interrupted my thoughts.

"The island of Luzon, January of 1945. We, that is the 11th Airborne Division, had made an amphibious landing on the beaches at the village of Nasugbu. The Japanese were entrenched there and more importantly, they were occupying Manila.

"This story, however, is less about the invasion by the 11th Airborne Division at Luzon and more about our experience with the hospitality of the people we met there afterwards. They looked at us almost like gods.

"Although the war was yet to be won, in their eyes, we were already heroes. The Japanese had been there since December of 1941, when they invaded the island of Luzon and took possession of Manila. The Allied Forces led by General Douglas MacArthur had counterattacked, but had been forced to retreat in May of 1942, after promising to return. We came back in January, 1945.

"Some of the men couldn't handle being worshipped and couldn't keep their pants zipped. Many of them were away from home for the first time. Others just couldn't stay put and went AWOL after some little Filipino girl. When that happened and my soldiers didn't return, I sent the MPs out to get them.

"Anyway, once the beaches were cleared, we remained at Nasugbu for a brief rest en route to Manila. While we were there, the mayor of this little village invited all of us to stay overnight at his house. The Filipino people considered it an honor to have us, and they took very good care of us during our brief stop.

"In their four years of occupation, the Japanese had treated the natives like servants or even slaves, so they were very happy to be liberated. I decided to accept the mayor's offer of hospitality, but I did have some concerns. 'Be sure that you don't let your men get so drunk that they can't walk away,' I told my lieutenants, 'because we're not leaving anybody behind. They better be able to move out tomorrow morning.' We had no vehicles to transport them. They would have to walk to Manila."

"Why couldn't you stay longer?"

"By remaining at Nasugbu, we were giving the Japanese an opportunity to regroup and counterattack at a time when we would be most vulnerable." My uncle spoke reflectively. "We were also putting the people in that little village at risk. Then there was the issue of company morale and our mission. The longer they stayed there, the more likely the men were to forget that our mission was to liberate Manila, the capital city. We had a long, hard march ahead of us. Manila was 75 miles away.

"The next morning before light, the people of Nasugbu served my men breakfast. I remember hearing a rooster crowing and listening to the early morning sounds of preparation in the mayor's house. I went outside to join the men where they were waking up to the smell of coffee, real coffee, not this stuff we pretended was coffee when we were marching. We had eggs, sausage, and bacon—all kinds of breakfast food and very fresh. The chickens that had laid the eggs were just getting up and running around the mayor's yard, pecking and scratching. I let the men eat until they couldn't hold any more.

"Before we left, the mayor had us file through his kitchen pantry and fill our packs with any of the canned goods that were there on the shelves. The men got peaches, beans, all kinds of veggies—anything canned that you could think of and anything we thought we might use later. We pretty much cleaned out his storehouse. A company of hungry men can make a considerable dent in even the most well-stocked pantry.

"It was about sunrise when we left the mayor's house, moving out in a column of twos on each side of the road. Highway 17, the road to Manila, was a very narrow, poorly kept asphalt road, but it was better than the muddy footpaths of Leyte. Our cadence was 120 steps a minute, and we were able to make good progress.

"As usual, while we were marching, I listened when my men talked, and I paid attention when they didn't. What men normally talk about among themselves is what they did last Saturday night, or for the weekend. When in combat, they'll discuss maybe what they are looking forward to when they get home. But when they've been on the battlefield for thirty or sixty days, that runs out, and the longer they are away from home, the less there is to talk about. It can be very quiet on the line within the company. This time they had something to say, some of which probably should not have been discussed.

"We pushed on as fast as we could, engaging the enemy at all times. There were heavy casualties on both sides. But the specifics of those skirmishes are not what I want to tell you about.

"I want to say that during that march, we would use our bayonets to open the cans of food that we had collected from the mayor's house. When we could, we heated the food in our helmets or right in the cans over an open campfire. Everybody shared what he had. Nobody tried to keep anything just for himself. There's a sense of community that's created under these conditions that is impossible to duplicate.

"The canned food was a most welcome addition to our C-rations. By comparison, it was delicious. The food nourished our bodies, but it nourished us in another way as well. Every time we opened a can, we remembered how we had been received in Nasugbu and how much the Filipino people appreciated us."

Night drew close around us and the woods that circled the house were indistinguishable from the lawn. My uncle took the afghan from the back of his chair and spread it carefully over his lap, smoothing out the wrinkles. He glanced toward the basement steps, which led to Jane's office. Thinking he was finished, I stood up to leave.

"Wait. There's something else I want to tell you about Nasugbu. Sometime much later, when I was stationed in Germany, Genevieve and I were vacationing in Rome. We were on a tour and had just gotten off the bus. A Filipino lady who was with the group followed us out into the street. In very good English, she asked me, 'May I hug your neck?'"

My uncle grinned. "Of course, I said 'yes,' and it was only after she let go of me that I asked her why she wanted to do this. She explained that her father was the mayor of Nasugbu, and that she had fed my men breakfast while they were there. She had recognized the 11th Airborne Division insignia that I was wearing on my right sleeve, and she wanted to thank me.

"'You are more than welcome,' I said to her, 'then and now.' I think Genevieve was quite jealous at the time. At least that's what the expression on her face told me."

Uncle Legs shrugged his shoulders and raised his eyes to meet mine. They were as clear and untroubled as the sky on a warm day in winter. "I said to my wife, 'She was just one of the many little Filipino girls running around serving us during our brief stay at her father's house. She was just a child at the time.'"

Jane entered the room with his night-time wine. He looked up at her. "Now there's a pretty woman." She seated herself to his left where I imagined they spent most evenings together. If Jane had heard anything of the story, she said nothing.

I hugged her goodbye "Thank you for the time you've allowed me to spend with him."

"Thank you for coming. Legs looks forward to your visits, and so do I."

"Love you both," I said. My uncle patted his cheek, and I leaned over to kiss him. Jane walked me to the door.

Contrasts and Contradictions

*"Thinking you've been shot and being shot
are two entirely different things."*

—Lieutenant Col. Lehman H. Johnson, Jr.

"I'll be 93 this month, and I still remember these names and the events that are attached to them as clearly as the people I saw yesterday," Uncle Legs said to me, in January of 2009, from his seat in the den. "In some ways, they are more a presence in my life than those I pass and repass on a daily basis. They are always in the back of my mind." He crossed his legs and looked out the window, away from me.

I wanted to see what he saw out beyond the trees bare of leaves and exposed now. Together we could see glimpses of the highway beyond his house.

"I've already told you about Nasugbu and the stop we made there on Luzon."

I nodded.

"There were actually two assault attacks on the island of Luzon—one from the southern end of Batangas and another at the northern end of that province. Our first mission was to capture and occupy Nichols Air Force Base and our second was to secure the uninterrupted march of the main body of the 11th Division, 187th

Regiment—about 6,000 troops—to Manila. It was on this march, I think, that I became most aware of how differently men react when they're under the gun.

"I know of at least one instance of a man shooting himself in the foot, so that he could get sent home. The injury was not life-threatening, but he was doing a lot of loud moaning and groaning. Everybody knew but nobody said anything to the man, who will be unnamed. Even the medics took their own sweet time in getting around to treating him. To have a self-inflicted wound was a very disgraceful thing, and it would be a source of shame to his family today if his identify were known.

"Getting sent home for a minor wound or a sickness that could be treated on site was nothing to be proud of either.

"It was our first day along Tagaytay Ridge, on the road to Manila, and so far, it had been uneventful. My company had seen no Japanese, no snipers, and met no artillery fire. We had just caught up with Company L, from the 188th Infantry Division, when somebody hollered out at me.

"'Captain Johnson!'

"I stopped and turned in the direction of his voice. The company commander was sitting beside the road with a medic next to him. His right leg was bandaged, and he was all smiles.

"That's strange, I thought. He looks so happy and they have obviously just encountered some resistance from the Japanese. His men were using the break to drink from their canteens, but I noticed that none of them were relaxed. Each man had one hand on his weapon and the other held his canteen.

"'I got the go-home wound,'" he said, pointing to his leg. 'A piece of shrapnel broke my leg.'

"I couldn't stop to find out exactly what happened because my company was moving on ahead. I wondered what we were walking into. All I could say to Dave was, 'Give my love to your family,' as I briefly shook his hand and then ran to catch up. We were good friends. Genevieve and I had shared living quarters with him, his wife Dottie, and their daughter back in Pinehurst, North Carolina, while they had waited for housing. We had both been stationed at Fort Bragg before our deployment.

"We didn't see any action that afternoon. That came later. But Dave was certainly on my mind. I had some very mixed feelings about his situation.

"Another instance that I remember was truly minor. Another soldier, one of mine, had received a grazing wound just over the top of his right eye. For that it was determined that he was unable to carry out his duties. We called an injury like that 'a million-dollar wound.' That meant you had an injury that would heal with no lasting effect, but it was enough to get you to an area hospital and then home from there. This man never showed up again during the war. I recall his name, but will not say it here.

"The next time I saw him was after the war at Ft. Benning, Georgia. He had been sent down to be my communications officer. We never spoke of his wound or the fact that he had been sent home. I think he was embarrassed."

"How did you feel about him at that point?" I asked.

Uncle Legs shrugged his shoulders and glanced toward me. "What the hell—the war was over by then. He had to live with it, not me." His face relaxed into a smile. His eyes were as clear as the sky that day without even a passing cloud.

"I was never wounded, except in my canteen, so I can't really judge. Thinking you've been shot and being shot are two entirely different things."

We sat in silence until Jane came in with his coat over her arm. "You know it's time for us to eat," she said, holding the full-length overcoat so her husband could slip into it.

At Huey's, my uncle hung his coat and hat on the rack beside the door. "We haven't gotten to the best part, the part about the men who made it possible for me not to get shot."

It was a cold day, and we could hear the wind whispering outside the window at our booth. I welcomed the heat circulating in the room and the pleasant sounds of community in the kitchen and dining area. The war was still there, an undercurrent waiting for our return, and I could feel its presence leaking through the blinds, in the same way I could feel the chill in my soul.

The food at Huey's was comforting. As we ate our barbecue, pork chops, and fried chicken, Uncle Legs said, "Getting to Manila was definitely a company effort, but I want to remember two men who were able without fail to advance our purpose. If either one of them had concerns about his personal safety, those never came before protecting the company.

"E.M. (Fly) Flanagan, Jr. was the commissioned officer who served as the forward observer for both the 187th and 188th Regiments. Battalion headquarters assigned him the task of moving his men as a section between these two regiments, depending on where the need was. He was in charge of the heavy weapons fire support, the artillery, specifically the 75mm Howitzer. Fly was an exceptionally confident, out-going person, very expressive—always on the go, always ready for action.

"I can't recall a single instance when Fly turned down an order to fire, although he could have. You see, ladies," my uncle said, nodding across the table at us, "the relationship between the artillery and the infantry had to be reciprocal. The infantry, of which I was a part, was between the artillery and the enemy. Orders to fire needed to be given only when a target was assured. Otherwise, the artillery would not be so willing to expose their men to enemy fire."

Uncle Legs took a napkin out of the holder and with his pen drew their respective positions. "It looks like this," he said, showing Jane and then pushing the drawing across the table to me.

"I see."

He laughed. "We had such close fire support from Fly that occasionally I had to ask him to call it off. In other words, it was falling on us!" My uncle drew sparks with pen on the napkin to demonstrate the effect.

"We were very fortunate that Fly was exceptionally good at his job. Since the war, he has written a number of books about his experiences. I highly recommend them."

When there were no dessert orders, Uncle Legs paid the check and then made his way to the coat rack, occasionally touching the tops of the unoccupied booths as he passed them. It was then that I realized he had left his cane, as well as his coat, on the rack.

Taking his overcoat down, he pulled the sleeves through. "This coat is reversible. That's why I like it," he said. "One side is waterproof. The other side isn't. It isn't raining, so I'm going to wear it this way."

Jane went to get the car, and I waited with him. "There's more than one side to many things." I took his arm, and he did not pull back.

When we were back in the den, he said quietly, "I want to tell you more about Lee Holstein, my mortarman. I've mentioned our friendship, but I want to explain the basis and tell you why I think so highly of him."

"Lee Holstein was the sergeant in charge of the 60mm mortar section. The 60mm mortar was the weapon we used to destroy any resistance we encountered. Lee literally had our lives in his hands, and he became an expert at what he did.

"Although he had no military background before being drafted, Lee was an exceptionally effective soldier. He never faltered at any mission he was given, and I was very glad he was in my company.

"Here's what Lee did. Whenever we would find a position where the Japs were firing on us, I would send word to Lee. He would find the enemy in his field glasses and calculate the range expectation and determine the target destination. I can see him now, a small man, walking out about ten to fifteen paces and setting up a stick—that's what we called the men who would assist. Then he would line up the gun and fire. He was a very big man behind that gun.

"Lee was aggressive enough to know just how far he could go, but he wasn't cocky. Sometimes he would allow the enemy to come within five thousand yards of where we were camped. The closer they were when he fired, the more damage he was likely to do. But he did not take unnecessary risks. He wasn't a 'yes' man, but when I gave him instructions, I didn't have to worry about things getting done.

"Usually, Lee would get the target out of the way the first time he fired—poof—just like that. Occasionally, it took two rounds, but the Japanese would soon be destroyed. Because of this talent, Lee was very well respected within the company. I've already told you that he was Jewish, but I never witnessed any prejudice toward Lee among the men. Like me, they appreciated his skills and were confident in his ability to remain calm under fire.

"Lee and I have remained lifelong friends. He was with me through the occupation of Japan. When we get together, we talk about it. There's something about those kinds of experiences that press out any seeds of difference, so dissention never sprouted."

Jane entered seamlessly from her office and sat down across from me. "Lee and his wife Selma visited us once or twice a year, as long as Selma's health permitted them to travel.

"I remember once that we were going to take them to a golf course here in Raleigh, where Legs and I had a membership. We drove up to the pro shop and parked right in front of a sign that said, 'For Members Only and Their Guests.' Legs and I got out of the car. Lee hesitated.

"Legs opened the door to the back seat where Lee was sitting. 'Is there anything wrong?'

"For a moment, there was just silence. Then Lee said, 'I'm not allowed to play here.'"

Uncle Legs' feet hit the floor from the stool where they had been resting, and he picked up the story from there. "I said, 'What do you mean?'

"'I'm Jewish,' Lee said. I can see him looking me right in the eye that day. 'They don't allow Jews to play here.'"

"I was absolutely mortified," Jane said. "We had no idea."

"Lee didn't want me to make a big deal out of it," Uncle Legs said, "but after his visit, I went back to see if what Lee had said was true. Neither Jews nor blacks were welcome.

"Jane and I dropped our membership. And I told them why," he added.

My uncle was angry. "It was a good course, but we decided we could play elsewhere. If a decorated Army veteran wasn't welcome, then I didn't want to be there either." A muscle in his cheek twitched.

"If you don't mind," Uncle Legs said to me, "I think I'm going to sit up a bit."

Jane and I both rose to leave him. "I'll be in bed, Sir," she said and went down the hall, leaving me to say good night.

I gave him a quick hug and wondered if it bothered him that blacks were excluded as well as Jews. Looking at the set of his jaw, I decided against asking. I went upstairs and left him to his thoughts.

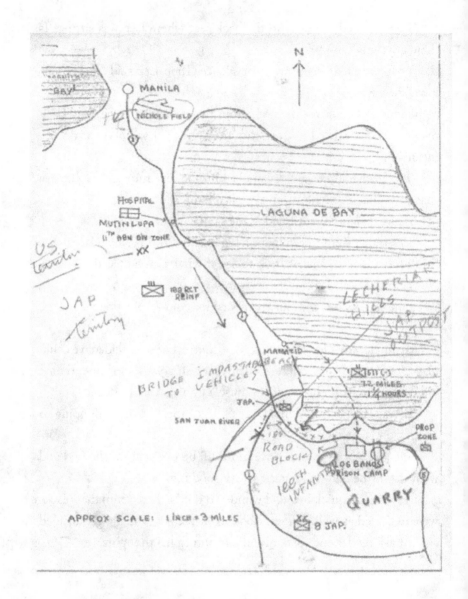

Company B of the 511th Parachute Infantry Regiment, 11th Airborne Division, jumped on Los Baños on February 23, 1945, securing the release of 2,147 prisoners of war. This was accomplished without the loss of any American lives or casualties among the detainees. Uncle Legs' role was in directing the repatriation of the Los Baños internees.

A Daring Rescue

"Public opinion is a strange animal."

— Lieutenant Colonel Lehman H. Johnson, Jr.

Back from church and Sunday lunch, Uncle Legs began our afternoon session philosophically. Jane had already left for her afternoon church meetings, and he and I were alone in the den.

"Take those guys returning from Vietnam. They weren't welcomed back, at least not the way we were. There were no parades and some people, those who didn't support the war, were downright hostile to them. Public opinion is a strange animal.

"Politics shouldn't have anything to do with it. Those men were drafted just like we were and fought just as hard as we did. I wasn't drafted, but many were."

I waited for my uncle to cross that bridge in his thoughts. He took a deep breath.

"Take Los Baños, for instance. The take-over of the prison camp was pretty smooth. It was no big hullabaloo, but the events made headlines back in the States. The Japanese guards were exercising on the parade grounds and didn't even go for their rifles. It was a cake walk. I don't know if that was just luck or not, but we didn't lose a single man.

"Strategically, Los Baños was important because of the timing. The prisoners there were in mortal danger because the Japanese were vindictive. Manila had been secured on Feb. 5, 1945, and MacArthur was anxious about the thousands of prisoners, including many civilians, who had been rounded up and incarcerated by the Japanese in various prisons located throughout the Philippines. Here's how that came to be.

"Before the war, many international companies had overseas operations in and around the major cities of the Philippine islands, including Manila, so many Americans were living there with their families. When war broke out, the Philippine government didn't know whether these international citizens would be on their side or on the side of the Japanese. So they had these people put in prison to control them. When the Japanese moved in, they took over the prisons. There were locations at Los Baños, Santo Thomas University, Bilibid, and Cabanatuan. Rescue operations took place at all of these camps."

"Can you tell me something about the involvement of the 11th Airborne Division?" I asked.

"The soldiers of Company B (511th Parachute Infantry Regiment, 11th Airborne Division) jumped on Los Baños on February 23, 1945. MacArthur's orders to that company as issued through General Joe Swing were to drop on the prison camp at Los Baños and secure the release of the internees."

And where were you? I wondered. Then I remembered from Lee Holstein's recorded interview for the Library of Congress (August 5, 2003). "We (the 187th Infantry Regiment) had to keep the Japanese busy," he had said. "We were strictly Infantry—always pushing forward (in Southern Luzon)...Otherwise, they (the 511th Infantry Regiment) wouldn't have been so successful (at Los Baños).

My uncle continued. "Company B of the 511th parachuted in about 6:00 a.m. and surprised the Japanese. The 188th Regiment was already there supporting the operation on the ground. The prisoners were not alarmed because they had been informed by the Filipino guerillas that there would be American troops in the area. When we attacked, they secured themselves pretty well, and to my knowledge, none of the detainees were killed or injured.

"We don't really know why the Japanese hadn't already executed the prisoners before we got there, other than they just hadn't gotten around to it. The information that we had through these same guerillas was that the man in charge, a Captain Sadaaki Konishi, a brutal man, had every intention of doing so. Under Konishi's command, rations, even for infants and children, had been drastically cut, while the guards were well-fed, and the storehouse was full. Unfortunately, Konishi escaped with six or seven other Japanese when we attacked. The others were killed or captured." My uncle allowed himself to rest briefly before he relived the rest of his assignment.

"We were then to organize the prisoners, so that we could march them to a point where they could be evacuated. In all, there were a total of 2,147 prisoners of war and civilian internees at Los Baños, so that was no small task. But I am satisfied that we did the best we could by these people, even though I had never done anything like this before."

"Like what?" I asked.

"Set up a process of repatriation. My orders from General Swing were to 'Go clear out the prison, Johnson.'—not an easy task, considering most of the internees were slow to gather themselves and did not understand that they were still in immediate danger from the Japanese. For starters and for their safety, we moved the prisoners across the lake to Mamatid and set up camp.

"I had an administrative monkey by the tail so to speak—not a good place to hold on to a monkey. There were so many people that we did not even have enough paper to write their names on. We started writing on toilet paper and paper wrappers when we ran out."

"How did you manage?" I asked.

"I set up a process by using the people in the prison to help with the organization—those that had kept their sanity, of course. Everyone was not so fortunate, but they were already familiar with each other, and for the most part on good terms.

"Then we asked the newly liberated prisoners some general questions. My officers and assistants were instructed to ask, 'How have you been treated? What kind of food have you been eating? Are you sick? Do you need medical treatment?' We had some nurses there in the prison from the East Indies who could help with the health issues.

"The lack of food appeared to be the most serious issue. In recent weeks, a doctor who had been imprisoned there in the camp, Dr. Dana Nance, listed malnutrition as the cause of death on most death certificates, although he had been warned by the Japanese not to do that.

"People had lost weight because they hadn't had three squares every day. Mostly what they had had to eat before we came was the same as what the Japanese soldiers had, although they had less of it—GI rations. Until Konishi put a stop to it, those prisoners who still had money could buy produce from the natives who came to the gate. Of course, even at the beginning of their imprisonment, everybody didn't have money. There was some dysentery, but they had not been beaten or tortured, as far as we could tell.

"Many of the bridges and roads leading from Los Baños had been destroyed, so we determined that the safest evacuation would be by amphibious tanks, 'amtracs,' across Laguna de Bay to Muntinlupa. The facility, formerly a Japanese prison, was now a hospital for the American Army. Conditions were not bad. There were bunks and open doors. Nobody was in confinement.

"The detainees fixed their own meals, just as they had before our coming. They ate what we ate, which was whatever the quartermaster had. Sometimes the Philippine people brought fresh fruits and vegetables and left them in our camp. We were very grateful."

My uncle moistened his lips and smiled. "Fresh pineapples, bananas, coconuts, anything they might have grown in their gardens. Everybody shared, and I don't recall any dissention over the distribution of these gifts."

He stretched and got up and went to the kitchen, returning with a box of Cheese Nips. "Have some," he said handing me the box after he took out a handful. He lowered himself carefully back into his chair.

"We needed to move quickly. By February 1945, Hitler was in hiding, but the war was not over yet. There were still pockets of resistance in the area—and of course, we had to feed and clothe all those people. There was also the very real problem that many of the former prisoners didn't know where home was any more.

"'Home. Where's home?' we asked them.

"Some of them had been in prison for as long as four years, and before that, many had lived and worked in the Philippines for decades. There were whole families, including children. They considered the Philippines to be their home. That was no longer the reality." My uncle popped a few of the crackers into his mouth and munched thoughtfully.

"The only person allowed to stay was Charles Armstrong. He was the adult son of Americans who had moved there. He had been born and reared there. As a liaison with the Philippine government, Charles was invaluable. Previously, he had commanded a guerilla force, and he spoke their language—Tagalog, as well as English. There were many dialects, but this was the dialect spoken around Manila and on Luzon. To my knowledge, Charles was the only exception.

"We asked a different question when the internees would say they didn't know what country they should go back to. 'Do you know anybody in the United States? Do you know anybody in England?' We went down a whole list of countries willing to take them. If the answer was 'Yes' to any country, we would send them there.

"Fortunately, we had good support from the Navy. They kept us informed about where the ships were that were coming to take the prisoners home and how fast they could get to us. We set it all up in a processing line, and once things started moving and the prisoners accepted that they could not go back to their former life, they were ready to go. The whole process of repatriation of the Los Baños prisoners took about two weeks.

"Then we left, and unfortunately, after we withdrew, the Japanese came back. Konishi disguised himself as a farmer and recruited the scattered Japanese soldiers who had also escaped. They massacred thousands of Filipinos before he was captured." My uncle sighed, a long breath of regret, and stretched his legs. "Konishi died of cancer before he could be executed for his war crimes. I hated that."

Uncle Legs bowed his head and was silent. When he looked at me, his gaze was as steady as a sure-footed goat scrambling over a rough place in the road. "The truth of the matter is that there were many guerilla troops in the area that had supported the Americans and the prisoners at Los Baños. Many of the residents of Los Baños and these guerilla troops felt that they had been betrayed when the American troops were withdrawn. They were at the mercy of the Japanese.

"But the 11th Airborne Division did not forget. To express our gratitude, we now sponsor the Los Baños Liberation Foundation. We established the foundation in 2003 at our reunion. Each year we give scholarships to twelve students at the University of Philippines Rural High School." My uncle sat up a little straighter in his chair. "This is the same high school that was located on the campus of the Los Baños Prison Camp. We remember, and we want them and their descendants to know that we appreciate their sacrifice."

I stood up to leave.

"Wait, please," he said, raising his hand. "Before you go, I have a very personal story that you won't read or hear anything about anywhere."

"Until now," I said, and sat back down on the sofa.

"You remember that after I was retired, I taught history for a while at Broughton High School in Raleigh."

I nodded.

"Mrs. Mary Sue Fonville, another history teacher, had asked me to give a lecture on my time in the Philippines to our combined history classes. I had ended my talk with the account of the rescue and repatriation of the prisoners at Los Baños. We were in the auditorium.

"When I finished, I looked up and saw Mrs. Fonville, coming down the aisle toward me with tears streaming down her face. I quickly dismissed the students and came down to meet her. I had no idea what was wrong.

"'I never knew until now,' she said, 'who repatriated my sister. Catherine Taylor Hodges is my sister.'

"She threw her arms around my neck and hugged me right then and there."

"That seems to happen to you a lot," I said. He laughed.

"A few of the students turned around and looked, but she didn't care. 'I just want to thank you,' she said. While I was speaking, Mrs. Fonville had put the date of the Los Baños Raid (Feb. 23, 1945) together with my account of the role of my division in the liberation of the prisoners (Company B, 511th Parachute Infantry Regiment, 11th Airborne Division).

"It was on that date that Catherine and her husband Harry had seen the 'white umbrellas' that were the parachutes of the soldiers of Company B who were jumping on Los Baños. She had told her sister about their release.

"You see, Mary Susan, at the time operating and living costs were lower on the islands than in America, and large American companies frequently outsourced parts of their operation there. Catherine's husband Harry had been a representative of McCormick-Deering, a heavy equipment company, and they had been living in the Philippines.

"Many of these businesses had already brought their people home when things heated up in Europe, but apparently McCormick-Deering did not. The Hodges were stuck there when the war broke out, but Harry said later he never thought they'd be bothered. They just wanted to be left alone to conduct their business. Instead, the Philippine government became suspicious and confined them to the prison camp at Los Baños.

"I knew all this because Harry had made himself known to me at the time. We had been classmates at Oak Ridge, although I did not recognize him at first in the prison camp. Even though there was a personal connection, Harry and Catherine were processed like everybody else. We couldn't let them out until we had determined their destination and set them up with transportation. All Americans were treated the same way—a one-way ticket home when the Navy could arrange it. Until then, they stayed in the camp.

"Government representatives from the United States and other countries came to escort their repatriated citizens home. There were officials from Indonesia, England, Australia, New Zealand, and many other countries, who came to get them. It was quite a conglomeration of nationalities."

"Did you take anybody home?" I asked.

"I did not. Some countries were more hospitable than others, and I did not want to get tangled up in any kind of international mess. There was no way to verify who actually belonged where or to establish citizenship. All we had was word of mouth and the records we created.

"Besides, my job was to process the detainees and to do so as fast as possible. I could not afford to get emotionally involved with helping people get settled and still accomplish my mission."

"What about Mrs. Fonville though?"

"What I felt that day was gratitude that I had been able to participate in such an event, and I was very happy that her sister and her sister's husband had survived the war. I had not known about this connection with my social studies chairperson until this moment. It was a very good feeling."

"Did you ask Mrs. Fonville about how Catherine and Harry had managed after the war?"

"I most certainly did, and I was gratified to learn they were doing well and that they were happy to be back in the States."

"Connections," I said.

By this time the darkness outside had circled the house and was hugging the doorstep in an embrace that would last until morning. I had to go, so I wrapped my arms around my uncle's shoulders and hugged him. He hugged me back.

"Yes, connections." He had the last word this time, and I was glad.

TOKYO

OKINAWA

On August 12, 1945, Uncle Legs' regiment left Manila for the occupation of Japan. They headed to Okinawa, en route to Tokyo. The plane he was assigned, a C-46, crashed on landing;
everyone was killed. Because a friend had asked to take his place, my uncle flew in later. "I
had to go and see the chaplain and discuss this," he said.

Feeling Small and Walking Tall

"They had survived the jungles and the Japs and now all twen-ty-four men on that C-46 were killed in a plane crash."

— Lieutenant Colonel Lehman H. Johnson, Jr.

I found Uncle Legs seated in the den huddled under the throw that usually rested on the back of his chair.

"I'm cold all the time now," he said, pulling the cover up under his chin, exposing his sock feet. "Before you sit down, could you turn up the gas logs? Jane is already out, and I never fool with the darn thing."

It was February, and the camellias that would be pink in the back yard were tentatively budding, their baby heads nodding back at me from the yard. The bushes, more like trees, were visible from the windows that flanked the fireplace.

I adjusted the dial on the logs, and the flame leaped up to illuminate the room.

"Catch me up, please." I sat on the couch where he could look directly at me.

Uncle Legs flexed his toes. They popped, the sound blending with the crackle of the gas. He drew his cover more tightly around him.

"We bombed Japan twice—Hiroshima and Nagasaki, Aug. 6 and Aug. 9. Japan did not officially surrender until August 15. But my regiment, the 187th Glider Infantry Regiment, took off from Nichols Field, Manila, on August 12, 1945, for the occupation. We were headed to Okinawa, en route to Tokyo, Atsugi Airfield."

Yes, the Rakkasans, I thought. You were with them—so named by the Japanese during that occupation tour, as the "men falling under umbrellas"—in their language, that was the closest they could come to "parachute troops." From my research, I know the 1st and 3rd Battalions of the187th Airborne Infantry Regiment are the remaining active units. The Rakkasans, 1st Battalion and 3rd Battalion, 187th Infantry Regiment, 3rd Brigade Combat Team, 101 Airborne Division (Air Assault)) are currently based at Fort Campbell, Kentucky.

My uncle's voice, raw with emotion, drew me back into his story. "We were loading for the trip from Luzon to Okinawa when a friend of mine asked if he could take my place on the C-46 to which I had been assigned for transport. I don't remember his name now or the reason for his request—maybe he was in a hurry to get there. I don't know.

"It didn't make any difference to me. We both had assignments relative to the occupation of Japan by the Allied Forces, and I was happy to accommodate another soldier. We switched the manifests which assigned us to specific planes. I took his place and he took mine. The exchange meant that I would come in on a later plane.

"For me the trip was uneventful. The C-47 in which I was riding landed without incident at Kadina Air Strip, Okinawa. I was on my way to turn in my manifest, thinking that I was glad to get to this point. Being there in Japan meant that I was that much closer to getting home to my family.

"Just before I got to the building that was serving as our headquarters, I spotted Tommy Williamson from Kenly, North Carolina, coming out the door. He was among the group of pilots who were flying us to Japan.

"When he saw me, he stopped dead in his tracks, so I stopped, too. He just stood there and stared. His eyes were big as saucers, and they got bigger. Finally, it looked like they couldn't hold any more.

"He came in closer for a better look. 'Why, why there's Major Johnson!' he stammered. 'How did you get here?'

"'The same as you,' I replied, eyeballing him back and pointing to the aircraft behind us.

"Then he told me that the plane I was supposed to be on, a C-46, had crashed on landing. A master list of who was supposed to be on board had, of course, been maintained. I was supposed to be dead.

"I learned later, much later, that these planes were known as the 'flying coffins' among the men who flew them. The Curtiss C-46 was the most massive twin-engine aircraft used during WWII. Let me show you something."

Uncle Legs got up and rested his hand lightly on the arm of the chair to steady himself, but he did not reach for his cane. Instead he stepped quickly to the bookcase and selected a volume entitled *The Army Air Forces in World War II*. When he brought the book back to his seat and opened it, I could see that page number 25 had been creased at the corner.

A muscle in his cheek twitched. My uncle read:

"From first to last, the Commando remained a headache. It could be kept flying only at the cost of thousands of extra man-hours for maintenance and modification. Although Curtiss-Wright reported the accumulation by November 1943 of the astounding total of 721 required changes in production models, the plane continued to be what maintenance crews aptly described as a 'plumber's nightmare.' Worse still, the plane was a killer ... From May 1943 to March 1945, Air Transport Command received reports of thirty-one instances in which C-46's caught fire or exploded in the air. Still others were listed merely as 'missing in flight,' and it was a safe assumption that many of these exploded, went down in flames, or crashed as the result of Vapor lock, carburetor icing, or other defects.'"

Uncle Legs slammed the book shut. He gripped it in his lap while I watched the knuckles of his hands turn white. "This particular crash was attributed to pilot error although other factors could have been involved. The plane landed short of the runway, killing everyone on board.

"They had survived the jungles and the Japs and now all twenty-four men on that C-46 were killed in a plane crash." He hit the book hard with the open palm of his left hand. "I should have been among them, but I was spared. Another soldier was dead.

"I had to go and see the chaplain and discuss this."

The silence between us got wider and deeper until I fell in.

"What did the chaplain say?"

The sigh that escaped from his lips was ragged on both ends as he placed the book on the floor. "The chaplain didn't have an answer for me any more than he had answers for other soldiers who probably came to him with the same question.

"I concluded that there were many things in this world that only God knows and which we're not meant to understand. I was able to go on because I had to, and I boarded a plane for Tokyo when it was time. This time I got on the plane I was supposed to be on."

Uncle Legs leaned back in his chair and closed his eyes. His breathing was deep and rhythmic; a seamless transition to what I hoped was relief and rest. At precisely 11:45, I heard the garage door open, and Jane was home. "Are y'all getting a lot of work done?"

My uncle's eyes flew open. "We certainly are. We're in Tokyo, occupying Japan."

"Finish up in there." Jane poked her head in from the kitchen. "The Reubens we're having for lunch will be ready by noon."

My uncle straightened his back and stretched. The chair exhaled. "The Allied Forces gave me an interpreter. The first thing I did when I got to Tokyo was to take him and call on the chief of police. The chief was a short man, like all the Japanese, and I towered over him. He asked me to have tea, which I accepted. We sat on the floor, but I was still taller.

"A Japanese woman, maybe his wife or a servant, poured our tea from the same pot. I waited while he drank first. Then I joined him. I asked the interpreter to relay the orders of the Occupation Forces of the United States Army, which I had been asked to deliver.

"There were other conditions, but one of those was that there would be a curfew. No one was to be out on the streets of Tokyo after six o'clock. I was very specific about that. I explained to him, through the interpreter, that anyone caught out on the streets after six o'clock would be shot on sight.

"I don't know if the man didn't believe me, or if there was a misunderstanding. Perhaps he didn't get the word out because the next morning my soldiers reported to me that there were now several dead Japanese lying in the street."

My uncle's lips curled in a smile, and he stood up. Swaying, he spread his feet apart to balance as he went down the hall, his left hand touching the wall. His voice floated back to me, his tone sure and even.

"After the first night, there was no more misunderstanding and no more problems with communication between us."

As my grandmother would have said, "The fox was in the henhouse."

It was 11:55. Our Reubens were ready.

NUREMBERG

REGENSBURG

BAVARIA

LANDSBERG

MUNICH

The Occupation of Germany: "We got the playground--Bavaria, southern Germany.'--Lieutenant Colonel Lehman H. Johnson, Jr. "Before the war, Bavaria had been like a resort. The wealthiest people lived there."

In August of 1946, my uncle received orders to help set up and run a displaced persons camp, and oversee the process of disbursement of Jewish refugees. There were camps in Germany, Austria, and Italy. Lieutenant Colonel Johnson was in charge of the one at Regensburg, shown on this map. During that time he lived in Bad Tölz, a small town about 92 miles west of Regensburg. Later he was assigned the duty of overseeing the execution of Nazi war criminals at Landsberg Prison. Landsberg is about 220 kilometers south of Nuremberg.

Occupying Germany

"I'm haunted by the children, their eyes with no hope,
by the young people who looked so old, and by the old
who looked like skeletons, the walking dead."

—Lieutenant Colonel Lehman H. Johnson, Jr.

"I was never in Germany during combat, but I was assigned to occupation duty with the Allied Forces. I had been in Japan for about a year when in August 1946, I received orders to the 1st U.S. Infantry Division in Regensburg, Germany. I was to serve as the assistant to Ray Riggin, the division provost marshal. I was excited about this assignment because it meant my family could join me.

"My particular job was to help set up a displaced persons camp and oversee the process of disbursement—either sending the refugees back to their homes or finding them a place to go. The details were handled by the officers who reported to me and by a Displaced Persons Committee."

"How long were you there?" I asked.

"The camps existed for four years. I was there for two and a half. During that time, which was supposed to be a period of rehabilitation, we were to supervise these people, educate them, and prepare them for different occupations, using the various skills they already had. I

315

felt, and still feel today, that more time should have been spent on re-habilitation and socialization. It must have been a tremendous culture shock."

"Culture shock?"

"Yes, culture shock—suddenly being freed like that and not having to be afraid, although they still were. But then there had to have been other fears as they faced life in a new country. The Jews hardly had time to clean out the cobwebs before they had to build new nests. The average length of time spent in the camps before deportation was only two to three months—certainly not long enough to accomplish what we said was our mission."

The flame from the gas logs had subsided and the shadow from it now played across the rug. The early afternoon light sifted in through the blinds and illuminated my uncle's face. He was not an easy man to read.

Without turning to me, Uncle Legs said, "I'm haunted by the chil-dren, their eyes with no hope, by the young people who looked so old, and by the old who looked like skeletons, the walking dead. They come to me in my dreams." He shuddered. "There was a constant river of people cycling through every few months.

"It was quite an experience, not the least of which was figuring out how to get to work. Before the war, Regensburg had an aircraft factory and an oil refinery. The allies had bombed both strategic locations, and the Germans hadn't done much cleaning up. I had to get a bulldozer to clear the streets of Regensburg, the location we had selected for the displaced persons camps.

"But the politics of what we were doing was the real hot potato. The Jews who had survived the concentration camps had to go somewhere, and they weren't necessarily wanted anywhere, including the United States and Britain. Many were afraid to go home. They came from Austria, Poland, and various locations in Germany by railroad boxcars and in trucks to wait for deportation at Regensburg."

My uncle threw up his hands. "So what were we to do? The creation of a Jewish state in British-controlled Palestine was a popular choice among the refugees. But the idea was not popular with the British.

"We set up these camps in Germany, Austria, and Italy—minimum security facilities to be run in a military manner while we sorted these people out. Regensburg was the largest displaced persons camp in Germany. We had a staff of officers and enlisted men who took care of the day to day operations. Our job was to perform control inspections, maintain personnel accountability, assign jobs, like sewing or carpentry work to the refugees, and in the beginning, to set immigration quotas. The refugees did not give us much trouble, even about the quotas. They were just glad to be alive.

"We had dormitory-type barracks, most of which held one thousand to five thousand people. The refugees had no place to eat, get clothes, or other necessities, except in the camps, and many were nearly starved. We had tried to get to those who were in the extermination camps first because they were most likely in the worst physical shape.

"The situation was so bad that I know of one division commander who cut the rations for his own troops by one half and gave the other half to the Jews who were flooding into our camps. No one told him to do that. He was operating under what we call in the military, 'field expedience'—doing what a particular situation calls for without waiting for orders. We all want to survive, and he knew that. No one questioned his decision or tried to stop him.

"Another area where we had free rein was in setting immigration quotas to various countries. A U.S. senator, who will remain unnamed, publicly made the statement, 'Damn if any of these bastards were going to the United States.' In fact, if all the Jews who wanted to come to the United States had been sent here, they would have flooded the job market and thrown our society out of balance. We were aware of that and we didn't really want President Truman trying to influence policy that the military had already written. But in 1948, he did just that by supporting the Displaced Persons Act."

"How did you feel about that?"

My uncle rubbed his hands together and spread his fingers out in front of the fire. Yet beads of sweat were visible on his forehead.

"The process was handled as efficiently as possible with each adult being asked a series of questions for placement.

"'What country are you from?' was first.

"For most, the answer to that question was 'Germany,' and of course, they couldn't stay there.

"'Where do you want to go?' was next.

"'To America,' was usually the answer."

My uncle glanced over at me. "I had to ask the questions and decide what to do with the answers."

I nodded.

"This is how I usually continued the conversation.

"'If I send you to America next year, what are you going to be?'

"'I'm going to be a Jew.'

"I'd respond. 'If I send you to Israel next year, what are you going to be?'

"The answer was always 'I'm going to be a Jew.'

"Then I would say, 'Why do you think I'd send you to America to be a Jew? If you get there, you're going to be an American,' and that was that. Most were sent to Israel."

Uncle Legs picked up a *Military History* magazine from the stack on the TV tray beside his chair and began to leaf through it. He wasn't reading it. Instead, he was staring straight ahead at the bookcases on the wall behind his big screen television, at titles such as *A Complete History of World War II*, *The 11th Airborne*, and *Bush at War*. He wasn't seeing those either.

"In fact, ninety percent of the Jewish people that we liberated went to Israel, which was, for the most part, their second choice. Some were sent to other countries that were members of the United Nations. A few were allowed to come to the United States, based on their level of education and profession.

"Having a relative already in the States helped. In fact, immigration by the Jewish refugees to the United States was very limited and very closely controlled by the military—at least until 1952. The Displaced Persons Act was amended that year to make immigration to the US more favorable to the Jews."

Uncle Legs took out his handkerchief and wiped his brow. Then without seeming to notice, he dropped it, a damp wad on the floor between us. "It wasn't intentional, but I suppose that through these proceedings, we were, in fact, really carrying out one of the things that Hitler had tried to do—that is to purge Germany of the Jews."

Uncle Legs was gripping the arms of his chair, rigidly silent in the now dim natural light. I was groping for soothing words, some balm to apply, when the kitchen door slammed shut behind Jane. A draft of cold air swept into the room. The silence was shattered. "It's five o'clock. Where do you want to eat, Legs?"

He held his hand up at her. "Five minutes, please." His tone was distant and strained.

"As you will, Sir," she said lightly, giving him a peck on the cheek. "I want to change my blouse anyway."

Uncle Legs turned toward me. "These people, the Jews, were, of course, traumatized and were still very much afraid, even though they were now safe in these displacement camps. Hitler had believed that the Jewish people were the greatest threat to the German nation's so-called purity, and he was executing them as fast as possible. Hitler buried them, burned them, hung them, whatever he could do to destroy them. The survivors were recovering from horrific experiences."

"I do know that. But I don't know it in the way that you do."

He continued. "Part of my job was to collect any unauthorized weapons that had been brought to camp. There was no real privacy in the camps, and even though we had the right to search anybody and everything, I would always ask first. Through an interpreter I said to the men, 'Do you have any weapons?' I didn't bother with the women, and I didn't ask the children, although we found that some of them did have weapons—guns, clubs, knives, the usual kinds of things that people keep when they are most afraid.

"For the most part, the people surrendered these things willingly. Even when they gave them up, we searched anyway and usually found more in the bed clothes, under the beds, and in the closets. When they said, 'No. No weapons,' we were especially diligent and searched them. It felt very wrong to do that, after everything they'd been though, but we couldn't let them keep those weapons.

"Fear is contagious and can turn on itself. No one was punished when we found these unauthorized items, but it still took the Jewish people in these camps a long time to trust us, to trust anybody." The lines around my uncle's mouth became a frown that dragged his whole face down.

I studied him and thought, *fear is like something sticky that has been spilled, staining everything and everybody it touches—even you, in spite of your efforts to stand apart.* My uncle's voice was firm when he spoke.

"On purpose, I had no personal conversations with the people I was supervising, other than the questions I've already mentioned. I could not afford to get emotionally involved and still be objective."

Abruptly, he asked, "Did you learn in school how Germany was divided after the war?"

"No."

"We got the playground—Bavaria, southern Germany. The British got the industrial area, the northern part, and France got what was left over."

"The playground?"

"Yes. Before the war, that part of Germany had been like a resort, and it was where the wealthiest people lived. There had been many fine homes, and the occupation forces took over those that were still standing for our officers' accommodations. The owners, if they were still there, were relegated to the servants' quarters and enlisted to serve the new occupants. My family, that is Genevieve, Lee, Jule, and I, lived in such a house in Bad Tölz, a pretty little town in West Germany — about ninety-two miles from Regensburg.

"We, that is the United States, acted on the basis of political expediency — what advanced our own interests. I was part of that. We do things all the time in the military that are applicable to that concept." He sighed.

"Speaking of expediency,..." I said.

"Jane!" Uncle Legs glanced at his watch and called down the hall. "Are you dressed yet?"

"Been that way," she said, entering the room, smiling. Uncle Legs took the sports coat she handed him and got unsteadily to his feet. When he swung around to put it on, I breathed in the scent of Old Spice aftershave that had been absorbed by the wool.

He reached for his hat. "Who's picking the restaurant tonight?"

"Who usually picks?" Jane tossed the question back over her shoulder as carefully as she was now winding a cashmere scarf around her neck.

"You do."

"Legs, you know you always make that decision. You should be ashamed!"

He was not. I looked back to see my uncle turning up his collar as a defense against the wind. He looped his cane jauntily over his arm and then held the door.

Jane preceded her husband down the steps. "To your credit, you always pay," she said. I followed her.

"And for that, you are just as welcome as the sunshine and the rain."

It was a little past our usual appointed dinner time. We would make an entrance at Huey's because people in Mebane would notice.

Getting Picked and Getting Bill

*"I would always reply, 'You know I can't sell my dog, and you un-
derstand why I can't sell my dog.'"*

—Lieutenant Colonel Lehman H. Johnson, Jr.

That evening Uncle Legs had directed Jane to Huey's and as soon as we
were seated, he continued, "When I was in Germany, Ray Riggin, the
provost marshal, called me in to division headquarters in Bad Tölz and
said, 'I've got one special job for you, Johnson.' He made his announcement in front of Col. Frank Murdock, our chief of staff, and the way he
said it made my next assignment sound very exciting.

"'What's that?' I asked, feeling proud to be singled out this way.

"'I want you to execute some Nazi war criminals,' was his response."
Heads in the restaurant swiveled toward us. There was a partition between the booths and the tables. Rather than speaking in audible tones,
people on our side began to whisper.

My uncle's voice filled up the room of the small family-owned
restaurant. The smell of cigarette smoke coming from the other section
wafted our way. Someone dropped a fork. Suddenly, I felt we were
being sucked into a vacuum of silence. All conversation in the booths
close to us had ceased.

Jane cleared her throat. "Legs," she began, "unless…" Her voice trailed off.

"Darla!" My uncle raised his hand. "We'd like to see a menu."

Darla carefully placed a laminated bi-fold menu in front of each of us. "Specials are on the back." She retreated to the kitchen to give us time.

"I'd like the ribs tonight." Uncle Legs closed the menu decisively. "I'll tell you about Bill, my German Shepherd, and save the other story for later."

Jane smiled. "I'd like the ribs as well. What about you, Mary Susan?"

"We'll make that three."

Darla was back. "Did you say three ribs?"

"Yes," and Darla left to turn in the orders. My uncle began to hold court.

"I got the idea while we were in Germany that I wanted a German shepherd dog. I suppose I got that from Bob Ziles, the counterintelligence corps agent, who worked with me. It was our job to search the caves and other areas in Berchtesgaden for artifacts, weapons, and explosive devices. This was the other part of my provost marshal duties. Bob took his dog along when we went out on assignments together.

"Berchtesgaden was where Hitler had carried his girlfriend when he wanted to be with her. His living quarters, which I saw, were furnished with valuable artwork and other expensive things. Many of these had been taken by the Nazis from the homes of Jewish citizens. I had the opportunity to decorate our home with the finest pieces of great historical significance, but I always immediately turned what I found into the European command. A lot of soldiers took things, but not me.

"Bob's dog was trained to sniff out explosive devices, and I was most grateful for her services on more than one occasion. Besides being smart, she was beautiful. She was also very protective of Bob, and I knew as long as we were together, I was safe. However, I could start for the car without him, and Sheba—that was her name—would growl at me or anyone else who approached without permission. After Bob spoke to her, I could get in the jeep without incident. She was very well-trained and answered to commands in both English and German."

"You had a German shepherd?" Darla was back at our table with our orders. The other diners had resumed their personal conversations and were no longer involved in ours.

"I did." Uncle Legs answered her, "and if I had a dog, I would want another German shepherd. There are two reasons why I don't have another one now. One of those is sitting across the table from me." Jane nodded.

"I'm sorry. I just can't have a dog in my house," she said.

"The other is that it would be impossible to find another dog that would compare to my dog Bill, and I just wouldn't be satisfied with anything less. I sit out in the yard now sometimes and my neighbor's German shepherd comes over to visit. I pet him and talk to him, but he's nothing like Bill."

Satisfied that the food was in place, my uncle said the blessing during which he thanked God for all His present and past gifts, including Bill. Then he turned back to us.

"When I decided to get a German shepherd for our family, I asked my housekeeper Seine to find me a kennel. She went with me to get the dog and to translate. I asked her to tell the owners, 'I want the best.' Then I held up a fistful of American $20 bills. That part didn't need any translation, although I directed Seine to say, 'Take as many of these as it takes to get the pick of the litter and I want you to train him.' They chose Bill.

"Bill joined our family when he was about nine weeks old, although he still spent time with his trainers. He understood both German and

English, but he preferred German commands, because his handlers were German. He had a wonderful temperament, and he learned very quickly. The older he got the more protective he was. It became Bill's responsibility to go around the house each night before we went to bed and check for intruders. When he was satisfied that there were none, he would come back to where I was waiting, lie down in front of me, and wag his tail.

"One night in our house in Germany was an exception. There was somebody in the basement, and we heard him. Bill heard him too. A line of hair stood straight up on his back, and he was growling. 'Sic him, Bill!' I said, and that was all I had to say. Very shortly, we heard the awfulest racket coming from the cellar. Then things got quiet again. Bill returned, laid some scraps of clothing at my feet, and wagged his tail. When I checked the basement, there was no one there, but the trap door to the outside of our home was wide open. Apparently, our uninvited guest had left quite suddenly, the same way he came in.

"Another incident occurred when my son Jule was approximately three and a half. He accidentally stepped on Bill's tail, and Bill snapped at him. I, in return, immediately hit the dog with a swagger stick. Then I had Jule start at the tip of his tail and walk all over him. Every time Bill raised up, I hit him with the stick."

"That seems harsh," I said.

"Perhaps. But he learned that day that the boys could do anything to him, and he was not to react. He never snapped at them or offered to hurt them in any way again. The children were crying the whole time this was going on. They didn't want me to hurt their dog, but I felt that it was necessary.

"After Germany, my next assignment was at Gulfport, Mississippi. Getting Bill out of Germany and into the States was a problem easily solved when Mother agreed to keep him until we could get settled and pick him up. We certainly had no intention of leaving our dog behind. We shipped him to Kenly.

"When Bill arrived at the train station, the agent on duty read the tag and immediately called my mother. 'There's a BIG dog down here shipped to you from Germany! Can you come and get him now?' This was not an everyday occurrence in Kenly.

"The agent was afraid to take Bill out because by this point, he had been in the crate for seven days, including the time it took to get him through customs, and he was barking and growling. But Mother had no problem with Bill. She had a way with dogs and, in fact, raised and sold Boston terriers. She reached in and led him out into the station without any incident. They made their acquaintance, and Bill jumped right in her car. He stayed with my parents for about two weeks during which time he made himself quite at home. He did not go to the pen with her terriers and Daddy's bird dogs, but instead stayed in the house. Mother enjoyed Bill and hated to see him go. 'A most unusual dog,' she had said when I came to get him."

My uncle glanced at our plates. "I see that you are almost done. I've been doing more talking than eating. Would you like coffee while I finish up?"

The diner was almost empty. "Regular or decaf?" Darla asked, appearing at my uncle's side.

When she returned with our coffee, Uncle Legs said, "You can go ahead and bring us the bill. We'll be leaving shortly."

"Does this mean I don't get to find out what happened to Bill?" Darla asked, returning with the check.

My uncle shifted slightly in the booth, causing the Naugahyde upholstery to crackle. "I'm afraid not. It's a sad story and not a really good story for here." Darla nodded and left the check.

Between bites, Uncle Legs continued. "At Gulf Coast Military Academy, where I was teaching, it was Bill's habit to walk Lee and

Jule to their school. The academy had an elementary school, as well as a high school, and we lived on post. Normally, Bill would return home and wait on the porch during the day until they returned.

"But on one occasion, Bill decided he would go back to school and find them. Genevieve had no idea he was gone. Somehow Bill had gotten inside and gone all the way through the school until he found Lee. He stood beside Lee's desk and refused to move.

"Genevieve got a call from the teacher. 'Mrs. Johnson, your German shepherd is entertaining my class, and I can't get a thing done! He won't leave.' Genevieve, of course, called me, and I went and got him.

"Our youngest son, Steve, was born in Gulfport. Genevieve would put him out in the yard in his playpen with Bill to stand guard. She could be in the house, doing whatever she needed to do because nothing came near that playpen or Steve while Bill was on duty. One day I came home, and Genevieve said, 'You need to go clean up the mess.' When I went outside to see what she was talking about, I found two cats, a chicken, and a little dog, all dead beside his playpen. They had all had the misfortune to invade Bill's territory.

"Bill felt that he was in charge of many things. When we would have our parades at the school, I'd be standing as the reviewing officer. Bill would sit right there and review the troops with me. Another officer was so impressed with Bill that he tried to buy him from me.

"'How much for your dog?' Captain Andrew Bass frequently asked me.

"I would always reply, 'You know I can't sell my dog, and you understand why I can't sell my dog.'

"He would then say, 'Oh, I understand. You can't sell your dog.'

"I could not sell my dog for any amount of money because it would have been like selling a member of my family. We never had another German shepherd after Bill's death. I did not think I could find another one that would meet those standards."

My uncle reached for the check, and I drained my coffee cup. On our way out, Darla called after us, "Thank y'all for coming." Her courtesy was as predictable as most everything else in Mebane.

"See you Tuesday," Jane said. We always went somewhere else on Sundays, and Huey's wasn't open on Monday.

Lessons from Landsberg

"We offered death by hanging and by firing squad at Landsberg."

—Lieutenant Colonel Lehman H. Johnson, Jr.

Sunday afternoon found us facing the firing squad of memories that Uncle Legs still felt trained on his mind's eye. Those memories never died, but instead resurrected themselves periodically to haunt him and cause him to question himself.

The afternoon sun entered the den from one of the windows beside my uncle's chair and glanced over his left shoulder, highlighting a copy of *The Rise and Fall of the Third Reich* that lay open on his lap, but Uncle Legs did not refer to it. There was no need, and he closed it with a resounding thump. "I'm going to talk to you about my experience executing Nazi war criminals," he said, slapping the cover with his open hand, "but if you need background information, this book is an excellent reference. You can take it home with you."

Uncle Legs leaned back and closed his eyes. *What did he see and what was he shutting out?* He began with the facts. "It was the fall of 1946, and I had suddenly become the officer in charge of the execution of Nazi war criminals at Landsberg Prison—not Nuremberg, you understand—Landsberg."

I nodded. "Yes, you executed the so-called lesser criminals."

My uncle's mouth twisted in a wry smile. Pleased that I had re-membered, he added, "Mainly, German nationals. The bigwigs, like Goering, the second in command of the Third Reich, after Hitler, were all put to death at Nuremberg."

"But I thought he committed suicide."

"That's right. He did. Goering was scheduled to die on October 16, 1946, along with ten other prominent Nazi leaders who were hanged. But he committed suicide in his cell by swallowing a cyanide pill which he had somehow concealed for that purpose. Martin Bormann was also sentenced, but he was already dead before the trials.

"The men I executed were condemned to die because they had committed a capital crime like murder. For the most part, they were following orders." Uncle Legs looked over his glasses at me.

"I could relate. When Col. Frank Murdock, chief of staff at division headquarters in Bad Tölz, Germany, said to me, 'You've got the job of executing Nazi war criminals, Johnson,' I said, 'Yes, Sir.' I did not say, 'I'd like to think about this, Sir.'"

"I believe that the term used during the trails was 'crimes against humanity.' What were some of these?"

"The German soldiers I executed did not make these decisions, but they had orders to murder, dehumanize, massacre, exterminate the Jews...." My uncle's voice trailed off, and he sighed.

"The German forces in World War II were probably the best disci-plined and best trained soldiers in the world at that time. The German army was trained to obey. But understanding all that was really beside the point. I was neither the judge nor jury. I was the executioner, and what I was told to do was carry out these executions 'by the book.' There was an actual Procedure of Military Executions manual, and I had to get it down and study it to make sure that I followed protocol. Protocol included making sure that there was no prolonged physical suffering as part of the death sentence. Nothing was said about mental anguish. Our doctor, the same doctor who would later pronounce them dead, sometimes prescribed sleeping pills for the German soldiers, days before, so they could sleep while they waited for their own deaths."

My uncle got unsteadily to his feet and shut the blinds, instead of calling for Jane or asking me. "We don't need this light," he said before falling back exhausted in his chair. A few minutes passed before he continued.

"We offered death by hanging and by firing squad at Landsberg. They didn't have a firing squad at Nuremberg, and we did at Landsberg. The orders from the general headquarters commander included the type of execution in the sentence for each prisoner, so if a man was to be executed by firing squad, he came to us.

"It was my job to select the men for that firing squad. I always had twelve. All the firing squads I learned about at Oak Ridge had twelve men, and I saw no reason to make any changes in that respect. As for the men themselves, there were plenty of volunteers among both the U.S. and the Allied soldiers.

"I know that you want to know how I selected them." My uncle glanced sideways at me, and then stared straight ahead. "If a man wanted to serve on my firing squad, the first thing I did was check his 66-1, his official record of service, to determine his skill level with a rifle. I didn't care about his rank. I was looking for men who were expert shots. Expert status meant that soldier could put a bullet through a ten-inch disk seven out of ten times, at a thousand yards. I also tried to choose men who had been in Germany more than two or three months.

"After I had my firing squad, I reviewed the procedures with them. The first thing I said was, 'Do you expect to get a blank round?' Then I would wait for any response. There was never any, so I would continue. 'That's a myth, at least here, that only one person has actual ammunition. If that's what you thought, you can fall out right now.' No one ever left.

"Everybody in my firing squads got a live round. I learned that sometimes a so-called 'conscience bullet' would be included in one man's rifle. That was so each man could say to himself that perhaps his would not be the fatal shot, and it would be easier for him to fire. We had no such thing.

"I expected all twelve men to fire, and they fired standing, although they had qualified as experts on the rifle range in standing, kneeling, and prone positions. Standing is actually the more difficult position, but to tell you the truth, I didn't want them messing up their uniforms by kneeling or lying down in the dirt.

"In order to perform the execution, we dug a hole in the ground and planted a pole. I clearly recall one day when I had five prisoners to execute by firing squad. There was no use in digging five holes in the ground for five poles, when you could reuse the one, and this is what we did — five times. In turn each condemned man was tied to that pole and blindfolded. A circle that had been drawn on a white three-inch square of paper was pinned over his heart. I then called for the firing squad to advance. They took their positions and I called out to them, 'Ready. Aim. Fire!' My uncle cupped his chin in his hand and shook his head. "We shot them one at a time, brought each one off on a stretcher, and brought the next one on.

"I knew that some of my soldiers lifted the barrels of their guns and shot over the prisoner's head rather than aim for the heart. They were experts, and if they completely missed hitting the German, it was done on purpose. I knew by the number and pattern of the bullet holes when this happened, although I could never tell exactly who was guilty. I did wonder though about what second thoughts they might have had.

"I also knew that some of the men kept the rifle shells as souvenirs. That I understood, and I didn't care. It never crossed my mind to count the shells." My uncle sighed heavily.

"It was also my responsibility as the commanding officer to examine the prisoner to see if there was lingering pain. If so, I was to administer the 'coup de grace.' On these occasions, I was a bit of a showman, slowly approaching the body with my '45' cocked, staring down at the prisoner who was now lying still on the ground. Sometimes there was a little blood, but not much. If by chance the man was still alive, I was to complete the execution by pulling the trigger. That occasion never arose, but I questioned myself each time, 'Can I do it?'

"The answer was always the same. 'Sure, I can do it.' I would have shot the prisoner in the head and not thought twice before doing it. Why? Because I was just carrying out my orders. That was my job. Reminding myself of that fact allowed me to block out any personal feelings I had about what I was doing. It bothered me, and still does, that under similar circumstances, I could have been taught to do the same things as the men I was executing.

"Because we were not trained to tell when a person was dead, I requested two doctors from the regimental commander who were to be assigned to the executions that I was supervising. They did not know what their job was until they stood before me. One of the two who had been given this duty became squeamish.

"We had just performed an execution, and one of my soldiers went over and looked at the 'body.' He called out, 'We've got a live one over here.' The executed man was obviously still breathing. We all rushed over, but the man stopped breathing almost immediately. We did not have to take any action to finish him off.

"Within the hour one of the doctors approached me. Apparently, he was experiencing some conflict between what he saw as his duty as a doctor and his duty as an officer in the United States Army. Standing before me with his head down, he said, 'I do not want to do this anymore.' He meant that he did not want to examine the prisoners after the executions or to pronounce them dead. Part of the Hippocratic Oath is that a physician will 'first, do no harm.' I believe he saw his participation in these executions as a violation of that oath. That I could not help.

"'Do I have to call your commanding officer and press charges against you? You're going to do it or you are going to be court-martialed. Do we have to have this conversation again?' I said all this to him.

"The good doctor and I didn't discuss the issue at any other time. The subject never came up." My uncle folded his arms across his chest and was silent.

I don't know how Jane knew that her husband needed his evening toddy, but I heard her coming up from the basement. At fifteen years his junior, Jane took the stair steps one at a time, each foot lightly touching a step as she emerged.

She entered the room from the kitchen and handed the wine glass to my uncle. "Here you are, Sir," she said. She opened the blinds and then turned as if to go. "It's awfully dark in here."

"Do you want to hear this? I'm about to finish the conversation I started at Huey's about the executions at Landsberg."

"I'll pass. I need to focus on my lesson for tomorrow." Jane's footsteps were a crescendo on the stairs, trilling as the classical music and hymns she sometimes played on her baby grand before bedtime. There would be no music tonight.

Uncle Legs looked at me. "Genevieve was the same way. Because of the nature of my duties, Col. Murdock had asked me if I would like to have the general's train for my commute from Bad Tölz to Landsberg. I was most appreciative, and I accepted his offer. The train was very luxurious with a dining car, a Pullman, a coal car, an engine, and a 'right behind' engine. I asked Genevieve if she would like to ride in with me to Landsberg—not to witness an execution—just to ride on the train. She refused, as did all my officers. No one, including my wife, wanted to get any closer than necessary to what I was doing.

"The man who assigned me this duty—to execute Nazi war criminals—was more curious. Col. Murdock never asked me about the firing squads, but he did ask me about the hangings. Maybe he was more familiar with the military protocol for firing squads.

"One day he asked me, 'How do you do that, Johnson—hang somebody?'" My uncle looked over at me, without blinking. "You understand he was asking a procedural question, not about how I felt about my assignment."

I nodded.

"My answer to him was, 'By the neck until dead.'"

This time Uncle Legs turned his face away from me and gazed out the window at a winter orange sunset. Only the light changed the perspective of what had remained the same throughout the day. The trees that had blended earlier with the landscape now stood out in bold relief against streaks of color. With the passage of time, it was the same with this memory. A muscle twitched in my uncle's right jaw. He took a deep breath and his shoulders heaved.

"Col. Murdock had already asked for volunteers for this job among the ranking officers and hadn't gotten any. That meant there were three officers available for Landsberg—a captain, a major, and himself. He wasn't going to dirty his hands by doing the job personally, so that left myself and the captain. Although I outranked the captain, I guess the colonel figured I had the experience and the stomach for it."

My uncle turned back to me and moistened his lips. "I had the experience." His voice sounded detached, like a helium balloon that had somehow come loose from its string, soaring off into the sky.

"Executions at Landsberg were to occur when we got orders from the European command, although everybody at Landsberg was not to be executed. At Nuremberg, when criminals were convicted, they were executed immediately. In some ways, I think that was more merciful.

"I made sure that each man was told immediately when the orders came. Those that were to be executed reacted very differently to the news of their sentence. These differences became more apparent the closer we got to the day of execution. I had to put a watch on some of the men to make sure that they didn't commit suicide. Some of them still tried. One man stood up on his top bunk and jumped off, head-first. It knocked him out for a while, but he came to, and was still executed.

"Another man had such a strong will to live that we had to tie him to a plank in order to hang him. He wouldn't obey orders. I guess he figured he didn't have anything to lose at that point. He was hung, still tied to that board.

"Being hung was the most disgraceful way to be executed, according to the standards of that time and place. Hanging was the method used for most of the Nazi war criminals. The sentence for most of the German nationals, as well as the Allied criminals, was death by firing squad. But as I've said, that decision had already been made."

My uncle stood, wine glass in one hand, cane in the other. "When I get back, I'll tell you how I went about carrying out the orders to execute by hanging. I had my own hangman." He disappeared into the kitchen, the cane hitting the floor with every other step.

Uncle Legs returned with a full glass of red wine and sank back into his chair. "We had two hangman's stands. I figured we could do two at a time as well as one, and there was nothing in the book to prohibit it." With his left hand, he held the goblet out in front of him and studied it. When he spoke, his words sounded like they were all stopped up in a narrow-necked bottle and wouldn't pour out, even when you shook it up.

"In May of 1946, we hung twenty-eight former SS guards from Dachau in a four-day period."

Uncle Legs glanced at me and then drained the glass he was still holding. "The stands were built by the prisoners themselves, and they were solidly built. Perhaps these were some of the same men who had served Hitler in a similar capacity. I didn't know nor do I want to know now.

"The hangman's stands were maybe six feet by six feet wide and eight feet high, with a drop door in the floor. I got inside the frames and tested them myself after they were built, making sure that the drop door would open, and the noose would support a man's weight. None of the prisoners would have been taller than myself although some of them were heavier."

Without looking, Uncle Legs placed the glass on the metal folding tray beside him. It was piled high with current issues of *Time* and the *Military History* magazine.

"Joe Norville was my hangman. I 'selected' him by calling all my sergeants together and asking, 'Is there anyone here who is willing to be a hangman of Nazi war criminals?'

"Joe was my man. Without hesitation, he stepped forward out of the line and volunteered. 'I am!' he said, and I was pleased with my choice.

"'Okay.' I said to him. 'Let's find us some Germans that know how to do this and get you trained.' The German police sent me to a civilian who, they said, had personal experience.

"I found the man at the address we had been given. 'How many have you hung?' I didn't ask him how or where he had acquired his expertise.

"'Sir,' he answered, 'so many I can't even recall.' Joe was well trained."

"For whatever reason, and I never asked, Joe seemed to take a certain amount of pleasure in carrying out his duty. Once we looked down the hole where the condemned man had dropped after the trap door covering it had been released. What we should have seen was the man dangling by the neck beneath the opening. I don't know what possessed us to look on that particular day, but what we saw was shocking, to say the least. There were arms and legs coming back out of that hole, like a spider.

"To this day, I remember exactly how Joe reacted. He was very calm and matter of fact as he stood back for a moment and watched the man struggle. 'I'm certainly not going to pull him up out of there,' he said. There was no order given, but what Joe did next was most expeditious.

"He solved the problem that was presenting itself by standing on the man's shoulders, thus putting two hundred and fifteen pounds of pressure on the rope that was still around the prisoner's neck. The rope was pulled tighter and tighter by Joe's weight. At first the man's breath came in gasps and then it was raspy. Then it was just a whisper. Then he suffocated. It was not a pretty sight."

Uncle Legs shaded his eyes with his left hand. He exhaled and reached for the wine goblet, which was still balanced precariously on the magazines. Forgetting that it was empty, Uncle Legs touched the glass to his lips and then set it back down.

"I want you to have some sense of the business we were about so I'm going to tell you one more Joe Norville story. Are you all right with that?" He took a deep cleansing breath.

"I am."

"It was our custom to ask every man on the platform who was about to be hanged if he had any last words that he would like to say. I suppose the purpose of asking was to give the prisoner one last opportunity to repent before he died. Incidentally, there were no Germans in my care who ever expressed any remorse. In fact, one criminal went to his death still expressing his hatred for the Jews. 'Go ahead and carry out what the God damned Jews have ordered.' The man's voice carried throughout the prison camp, loud and clear.

"Joe replied casually in a normal tone of voice. 'That's exactly what we're going to do, soldier.' Then he pulled the lever that released the trap door beneath the man's feet. Nothing else was said by either of them."

There were no stars that night. It was pitch black, and although I knew the trees were still there, I could not see them. Twisting around in his chair, my uncle now turned as far away from me as possible. He was looking out the window at nothing and for a while he said nothing. Then he spoke, but not to me.

"After an execution, most of the time, the closest relative would come by and ask for the body. These family members would present themselves to me in my office and ask, 'Did he have any last words?' You would think that maybe they wouldn't come — that they would be afraid of retribution. Instead it was rare when a body went unclaimed. But when that did happen, we buried them there, next to Spottingen Chapel, beside the prison. Their graves were unmarked." My uncle paused.

"Usually there was nothing to tell the dead man's next of kin. There's not much conversation going on in an environment like that, and what was said we didn't write down. We just had to remember it in case we were asked.

"The Germans were a very proud people, and they did not apologize easily, even if they thought they were wrong. I didn't have any confessions to report to the people who claimed the bodies. They just came and picked up their loved ones and left. I remember thinking at the time that the whole affair was most unnatural — this business of claiming the body of someone you loved who had been executed. How was their grieving affected by those circumstances?"

My uncle's gaze was straight ahead and unblinking. I wondered to myself how he had been affected by his own situation at the time. *Did he have what the Army psychologists call post traumatic stress syndrome? They certainly didn't call it that at the time and if he did, he didn't know it. He spoke now of a collective memory gathered like so many eggs in a basket without holding up a specific one to check for cracks.*

Neither of us had heard Jane come in, but she was there, closing the blinds and drawing the drapes against the night, shutting out the encroaching darkness. I should have been long gone, but Uncle Legs was not quite done. Jane came to stand by his chair. He bit his lower lip and blinked his eyes rapidly several times. Jane patted his shoulder, and he continued speaking.

"For the most part, I believe that the men I came in contact with there in the prison camp believed in what they were doing and that it was right. Human beings can be taught to do anything—including performing medical experiments on people, punishing others for their religious and political beliefs, running death squads designed to exterminate the Jews, using children in the military, and practicing the most inhumane methods of torture, among other unthinkable actions. They were executed for 'crimes committed,' but I believe they believed they were 'doing their duty.'"

Just like you, I thought. *That's a very uncomfortable association.*

He told me more than once that he didn't want that word "duty" in the title of this book.

Landsberg and the Press

"In one day, we literally moved the man and his wife out of their house and into a garage apartment that was on the grounds."

—Lieutenant Colonel Lehman H. Johnson, Jr.

"I got my fifteen minutes of fame—and infamy through the *Stars and Stripes*. Here, let me show you a copy. This is current." Uncle Legs and I were seated in the den. He handed me a newspaper with the *Stars and Stripes* blazing across the masthead. Underneath was the date, and in smaller print, The Official Publication of the United States Army. He reached over and took back the paper, held it up to the light, and snapped it open.

"How objective do you think the reporting is in that newspaper?" I asked.

Before he answered, my uncle ran his fingers over the creases before adding it to the stack of magazines beside his chair.

"Since the Army publishes it, it's a case of the Army presenting factual information in a way that the government wants it viewed. It's probably less that way now than it was when I was in service. This is a story about some very accurate reporting in this newspaper—a story that should never have been reported.

"I was in my office at headquarters in Germany, sitting at my desk

343

and drinking coffee, when I opened my copy of the *Stars and Stripes*. I had propped my feet up on my desk since I was alone, and I was leaning back in my chair. What hit me between the eyes was the front-page article. My feet hit the floor, and I spilled coffee on my desk. There I was in the lead article, identified by name, rank, and serial number as the officer in charge of executing Nazi war criminals at Landsberg Prison. That was me."

"I was furious. From the byline, I knew the writer was a public information officer, whose office was three doors down from mine. My reaction was immediate and forceful. I marched down the hall and into his office, walking on steam. His door was not completely shut, and I could see him through a crack, relaxing at his desk like I had been doing just a few minutes before. I kicked in the door.

"'What the hell is wrong with you?!' I asked him.

"He looked up in surprise, but his immediate response was feigned innocence. 'What do you mean what's wrong with me?' he replied as he backed away from me. I had caught him off guard.

"'You're damn right. What's wrong with you? Don't you have any courtesy about you? The very idea of you printing my name, rank, and serial number and identifying me as the officer in charge of executing Nazi war criminals at Landsberg Prison! Furthermore, if you don't like what I'm saying, we'll go higher up, and I'll say it there.'

"His response was that he didn't have any responsibility to anyone except to the chief of staff.

"I replied, 'Well then, right now I'm going to be that, so just listen.' He did, and when I finished with him, we both had an understanding of the impact of his article.

"Did I mention that before we had that conversation, I had hauled him down to the restroom and washed his face in the toilet while I flushed it?"

"No. You left that part out."

"I went to see Col. Murdock, our chief of staff, within the week. Unbeknown to Col. Murdock, this PIO had funneled information to the *Stars and Stripes* and written this article. The man knew he had a front-page story, and he did not concern himself with me or the potential effect of the publicity on my family. Had I been asked about an interview, I would, of course, have refused.

"When I told my story and what I had said to this officer, Col. Murdock was very supportive. He understood that I was afraid of retribution. My family and I were living in Bad Tölz, and as far as I knew, no one outside a close circle of military friends and associates knew what I was doing. Besides including personal information about me in the article, this reporter had also been very descriptive about the executions. This major had basically invited everyone in Europe to come and take a ring-side seat. The article was a security breach, and the exposure threatened the security of my family.

"Always a man of few words, the Colonel said, 'I don't blame you, Johnson.'

"For my part, I don't know when I have been that upset, either before or since with a fellow officer. Still, to this day, I bear him no ill will. I suppose he thought he was doing his job, but I bet he remembered me. The environment and the subject matter have a lot to do with what we remember about a time, a place."

Uncle Legs leaned back in his chair and looked out the window to his left. Across the lawn, there was a large forsythia bush, its tendrils brushing the ground and swaying in the March wind that swirled around the home on the hill. Jane was in charge of the gardening now, and I knew that most likely she had left the "yellow bells" unpruned.

"I don't care where you look out of this house, the view is breathtaking," Uncle Legs said, when he realized I was following his gaze. *A good thing that is*, I thought. *When the view gets dark within, we can always look out.*

"There were consequences for all concerned as a result of that article," he said. The major was the first to reap what he had sowed. Colonel Murdock took him apart in front of me. He told him that he had compromised the security of what was being done at Landsberg. As for myself, I asked to be relieved of my position of Officer in Charge of executing Nazi war criminals at Landsberg Prison. That didn't happen immediately, but my family was moved from one set of quarters to another within the week.

"Orders came down immediately to billeting that Major Johnson was on his way to pick out a set of quarters. I selected a half-million-dollar home owned by a German businessman and his wife. The house was about four and a half miles from Bad Tölz.

"In one day, we literally moved the man and his wife out of their house and into the garage apartment that was on the grounds. Given the circumstances, they were pleased to be allowed to stay. At least that's what I thought at the time.

"The man became our housemaster and gardener, and the wife became our maid and cook. The Occupation Forces wanted those serving in Germany to be as comfortable as possible, and in this specific situation, I was concerned about protecting my family and very little else.

"'To the victor go the spoils.' At least that's the way things looked on the surface." My uncle shook his head and then plunged on with his story. "I was still very edgy about my situation, and I had good reason to feel that way. I also learned the hard way that what seems to be isn't necessarily what is.

"I was at work one day when I got a phone call from the Army hospital. Genevieve had gone there some time after I had left for work, and the call was from her doctor.

"'Sir,' he said, 'Your wife is suffering from a nervous breakdown. She needs to go home, back to the States, to fully recover.'

"Mary Susan, I was completely blindsided. I had no idea. What I learned later was that the man and his wife, in whose house we were living, were threatening and intimidating Genevieve. Although I never got the whole story, I don't think there was any actual physical harm threatened, at least none that was verbalized. In front of me, butter wouldn't melt in their mouths.

"I learned later that when I was at work, things were a different story. The man would stand in front of Genevieve and not let her pass. Sometimes he would even hem her up in a corner and stand over her. When I was not there, the woman refused to serve her or take orders from Genevieve. At least once, my wife was not allowed to leave the house with the boys.

"Genevieve had stood it as long as she could. The Army doctor recommended that she and the children get out of that environment as soon as possible. Plans were made for them to go to her parents' house, where they always went when I was deployed, for an undetermined period of time. Genevieve, Lee, and Jule left as soon as transportation could be arranged.

"As for the man and his wife, I don't know what happened to them. They were dismissed. The Army moved me out of the house, and I doubt that they moved back in. At any rate, that was not my concern.

"My concern was the fact that this abuse had been going on for some time in what was my household. Genevieve had either been afraid to tell me, or perhaps she didn't want to worry me any more than was necessary. She knew that the work I was doing was stressful and that I didn't want to talk about it.

"Because of my deployments, like many soldiers, there had been long periods of time during our marriages when we led separate lives. That takes its toll. Couples have trouble reconnecting, and they don't always communicate like they should, even after they're together again. We never talked about this although I'm sure Genevieve told the Army doctors that she saw in the States what had happened. She fully recovered.

"Another very real concern at the time was how this report would affect my career. The Army expects its members to control their families."

"Control?"

"'Manage' might be a better word. Even now, I think the Army expects the man to see that the needs of his family are met. Not doing so can result in lack of promotions and reassignments that are less than favorable. If there are problems within your family, the Army expects you to solve them."

"What happened with you?'

"There is no record on my 66-S of this event. I was not punished in any way. Perhaps someone over me realized that this chain of events had begun with that ill-advised news story. I'm not sure. I had already requested a reassignment, and I got it."

"You went to Gulfport, Mississippi, as an instructor at Gulf Coast Military Academy."

"I did." My uncle smiled his pleasure at my being able to sequence his associated memories. "It was a pie job. And speaking of pie, it's time for dinner. Where's Jane?"

At some point in the afternoon, Jane had returned and was waiting for us in the kitchen, already making preparations for the breakfast she would leave for us on Sunday morning. She entered the room, smiling, and made eye contact with her husband. He smiled back, and we were ready to go.

We would speak of Landsberg again tomorrow.

Observations at Landsberg Prison

"This wasn't a circus, and I refused to be the ringmaster."

— Lieutenant Colonel Lehman H. Johnson, Jr.

My uncle looked at me over his glasses when we returned from church.

"After the war, in Landsberg, Germany, I was the officer in charge of overseeing the executions there. It's about 117 miles from Nuremberg."

I nodded, remembering. How could I forget?

Again, I took in the significance of his role although I could see that I was not going to get a history lesson. I learned later that during the occupation of Germany, there were 259 executions by hanging and 29 executions by firing squad at this facility.

My uncle's voice rose. "I carried out the proceedings on the basis of orders that came down from Nuremberg. We had one scheduled — an execution — for that morning. A German officer was to be hanged by the neck until dead.

"I was in the middle of making inquiries of my hangman regarding the sturdiness of the gallows, the prisoner's last meal, the visit by the chaplain, and any last words the prisoner might have shared.

"In walked this American colonel with his wife. She was all dolled up in a fur coat with earrings and high heels. There was an area in the

349

courtyard where officers, but not their families, could witness the executions. This couple was headed in that direction. She was leaning on his arm and taking little short steps beside him. She was prancing like a circus pony."

Uncle Legs looked sideways at me to see what kind of effect the story was having. I was speechless. I could not imagine someone wanting to see such a thing, even in the aftermath of the patriotism that followed World War II.

"It was military policy that officers could view executions at Landsberg Prison, but they had to come in uniform. The colonel had fulfilled that part of the policy as he was in full dress, but unless his wife was also an officer, she was not allowed in.

"I was astounded, but I did not hesitate to approach them. They never turned to look at me until I caught up with them. 'What in the hell is wrong with you?' I said to the colonel. 'You can't bring your wife in here to an execution.' This was not a circus, and I was certainly not going to be their ringmaster.

"'What do you mean I can't bring my wife in here? She's with me,' he said. His face was blood red, and the veins in his forehead were like rivers with the capillaries spreading out under his skin. I thought he might explode.

"But I did not retreat. I stood my ground between them and the spectator seats. 'It doesn't matter whose wife she is,' I said. 'She isn't coming in to view an execution. Only officers have that privilege.' The colonel said something to his wife while I waited. They didn't budge.

"I'm not sure how long we stood there before I called to the guards. 'Move these people out of here!' The uniformed soldiers were armed with bayonets, and they immediately left their posts at the entrance to do my bidding.

"As the guards approached us, the colonel pointed out to me in no uncertain terms that he considerably outranked me. 'I'm going to call your commanding officer,' he barked.

"'I'll give you his phone number,' I snapped. My visitor that morning was a full colonel, and he outranked me. I was a major, but that didn't make any difference to me. He was clearly in violation of policy, and I had a two-star general backing me up. I wasn't worried."

"Without accepting my offer, the colonel took his wife by the arm and led her toward the exit. They left without further incident, but this time she was dragging her feet—more like a mule. It was unbelievable that this officer thought he could use his rank that way. I blame his stupidity on the fact that he was Air Force."

"Was anybody else allowed to go in?" I asked, studying my uncle's face. Certain emotions are residual, anger being one of those. Memory might misplace them or even bury them, but I was learning that they could be brought to life again. The granite in his jaw shifted.

"Besides military officers, we let *Time, Newsweek,* and other comparable magazines send correspondents in to witness the executions. On one such occasion, a reporter had the unmitigated gall to ask me, 'Why don't you execute them, so they have some pain?'

"I don't believe this reporter had yet actually witnessed an execution. 'Would you like to see what it feels like to have that rope around your neck?' I responded.

"'You can't talk to me like that!' he protested.

"But I did, and I didn't stop there. Obviously, the man did not understand that even Nazi war criminals were human beings and that they had feelings." Uncle Legs shook his head and then closed his eyes for a good five minutes. I thought perhaps he was sleeping, and I wondered if I should tiptoe out and say my goodbyes to Jane.

While I was trying to decide, he opened his eyes. He had not fallen asleep. Tears veiled the steel in his eyes.

My uncle spoke softly, but his tone did not soften the sting of his words. "I asked that reporter, 'Why are you being such a horse's ass? Your lack of respect for the proceedings is appalling.' Then I asked the guards to show him out."

Uncle Legs sat back in his chair, exhausted. His breath came in one long, slow exhale. I stood beside his chair and leaned over to hug him. "Please don't get up." My cheek brushed his clean shaven one, and I smelled his signature Old Spice aftershave. His shoulders were rounded this time instead of braced.

"Thank you for coming," he said, looking up at me.

"I wouldn't have missed it." Normally, he would have walked me to the door. This time Jane appeared to show me out and wave me down the driveway Southern style, until my car disappeared around the first curve. The reds and oranges of a winter sunset faded in my rear-view mirror.

Bill's Death

"It was hard to believe that anything bad could happen to any of us under those pleasant circumstances."

—Lieutenant Colonel Lehman H. Johnson, Jr.

"It happened the day before I left for Korea." We were settled in the den. Uncle Legs still had on his black memory foam bedroom slippers when I arrived, and his feet were propped on the stool in front of his chair. Jane had turned up the gas logs and gone downstairs to review her Sunday school lesson.

"What?"

"Bill's death." My uncle pulled the afghan from the back of his chair and spread it over his outstretched legs. "I don't know why, but I'm always cold now," he said. "I had had losses before, but Bill's death was even more painful because of what I was facing—another overseas deployment and leaving my family. We had all gotten used to having our regular life together while I was stationed at Gulfport, Mississippi. Things had settled down after Germany. But we all knew we had to make the best of my new assignment.

"The United States was at war although we weren't calling it that. North Korea had invaded South Korea on June 25, 1950, by crossing the 38th parallel, the boundary with South Korea. President Truman sent American troops as part of the United Nations security forces on June 27, 1950. I got my notice for Korea on August 8, 1951.

"Since I had thirty days of leave before I had to depart the U.S.A., Genevieve and I and the children had come to Kenly to see my parents and visit hers in Stantonsburg." Uncle Legs crossed his feet at the ankles and stretched out like a cat before the fire, relaxing the muscles in his neck and face. He warmed to his story.

"It was beautiful outside, just a hint of fall in the air. The trees were beginning to turn an autumn red, orange, and yellow. It had been especially nice for the boys to have that time to play outside on their grandparents' front lawn and to be out on the farm. It was hard to believe that anything bad could happen to any of us under those pleasant circumstances.

"I was thinking about these things as I was sitting there in the barber's chair in Lucama. I could see the railroad tracks from where I was sitting, very much aware of the fact that I would be on a train tomorrow that would take me away from all this, but I had accepted it. For the moment, I was satisfied. I was getting my hair cut and enjoying all the small-town talk that was part of the package.

"All of a sudden Genevieve ran in the door of the barber shop, blood all over the front of her dress. The men who were waiting put down the dog-eared magazines and the newspapers they had been reading and stared. Just seeing Genevieve like that gave me quite a turn, not that it was the first time I had seen blood. My thoughts went immediately to my children and what might have happened to one of them.

"'Come quick,' she said. Her face was as white as a bleached sheet. She was breathing hard and fighting to hold back the tears. I knew whatever had happened was bad because Genevieve didn't come unglued like that. 'It's Bill!' she said, when she could get the rest of it out. 'You've got to do something for Bill!'

"I jumped up from the chair and threw the cape on the floor, scattering hair clippings all over the barber's clean-swept floor. 'I'll be back,' I said, over my shoulder. My haircut was not quite finished, and I hadn't gotten my shave yet so returning would be a necessity. I followed Genevieve outside, where she had parked her daddy's pickup crossways on the wrong side of the street.

"She led me to the tailgate of the truck where Bill, our German shepherd, lay panting for breath and wounded so badly that I knew from what I had seen in war, he wouldn't survive. I patted his head and did the best I could to make a couple of makeshift tourniquets from some rags that were in the floorboard of the truck. I moved him forward some because I didn't want him to fall out. I was never afraid that Bill would bite me—even as he was dying. He was so well-trained and loyal.

"I slammed the tailgate shut and jumped into the driver's seat. Genevieve got in beside me. She was crying now. I drove as fast as I could to our vet in Wilson. On the way, Genevieve explained that the farm hands had been mowing the grass on the side of the road using a sickle bar. Bill had made a game out of jumping in front of the tractor and then dodging out the way. Somehow, this time, the man had made a turn that Bill had not anticipated, and he had been run over. Bill did not make it, and I grieved for him. Losing him was a painful reminder that I would soon be facing many other losses."

At some point in the story, Jane had come quietly into the room and had placed a goblet filled with red wine on the table beside her husband. Neither he nor I had been aware of when that had occurred. Now both Jane and I were staring intently at him. He raised the wine glass to his lips with a hand that was not quite steady.

"But you had to go," I said.

"I did." My uncle carefully replaced the wine glass.

"When it came time for me to leave, I took the train from Kenly to San Francisco, my point of debarkation in California. I put the leaving off as long as possible and took the last train out. Mother, Dad, Gene-vieve, and the children saw me off."

Jane was staring intently at her husband. She reached over and pat-ted his hand. He continued talking although the expression on his face was as blank as the notebook in my lap.

"Leaving was especially hard because the boys were older. This was the first time that they had actually seen me go off to war. They were all crying there on the platform because they understood I was leaving to fight a war and that I might not come back.

"Candy, of course, didn't understand, but since everybody else was crying, she tuned up with the rest. Candy had been born on June 11, 1951, so my only daughter was just a couple of months old at the time. She was such a puny-looking little thing. The boys had all been big babies, and she was so little. I hated to leave her the worst in the world, but that was the job and I had to go.

"Genevieve told me later that Jule went to school the next day and told everybody, 'My daddy is gone off to war, and he's going to fight the enemy and get back home!' He was positive about it."

Uncle Legs sat back in his chair and sighed. "Jule was a lot more positive than I was about that. Bill's death made leaving even harder, and I took it almost as an omen. Things would never be the same."

The darkness outside the uncovered windows shrouded the lawn. Most likely there were deer grazing out there, but we could not see them. In the morning, we would see the evidence of nipped flowers and grass that would be shorter in spots.

"What do you mean things would never be the same?" I pressed him.

"Bill was dead. When I came home, he would not be there. I had no idea how long this next war would go on. In the meantime, my children were growing up, and I would not be there to be a part of their lives. I knew Genevieve and I would pick up where we left off when I got back.

"But suppose I didn't come back. Suppose I was wounded, changed in some sort of irreversible way? I knew that whatever happened, it wouldn't change Genevieve or her love for me. But what good would I be to my family, and what would we all do with those people and places that would make up our separate lives while I was gone? How far would we drift away from each other?"

"Do you want to talk about that now?" I asked.

"No." My uncle picked up his wine glass again and sipped from it. His eyes narrowed to slits, so it was impossible to guess at what memory he was bringing into focus. "What I want to do is sit up a bit."

Jane got up and kissed her husband goodnight on the cheek. I planted one on the other side.

"Good night, Legs," she said. "I'm off to bed."

"Good night, Uncle Legs."

He didn't answer either of us.

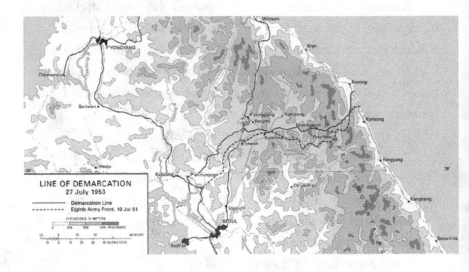

To earn his second Combat Infantryman's Badge, Uncle Legs requested he be transferred to the Mundung-ni Valley, just north of the 38th parallel — in the thick of the fighting. "I would be in the combat zone in a continual combat situation for the required thirty days."

(Map Credit: Center of Military History)

"Kiss My Ass Goodbye" in Korea

"Those of us who were sent privately called it a 'Kiss My Ass Good-bye' assignment."

—Lieutenant Col. Lehman H. Johnson

"Korea. Ah, Korea. It was a different type of war that I was going off to. There was nothing positive about Korea—except that I wanted to get there, get it over with, and get back home." After dinner, Uncle Legs spoke as though there had been no interval between the story about Bill's death and this pronouncement.

"There was no place in Korea for me in the 187th Regiment on the airborne team. They were running over with lieutenant colonels. So even though my Military Operational Specialty was 71542—an airborne infantry commander—I came under a different command.

"My assignment was to be the senior advisor to the command-ing general of the 7th ROK Division, Major General Lee Chung Il. As such, I became a part of the Korean Military Advisory Group (KMAG) in Tague, Korea. Those of us who were sent, privately called it a 'Kiss My Ass Goodbye' assignment.

"Korea was the first time that we as a country had gone into com-bat without being attacked first. We never officially declared war, but we went to Korea supposedly to stop the spread of communism. My feelings at the time were that we should let the Koreans run their own damn show, but I never allowed those feelings to dictate my actions. I was, in fact, committed to a cause I didn't believe in.

"So I left my children squalling and bawling on the train platform there in Kenly. I remember my father wiping his eyes with his handkerchief and how Mother pinched her lips together. Genevieve's bottom lip was quivering. She didn't like this assignment any better than I did, but she understood. When I got orders from the Army, I did what they said do.

"The train trip itself to San Francisco was intriguing and pleasant as I traveled first class in a Pullman car. I had never slept in a train bunk, but the bed was most comfortable. We picked up other military personnel along the way and we were all served and well cared for, although the food was certainly not the same quality as what I had enjoyed on those train rides from Bad Tölz into Landsberg, Germany.

"I had lots of time to think about that assignment, as well as what I might be facing this time. I gazed out the window of the train as small-town America passed by me in parade. The train cut a path through Tennessee, Arkansas, Oklahoma, New Mexico, and Arizona, and then finally, on to California. But that was just the beginning of my journey.

"I didn't even get to Korea before I faced a challenge. We arrived in San Francisco and prepared for departure. Those of us being sent to Tague were there for about three days until we got orders to make our flight.

"When we boarded, there were fifty-two officers on the plane. All of us were flying to Korea as replacements for the officers who were rotating back home. There were all ranks — majors, captains, and second lieutenants. I was the senior officer in charge on that flight, and everything was fine until we made a mid-flight stop for refueling at Wake Island." My uncle shook his head.

"Mary Susan, you probably know that Wake Island was attacked by the Japanese and fell to them almost simultaneously with Pearl Harbor. I wished I had never heard of Wake Island. Even though we were to be there only for the afternoon, I allowed the men to get off the plane for a little R and R. Control of the island territory had been returned to the U.S., and the native islanders were back in business. My thinking was that a few drinks, maybe a meal, would be a nice diversion. I designated a time for my officers to return and dismissed them. I stayed behind with the refueling and maintenance mechanics.

"The time for us to go got closer. The men were supposed to be back by four that afternoon. Departure was scheduled for 4:30, and I was waiting on the ground for my officers. They came back in groups mostly, sometimes with two or three supporting one who was drunk. As the men straggled back in, I did a head count as each one climbed back up into the plane. The fact that some of them had to be helped over the threshold wasn't the worst of it. Fifteen minutes after we had been cleared for departure, I was still short five officers.

"At that point, I called the military police there on post and requested that they check the bars and whorehouses to find my officers and have them report to me on the airfield. We were not leaving Wake Island without them. How could I explain that?

"They were not hard to find. Wake Island is not a big place, and I soon got word. The men had been found—no specifics about where they had been found—and the MPs were bringing them to the airport. The men came back willingly. No one was in handcuffs or anything like that. They hadn't meant to go AWOL—absent without leave. They just needed to be reminded of their duty." My uncle laughed and shrugged his shoulders.

"The men weren't so far gone as to forget to salute me and stand at attention—or the best they could do. 'Reporting for duty, Sir…ah,' the senior officer in one group said. There wasn't any breeze that afternoon, but he was swaying."

That word "duty" again, I thought. "What did you say to them?" I said.

"I didn't have much conversation with them. These men were derelict in their duty. There wasn't much point because most of them wouldn't have remembered it anyway. I was just glad that it was a long flight and that when we presented ourselves to the Korean Military Advisory Group, my officers would be sober.

"I do remember saying, 'Get on that damn plane, sit down, and be quiet. You can talk about where you've been and what you've done this afternoon among yourselves later, but not now. I don't even want the others to hear it.'

"Talking for the rest of the flight didn't present much of a problem. Most of the men were out cold before we were even in the air. If there was any conversation, I made sure I didn't hear it."

"Why do you suppose they acted like that?"

"Most of these fellows had never been in this type of environment before. I knew human nature. We had more than a nodding acquaintance, and I should have known better than to turn them loose like that under the circumstances."

At dinner that night, Jane ordered unsweetened tea for herself, and then spoke to Belinda, a new waitress at Huey's. Belinda was young, probably college-age, but she was learning fast. She had been at my uncle's elbow as soon as he sat down. "Be sure to make that unsweet for Legs, as well," Jane said.

To me, she added, "Legs passed out last week during our exercise program at Duke Hospital. He was riding an exercise bike and just fell off—passed out cold and hit the concrete. Fortunately, he didn't hit his head."

My uncle grimaced, then grinned, and rubbed his left shoulder.

"This shoulder, the one I always slept on out in the open, caught the devil—again. When I came to, I was in an ambulance, and there were some very pretty nurses giving me oxygen."

My uncle's shoulders looked thin beneath the wool sweater he was wearing that night.

"Will you go back next week?" I asked.

"Oh, yes. I was cleared for exercise. There are registered nurses and trainers right there within a few feet of all the equipment. I enjoy talking to them. Most of them are young. We have some interesting conversations."

Belinda brought three glasses of unsweetened tea to our booth and gave each of us a menu. For once it didn't seem to matter to Uncle Legs what he ordered. "I'll have the special tonight," he said, "whatever that is." He laid the menu down on the table without looking at it.

"Fried pork chops. What about you two?"

Jane had raised her eyebrows at the word fried, but said nothing except, "I'll have the same."

"Me, too," I added.

Uncle Legs added four packs of artificial sweetener to his tea and stirred it thoughtfully. "My position as part of the Korean Military Advisory Group was such that I was to serve as the go between for General Clovis Byers, the 10th Corps Commander of the United Nations forces, and Major General Lee Chung Il, the Commander of the 7th ROK (Republic of Korea) Division. This was a new type of assignment for me in that I would be in the company of generals and full colonels at staff meetings and social functions. These were men of an entirely different caliber than the officers I had previously been associated with. They were more educated, more dedicated to the military as a profession and a career they had chosen, not just as service. It was quite an experience.

"General Lee, as we called him, was no exception. He was an

interesting person, to say the least. He was a short man, but an impressive commander. When he stood before his men, he reminded me of a bantam rooster, strutting in front of a flock of hens. At the age of thirty-two, he was already a major general and had been in active military service to his country, starting in Mongolia at age sixteen. He spoke good English, with only a slight accent.

"I stood at attention before him at headquarters in Tague, Korea, only a few days after my arrival. I made sure that what I showed him was a poker face and that the distance between us was such that he wouldn't have to look up to see me. He gazed back at me without any expression whatsoever. You could never show any fear or anxiety in front of these guys.

"If they themselves felt any of these things, they never showed it. I saw it only once in General Lee.

"'Sir,' I said, 'For my first assignment, I'd like for us to go and inspect the front line units together.' I had the feeling that this suggestion was something that would please him.

"As Daddy would say, it didn't hurt to grease the axle wheels now and then, whether they needed it or not.

"I'm quite sure General Lee's pride didn't need puffing up, but he was definitely in favor of my request. He had the silliest little grin on his face. It did not match his expressionless dark eyes. I remember that he stood up on his toes and drew himself up to his full height of about 5'4". 'I'm glad you found out that I'm a front-line general,' he said.

"I don't remember exactly what I said to him, but I let him know that I understood.

"What he meant was that he was a general who kept in touch with what was going on with the men who were on the front lines. He was a very sharp man, and he understood other men.

"Those he commanded respected him, and he and I got along very well together. Although neither of us ever spoke of it, we both recognized that he needed me.

"Anyway, from that point on, we made it our daily routine to go out to the front lines first thing in the morning and see if we had what headquarters wanted. Then we had something specific to say to General Byers about the state of his troops and their readiness.

"It was a very cold day, with the early morning sun creating shadows in the valleys below, and General Lee and I were riding in a jeep on our way to report to headquarters. We had a driver to take us around the mountain. General Lee was sitting beside him in the front, and I, of course, sat behind them. The road was a solid sheet of ice, and sixty feet below, I saw there was a river of running water that I guessed was probably somewhere between 17 and 27 degrees below zero. It crossed my mind, as we were breezing along, that anybody who fell in would probably freeze to death before they could get out, if they were able.

"It was a prophetic thought. We were into a hairpin turn when we started skidding. The driver put the brakes on, but it was too late. The General started hollering, 'Sto...p, Sto...p, Sto...p!' Nothing else. Just that long word, echoing against the retreating rock on the side of the mountain, and the sound of the river racing below us. The distance between us and the drop was getting shorter and shorter as we were sliding toward the edge. I can still see General Lee's face to this day in my mind's eye, white, very white, like the underbelly of a fish, his eyes wide open, and his mouth a round O.

"My reaction was immediate and without hesitation. Without even thinking, I rolled out of the back of the jeep on my left shoulder, then back over a time or two, just in time to catch the rear wheel that was closest to me."

Rubbing his left shoulder gingerly, he checked in momentarily with me to see if I was enjoying the story. His gaze also swept over the room of regular Saturday night diners.

Thus far he had not touched the pork chops that were before him, and Jane and I, as well as anyone else within earshot, had stopped eating.

"It still gives me trouble to this day," he said, grinning, obviously delighted with his captivation of a wide-eyed audience. Without lowering his voice, my uncle continued.

"By the time I had caught the back wheel and stabilized the jeep, the right front wheel was already off the edge of the mountain and just spinning, spinning in the air. I was breathing hard, and I remember noticing that General Lee's breath punctuated the air with sharp little puffs of white smoke. He was sitting there like he was frozen, and that was a good thing since any slight movement could have sent the jeep into a free fall.

"I did think this time, but quickly. I had gotten both hands on the wheel, and I was holding on for dear life — theirs. I directed the driver to ease out of the jeep first and to the relative safety of the road since he was closest to me. Then he and I held on to the bumper while the general got out on the driver's side. General Lee was a very quick, light man, with excellent reflexes, so he leaped out with relatively little impact on the jeep's position.

"Then the three of us together pulled the jeep back onto solid ground. We got back in, took our same positions, and continued on to headquarters. It was a very quiet ride.

"Our breaths curled back white behind us in the wind like the smoke you see coming out of the chimneys in your neighborhood when you know you're almost home.

"Nothing was said to the driver. But you should have heard the General telling his staff officers about this event. It cemented our relationship."

Uncle Legs had been speaking out into the dining room from his seat against the back wall. Normally, he would have faced that wall with Jane and me on the other side. Tonight our positions had been reversed, so nearly everyone in the restaurant had gotten an ear full.

Now he looked at Jane and me. "Let's eat and then go home. Don't want to waste good food.

"I've thought of another story I want to tell you about Korea." We ate the rest of our meal in silence against the kitchen clatter heard through the swinging door and the hum of conversation that resumed around us.

Sitting in his favorite chair and sipping burgundy wine, my uncle held the glass up to the bulb of the one lamp in the den, which stood beside his chair. The wine acted like a prism, turning the soft golden reflection of the light, blood red.

"It's amazing what goes through your mind when you think you have a short time to live," Uncle Legs said, stretching his legs out over the stool and crossing them at the ankles.

I wondered if he was talking about then or now? Or both?

"Some time after the jeep incident, I did have time to think. How would I have been able to go back to division headquarters without General Lee? In my mind, I could hear one of his staff officers asking in an off-hand manner, 'Where's General Lee?'

"I could imagine his shock at my response — the only response I would have been able to make. 'Oh, he drowned back there. He's down in the river somewhere.' Such news would have certainly been a close call for me of an entirely different nature. It would have been just as well for me not to go back.

"You'd think I would have had enough," he smiled, uncrossing his legs and glancing over at me. "But I hadn't. Not yet. In my assignment with the 7th ROK Division, I knew that I would not be eligible to receive the Combat Infantry Badge. I had one and I wanted another one. There it is," he said, pointing a long bony finger at the glass-enclosed case of ribbons and medals that he had brought to this session. It was a silver wreath with a thin blue rectangle laid across it. In the center of the rectangle was a silver rifle. A silver star was attached to one side of the wreath.

"I got myself transferred to the regimental headquarters at Mundung-ni Valley, where there was just as much danger of becoming involved in combat as there was on the front line. I would be in the combat zone in a continual situation of finding, fixing, and destroying the enemy, as a 1542 MOS (Military Operation Specialist), for the required thirty days.

"From the Mundung-ni Valley, we, that is the United Nations forces, made limited attacks against the North Koreans and the Chinese and continued moving slowly into North Korea. Those we came in contact with, we killed. I don't recall a particular incident when I personally killed a North Korean or a Chinese, but I gave orders that caused people to be hurt or killed.

"I served as an observer and directed the field artillery. The Koreans didn't have any artillery assigned to them, except that which came from the U.S. Since the North Koreans were attacking our position, the South Koreans, of course, wanted artillery support. I had asked to be part of that. I was close enough to the action to see the North Koreans falling, without field glasses.

"I got the Combat Infantry Badge in World War II, and the star is for Korea. But I almost got killed there, and not from enemy fire. My fourth close call occurred in the spring of 1952, just north of Seoul, Korea, at an observation post on a mountain just above the Mundung-ni Valley, about 2,000 feet above sea level.

"I was to return to the 7th ROK Division, where General Willis B. Palmer, the new corps commander, wanted to see me. He had recently replaced Clovis Byers, and he was sending a helicopter to pick me up. I was waiting on the ground and shading my eyes against the sun and the tornado of dust that was being kicked up by the helicopter as it descended in front of me.

"The pilot landed, I got in, and he attempted to lift off the observation post. Unfortunately, neither of us noticed that the right, front landing gear of the chopper had hooked around a root where he had touched down. The chopper was now jerking back and forth like a toy on the end of a rubber band. We were on the ground and then off the ground, back and forth for several tries. I could see that his head, as well as mine, was bobbing back and forth with the motion of the helicopter. The pilot's hand was jerking the stick that controlled the landing gear back and forth. I remember how white his hand was.

"Our position was precarious at best. There were North Koreans to our north, south, east, and west, and we were momentarily stuck right in the middle of them. Finally, he broke loose, and we went off down the side of the mountain. Fortunately, none of the propellers hit the side, but it would be an understatement to say that the pilot was not in command of the helicopter.

"The engine had stalled, and we were falling without power, 1200 to 1500 feet to the bottom, to our deaths, I thought. We had just lost two L4 and L5 liaison aircraft that had been sent as forward observers, so I was familiar with what normally happens when a helicopter crashes. People don't usually walk away.

"The whole thing happened so fast that I hardly had time to pray. I have never felt so helpless in my entire life. In this instance, there was absolutely nothing that I personally could do except pray—unlike my previous near misses.

"It's amazing what goes through your mind when you think you have a short time to live."

That's the second time today you've said that, I thought.

He continued, "My prayers were for my survival, and my split-second thoughts were on how my death would affect my family. I wanted to spare them, if I could, by living.

"Finally, the engine caught, and the blades of the chopper began to whirl like an eggbeater—a most beautiful sound that oddly enough reminded me of my mother using hers to whip up some meringue for one of her delicious pies. We were just as safe as a mother's love.

"I didn't say anything to the pilot at the time, but I remember becoming conscious of just how tight the muscles were in the back of my neck. The sweat was pouring off my face, buckets of it, but I didn't notice until we were well on our way. The thought of what I would look like when I presented myself to General Palmer crossed my mind, but I brushed it away, as I wiped my face. At least I would be able to meet him, and I was not dead. I patted the person who was responsible for that, the pilot, on the shoulder.

"When we finally did land, I said to him, 'You did a fine job back there.'

"He replied, 'I know I did, and I'm very proud of myself that we're alive.'

"Nothing changed for me after these incidents. I went where I was supposed to go and did what I was supposed to do. You can't let fear enter your mind and mess up your mission, or you become ineffective.

"I always wanted to be where the action was, and I certainly got my wish. I had way too many things to worry about besides what was happening to me, and most of the time, I had my men to be concerned about—I survived and so did most of them."

My uncle leaned back in his chair, his head cradled in the indention that was already there, and closed his eyes. I waited for a few minutes and then left him as I went quietly upstairs.

I thought, *those of us who are privileged to be invited along for another's journey are better able to recognize our own milestones when we encounter them.* I was grateful.

Getting the Call

"Death was coming, and he wasn't about
to let it get the jump on him."

—Lieutenant Colonel Lehman H. Johnson, Jr.

"While I was in Korea, I got a granite mountain call—that's code for serious health concerns in the family." Uncle Legs made this announcement once we were back in the den.

The lesson in Sunday School that morning had been about the apostle Paul's 'thorn in the flesh' and what that might have meant in terms of his health and lifestyle. At lunch, this time at Cracker Barrel, the conversation had centered around my Uncle Leg's new physical limitations and Jane's increasing difficulty with her eyesight. There had been discussion of a possible move to Croasdaile Retirement Village.

The story of the afternoon was a natural bridge back.

"There's never a good time for that kind of news, but when I got that granite mountain call, I was at my observation post in Korea, observing an attack by the 7th ROK Division with General Lee. Word came from the Red Cross that my dad had had a heart attack and that he was seriously ill. Colonel Hokkum delivered the message personally. It was not a good message to receive, I tell you that. But he told me I did have permission to go home.

371

"My attention turned immediately away from the details of war and to getting home to the States, as fast as possible. Many times, when someone got that kind of call, the family member who was ill would be dead before they got there, and they would arrive just in time for a funeral. I didn't want that to happen to me.

"I called up J.C. (Hacksaw) Tarkington, a buddy of mine from Officer Candidate School, and asked him to get me a plane from Northern Korea to Seoul, so I could catch a flight back to the United States. We went all the way back to Oak Ridge. I knew he was in a position now to help me, and that he would.

"His response was, 'Legs, I'll have a plane to pick you up in an hour and a half to get you to Seoul.'

"Mary Susan, people outside the military don't understand the relationship of people inside the military — how they support one another in time of need." My uncle leaned forward, elbows on his legs, and relaxed his knees. His hands dropped between them. "I have done favors, big and small. I have invited 'strangers,' who had just moved, into our home to do laundry. Anyway, this time it was my time to ask for a big favor. And I got it.

"In a matter of a few hours, I was on my way back to the States. Settling into my seat on a plane bound for Houston, I remembered that all I had wanted was to get this war over with and get back home. Maybe God has a sense of humor. If so, I certainly wasn't laughing.

"These were not the circumstances I had wanted. But it was not the first time in my life that my situation had turned on a dime. Or even that my physical surroundings had been abruptly altered. But I was in shock.

"The fact that I had just been taken off the combat zone and hadn't slept in several days probably didn't help, so even though I was worried sick about Dad, I went to sleep almost as soon as I sat down on that plane. They had to wake me up to feed me although I would have moments when I would wake up, startled, and forget that I was no longer in charge of attacking the enemy. Maybe on some level I realized there was nothing I could do.

"It was nerve wracking because I didn't know who the enemy was anymore, or how he would strike. I had faced him before, of course, but not like this.

"I wanted to sleep because I was exhausted. The other part was that I wanted to escape from these thoughts and from my fears about losing my father.

"I was just drifting off again when the pretty little USO (United Service Organization) girl sitting next to me punched my arm to wake me up.

"'Hey,' she said brightly. 'Where are you back from?' Her red lipstick was almost blinding as I opened my eyes and squinted to see who was talking to me.

"She herself was just coming back to the States with a group who had been to entertain the troops. Leaning in toward my seat, she informed me of this fact before I could even answer. She was a honey and she was so close to me that I could smell her perfume. I guess she felt somehow entitled to ask me about my 'war experiences.'

"I have never wanted very much to talk about these experiences, but I especially was in no mood to talk right then.

"'Excuse me,' I said, more politely than I felt, and turning away, 'I've just come off the combat zone, and I'm going to take these four aspirins this nice stewardess brought me, and I'm going back to sleep. Please don't disturb me anymore.'

"She left me alone after that."

Uncle Legs leaned back in his chair and pulled the afghan off the back. He slipped his shoes off and stretched his legs out over the foot stool in front of his chair. Then he wrapped himself in the afghan and turned slightly away from me. I did not see when he closed his eyes, but after about fifteen minutes, he began to breathe deeply and snore.

The sound was a letting go of some inward pressure, like the carbonation that escapes from a bottle of soda when the lid is gently twisted. There was no gasping for air or choking, just the rhythmic exhaling of his breath. I let him be.

It was a warmer day, and I could see that the pansies were now upright and had turned their petals upward to face the afternoon sun. Time passed—maybe an hour, before my uncle awoke.

"What happened when you got home?" I asked.

Uncle Legs stretched and threw off the coverlet before he replied.

"The first thing Daddy said to me from his hospital bed was, 'Thank God you made it, son.' I wasn't quite sure how to take that." My uncle blinked his eyes to clear away any remaining fog of sleep.

"Then Daddy asked me, 'Do you have to go back to Korea?' I had to lean down to hear him. His voice was barely above a whisper. I wanted very much to put his mind at ease.

"'I don't know, Dad. I'll keep you posted,' I said. At that time, I had no idea, but it must have been enough to satisfy him. He closed his eyes and promptly went to sleep.

"I had thirty days of leave, and Dad was in the hospital the whole time. I was with him every day for as long as he wanted until he came home. We spent much time talking about current things and what was needed for the family—always the family.

"Daddy was convinced that what would be needed was a funeral. The doctors were monitoring him every day, and although he was improving slowly, the improvement wasn't enough to convince my strong-willed father. He was sure that he was going to die soon and that we needed to accept it and get ready. The doctor, Mother, and I all tried to convince him that his body would heal itself with proper rest, but he wasn't buying it. 'I want to see my preacher and prepare myself,' he insisted, raising himself up in his hospital bed, each time I visited. I was not about to argue with an almost dead man.

"So Mother and I spent a lot of time discussing the what ifs, to please him. Who would the preacher be? That was the only easy part. The minister would be the Reverend J.L. Jones, pastor of Kenly Missionary Baptist Church, where he and Mother were members. That left a few more questions. Who would serve as the undertaker? What about the church? What would the songs be? Would my sister Mary play, or would she be too overwhelmed? With Daddy's input, we started making tentative plans for his funeral."

Uncle Legs smiled broadly. Even though he was looking at me through his bifocals, I could see the twinkle. "I know this sounds morbid, but Daddy's perspective was in keeping with his character. Death was coming and he wasn't about to let it get the jump on him.

"Mother was very calm while we discussed these things. She just flat laid it out there, and that was how the funeral would be handled. Although we didn't know it, we wouldn't need those plans for another thirty years.

"It had not been that way with Mother earlier when we had first spoken from Houston, where I had changed planes on the way home. 'Tell me what happened,' I had said into the phone, just a few days before. All I had wanted to hear was that Dad was doing okay.

"But she was so worn out and on the peak of her emotions—happy that I was almost home, but so worried about Daddy that she handed the phone right over to one of the girls. It was like she was looking up a mountain and then back down again—like she couldn't find an easy resting place. I remember saying to my sister, 'Please put Mother back on the phone.'"

"I pleaded with her. 'Let me know the things you've been thinking about. Now that I'm almost there, you can tell me. I need to know what you've been going through.'"

"And so she did, even though every now and then, there were pauses in the telling. I had imagined Mother wiping her eyes in the silences that hung between us, between Houston and Kenly, reminding me of the time it takes to hear the explosion when the pin is pulled from a grenade.

"He had been at the cotton gin at the time, running the machine that was now providing most of their livelihood. He had fallen on the gin floor. The first person that came to him said Dad ordered him to 'Go over there and pull the lever and stop that thing!' The doctor came, and then an ambulance was called. My father didn't want to go, but he was taken to Wilson Memorial Hospital anyway. They found out that he had suffered a serious heart attack.

"People stayed in the hospital longer back then than they do now, and during that period of his recuperation, my father and I became closer. Mother had always had a soft spot for me although she tried not to show it. Dad never had that problem.

"We had some very deep conversations about life, and I got to know my father in a way that I had not known him before. Dad was real proud of me and the fact that I had served in two wars. But he had never wanted to hear any war stories, although I had asked him before. Since he had declared himself to be on his death bed, I thought now might be a good time to offer again. 'Only if you want to talk about them,' he said. 'I'm just glad you're back alive.'

"'Dad,' I said, 'I've been in some skirmishes where I thought I wouldn't get back.' This was not a topic I had wanted to discuss with anyone else, not even Genevieve, but I felt that I could talk about it with my father at that time.

"He just looked up at me. His dark eyes were almost burning holes in mine, and they were the only color on that white hospital pillow. I understood. Even though my father thought he was dying, he could not stand hearing about his son's near misses. He could face his own death, but not mine.

"So instead of talking about myself, I told him about the men in my company—about their courage and their survival. His response was that they were not old enough to do those things.

"'They're younger than me,' I said, 'but not by much, and some of them are home as veterans. Others are still fighting in Korea.'"

"Dad turned toward the wall. Was he wondering about what I had left out, the parts about me, or was he just tired? I'll never know.

"I did not go back to Korea. There was a regulation in place at that time that if you had served so many months in the battle zone and you were sent home for any reason, you didn't go back. Instead, I was sent to Fort Bragg, Fayetteville, only about an hour and a half from my parents and close to Genevieve's, as well. I was so happy. I had almost lost my father, but at least for a while, I could go see my parents whenever I wanted to.

"Mother depended on me, like she always had, but it was different somehow this time. I was to attempt to take Dad in hand—a most difficult assignment. Rest and time were the prescriptions of the day for a person who had had a heart attack, and my father didn't much want to take that medicine, so of course he improved very slowly. The way Dad looked at things, the biggest problem was that Mother wouldn't give him the car keys.

"Virginia Watson of Kenly had been hired to handle the bills and paperwork at the fertilizer office. She knew what do, and was very personable, but Daddy wanted to go to the office, and he wanted to take himself. 'Lehman,' my mother would say firmly, 'I've hidden the car keys, and I don't even know where they are right now.'

"Besides running the cotton gin, Daddy sold Weil's fertilizer. My parents had enjoyed a period of relative prosperity prior to Dad's heart attack, and he was worried, as always, about the family finances.

"It was six to eight months before Dad could go back to work, and even then, he couldn't go back to the cotton gin. There were stairs at the gin, and he wasn't supposed to walk up any stairs. Mother would tell him, 'Now you get well and do like the doctors say, and don't you try to climb any stairs.'

"I do not remember my Mother ever talking to my father like this before his heart attack, and I'm sure it was hard for her to have to say these things to him. But when he fussed about the restrictions, she just let him fuss on.

"At least for a time, Mother was now head of the household—no question about it. I did my best to back her up. But it wasn't easy—telling my father what to do."

"I can imagine that it wasn't," I said.

"Yes, I found myself in a strange position, standing between my mother and daddy. It was no secret in my family that Mother ran the household, but she and Daddy made all major decisions together. I had never seen them argue like this before."

The coolness of the evening had crept into the room, and darkness had laid a blanket over the pansies which were no longer visible from the window. Uncle Legs called out, "Jane, can you light these logs? It's cold in here."

I stood up to leave as Jane entered the room. She turned up the logs, and light illuminated the room and my uncle's face. "How about if I come back again this month?" I would come twice.

"Yes, please. Work out the details with Jane if you will."

I went out into the night.

My Last Close Call

"I looked up as I always did, expecting to see the beautiful canopy of my parachute. Instead, I was looking at the ground!"

— Lieutenant Colonel Lehman H. Johnson, Jr.

Perhaps T.S. Eliott was on to something when he talked about April being the cruelest month and the strange mixture of memory and desire that comes with spring ("The Waste Land"). Both of these were in full bloom, in the heart and soul of Lt. Col. Legs Johnson, along with the purple iris, that had pushed their way up through the hard winter dirt. They were lovely and dark as death in Jane and Uncle Legs' backyard.

He was sitting in the den with his cane across his lap that Saturday afternoon, huddled under a blanket. "I want to tell you about my last close call," my uncle said. There were no preliminary questions about family and no small talk. Instead he plunged right into the story.

"I looked up as I always did, expecting to see the beautiful canopy of my parachute. Instead, I was looking at the ground!" Without turning around, he gestured toward the large, framed photograph of a paratrooper that hung behind his chair, the one that wasn't him, but could have been.

"You see, Mary Susan, after Korea, I was assigned to the Joint

379

Airborne Test Board at Fort Bragg, North Carolina. On March 31, 1952, I began my new assignment, which was to review and test all airborne techniques and equipment. It was certainly a good assignment. It gave me a chance to get to Kenly often to visit Mother and Daddy, and I could get back into the tactics of airborne warfare at Bragg. There I was associated with all the airborne officers who had served in World War II. There were representatives from the British, the French, and, of course, from the U.S. I was in my element.

"One project we had was testing the value of dropping heavy equipment by parachutes where it might be needed. We would take a 75mm artillery piece, for example, and attach what would hopefully be enough chutes to land it without tearing the equipment all to pieces. Then we would take it up using a C119 or the clam shell of a C119. The equipment would then be released off the back of the plane. Our purpose was to find out what parachute and what platform would work for specific pieces of equipment. Some made it. Some didn't.

"It was there at Fort Bragg, Fayetteville, North Carolina, that I almost didn't make it after having fought in two wars. You read about these things—men who have survived war and then they are killed in a car accident once they get home. It doesn't seem fair somehow."

My uncle cupped his chin in his hand and leaned toward me, reflectively, before he continued.

"Anyway, another project that I oversaw was to test what size drop zone was needed for aircraft of a particular size. At times, I had fifty men jumping in tandem out both sides of the airplane. I would have to find a long, deep jump zone—a field that is long enough and deep enough for a drop. If that kind of space was not available, the men would be dropped into the creeks, trees, and everywhere else. An entire regiment of two to five thousand men could be moved quickly this way. It was the most efficient way to get to a place. You didn't have to drive trucks in, and you didn't have to march in. You just dropped the men out of the plane.

"As a junior officer, I was still required to do a number of routine jumps, and sometimes my commanding officer, General Bill Harper, would ask me to jump with him—which I did, of course. Usually, he and I would go out the back door of the airplane running—an easier method for me than jumping out the side where, at six feet, four and a half inches, it was easy for me to hit my head on the way out. The back-door method was good for practice. We would fall spread eagle and then the chutes would open up. There were no injuries that I can remember.

"What was almost my last jump, however, occurred during an air show and demonstration at Fort Bragg. It was the first and only time that Genevieve and the children came out to see me jump. I was out of the plane and falling at 75 feet per second. I pulled the string and looked up, as I always did, expecting to see that beautiful canopy. Instead, I was looking at the ground!

"My feet were tangled in the lines, and I was falling to my death in front of my wife and children. I remember saying to myself, 'Keep your cool, Johnson. Keep your cool.' I was not close enough to hear the gasps of horror rising from the stands on the parade ground. Genevieve told me about those later and the moment she realized what was happening. I was only dimly conscious of a cold rush of air past my cheeks, ears, and hair. I tuned out every sensation except survival and what was to be done at that moment.

"Miraculously, I was able to pull my knees up into my chest and reach my feet, just in time to untangle them so that my chute could open. It was just in time to slow my descent, but I still hit the ground hard. I landed backwards on a bank, on the base of my spine, not where I was supposed to land, in front of the crowd and to their applause.

"I could hear the gasps when they realized I was injured, and then how quiet it got as the medics rushed out to me. I was in so much pain I thought I had broken my back. I could not get up. The medics put me on a stretcher and took me to the post hospital, where I was x-rayed from head to toe.

"Genevieve followed me to the hospital, children in tow. She did not have to tell me what a potentially traumatic experience my children had almost just had. Lee was about 10, Jule was 8, Steve was 3, and Candy was a little over a year old. They weren't crying, but they all had these big eyes when they gathered around my bed. I remember thinking that they were afraid to get close to me. The older three, Lee, Jule, and even little Steve probably thought I was dead. Genevieve was holding Candy, the baby."

Studying my uncle, I remembered, "This has happened to you before—during jungle training."

"Keep your cool, Johnson. Keep your cool." He had said the same thing to himself, in the telling of that story. But the breath of death had been worse this time because his wife and children were present.

"Yes, and I had not forgotten. Fortunately, there were no broken bones, but I had a tingling sensation in my feet and legs for the next few days. The other thing that I had was a renewed awareness of just how fragile life is. It was a lesson that I had already learned many times over, but that day was a reminder. The only conclusion I could come to was that it just wasn't my time yet. But I took it as an omen.

"Speaking of omens, my stomach is growling. Where's Jane? It must be time for dinner." My uncle got unsteadily to his feet and balanced himself between the cane and the arm of his chair. He ignored my outstretched hand. Jane entered the room on cue and took his arm.

We were on our way to Huey's. At least that was the same.

Church at Home

"Somewhere out there, I was convinced, was a bullet with my name on it. I was not anxious for it to find me."

— Lieutenant Colonel Lehman H. Johnson, Jr.

Uncle Legs was uncharacteristically late for breakfast. There had been nothing said the night before about not going to church, and we were going to be late if he didn't come down soon.

I realized while I waited that there had been no more stories last night, before or after Huey's, just a few scraps to add — bits and pieces of reflections that we had already packed over with stuffing and sewed into the quilt of his life's story. That was fine. They would serve as reinforcement and finish off the seams so that there would be no ragged edges, no disjointed episodes that didn't fit.

After dinner, when we were back in the den, Jane had said that there had been another episode at the Duke Hospital exercise center. Uncle Legs had fallen again, this time from a cross training machine to the floor, and he had hit his head on the concrete. The nurses and trainers who were in the area had rushed to his side, but they were not quick enough to break his fall. Another trip to Duke Hospital Emergency Room had been the conclusion of their three times a week, morning exercise routine. The ER doctors determined that my uncle had a mild concussion. There was a purple and yellow bruise still visible above his left temple and the skin around it was red and angry looking.

Uncle Legs had fished out a piece of paper from somewhere between the magazines overflowing on the TV tray which he still kept beside him. Waving it in the air between us, he said, "I got a letter." The tone of his voice was as flat as a pancake made with old self-rising flour.

"Legs can't go to Duke to the exercise program anymore," Jane added.

"Liability issues," Uncle Legs had explained. There was no judgment or complaint in his voice. But I remembered now, sitting there in the kitchen, that I had thought he sounded tired. Should I go in and check on him?

Then he was there, standing before me in the soft morning light which made artificial light unnecessary. He still looked like an eagle, with his neck sticking out of the collar of his bathrobe and his nose jutting out like a beak. But not one that was about to soar. He was still in his multi-striped silk bathrobe and looked bedraggled. His eyes were alert and watchful, but his heavy lids made them look hooded. My uncle sat down at the breakfast table and crouched over the coffee I brought him.

"What do you say we go to church at home?" Uncle Legs asked.

"What do you mean?"

"We can turn on the television and watch a service that way. I do that when I just don't feel like getting up and getting dressed. Yesterday took the starch out of me, and this morning I feel like I've been hung out to dry."

Jane told me later in private that "church at home" had become more frequent. "Yes, Legs stays home now on Sunday mornings. I come in from church and he's asleep in his chair with the television still on. Sometimes, it's not playing, and I don't think it's even been turned on. He still goes to church sometimes though, when he's up to it. He rides in early with me because I have choir practice. He sits out in the hall to his Sunday school class and talks to whoever comes by."

That Sunday morning my uncle and I did not go to church at home. He wanted to talk to me, and I was more than ready to listen. At his invitation, we retired to the den and took our accustomed places.

"There were two honeymoon assignments after Korea. I've already told you about Bragg."

I nodded. "Yes, and you also told me about getting tangled up in your parachute and the fact that the honeymoon almost ended right then and there."

"Well, it didn't." A trace of a smile played across my uncle's face as he reached for the afghan that was now draped across the arm of his chair. The veins in his hands seemed to be more prominent, but perhaps I had just noticed them.

"I had been trying for some time—eighteen years in fact—to get myself assigned to the Army post in Hawaii. I had done everything I could to get my card punched. After Fort Bragg, instead of my first choice, I was sent to Fort Benning, Georgia.

"That certainly was not a bad assignment. We lived together as a family there on post on what was then called Rainbow Avenue. That was very pleasant—being with my family, that is. Our house was pink at the time, and our quarters joined the number two hole on the golf course that was right behind our house. It was very convenient for me. My work was mostly administrative—some teaching—and I had time to play golf.

"Rumors were flying around about that time that, without a degree, you wouldn't be on the promotion list, no matter how much action you had seen. You would not be considered for any of the plum assignments either, so while we were at Benning, I completed my four-year degree at the University of Georgia at Athens. I wanted to make sure my John Henry got at the top of both lists.

"All good things come to he who waits." My uncle laughed and then coughed several times. He reached into the pocket of his robe, but there was no handkerchief there. Instead, he got the one that was crumpled on top of his magazine stash, the plaid one I recognized from yesterday, and coughed into it again. When he had cleared his throat, he added, "It doesn't hurt to be working while you're waiting though. In June of 1956, following my graduation, I was sent back to Bragg.

"Anyway, I strolled into my office at Fort Bragg one morning and found my orders sitting there, waiting for me on my desk. I ripped open the envelope and read them. I couldn't believe my eyes. I guess my card had been punched because Uncle Sam was sending me where I wanted to go. I was being assigned as an advisor to the Hawaiian National Guard in Hilo, Hawaii.

"I couldn't get home fast enough to tell Genevieve. She was surprised to see me. 'Legs, you look like you've just swallowed a canary,' she said. 'What is it and why are you home in the middle of the day?' When I told her, all she said then was, 'Well, I'll be doggone. You've been waiting for it long enough.' Then in the next breath she said, 'When is the quartermaster coming to pick up the furniture?' Genevieve was ready to go. We were en route to Hilo by March 23, 1957.

"Part of my job in Hawaii was to travel to all of the islands at least once a month to ensure that the National Guard was carrying out their training responsibilities for each unit. I carried my golf clubs every time I went to one of the islands. Courtesy of the United States Army, I had the privilege of playing golf on every major course in Hawaii. Although I can't play anymore — my balance isn't good enough even to ride in the cart and get out — I have enjoyed chasing that little white ball. Nice work if you can get it, and I was very happy to have it." My uncle's head fell forward on his chest and he stopped talking. Then he yawned and lifted his chin.

"Would you get me another cup of coffee, please ma'am?"

"Of course. Sugar and cream?" I already knew the answer. Although the coffee was decaffeinated—Jane always made two pots, one for me and one for him—I knew he was trying to stay awake.

"Yes, please."

When I returned, Uncle Legs was asleep. I straightened the magazines, set the coffee cup down on top, and sat down to wait. His snoring sounded rattled, and after a while, he caught his breath. His eyelids flew open, like when a window shade doesn't catch in place and instead flies all the way to the top of the casing. He sat up straight but didn't taste the coffee. Instead he picked up his story.

"Genevieve and I decided Hawaii was the best place we had ever lived. We were there for three years. It was a very calm and relaxing time for our family. It was certainly the best place to raise children. Lee was fifteen, Jule was twelve, Steve was seven, and Candy was five. They loved to go to church in Hawaii because they didn't have to wear shoes, and Candy could hula like a native. Life was very informal and the people there were so family-oriented and friendly that we hated to leave."

Uncle Legs looked directly in front of himself at the television, but of course it wasn't on. "All good things come to an end.

"I departed Hawaii, on July 7, 1960, and on August 22, 1960, I was assigned to the 101 Airborne Division, at Fort Campbell, Kentucky. I remember those dates exactly because it was quite a change for my family. Nobody wanted to leave, but we had to go. Genevieve and the children packed up their hula skirts and we left for Kentucky. We still went to church at Fort Campbell, but the children had to wear shoes. Everything was different. There was also the added pressure of what was next for me in terms of assignments.

"We were the 35th Infantry Regiment, and we had been alerted three times. Vietnam was a smoking gun, and it looked like I was headed there. Our losses were heavy. Somewhere out there, I was convinced, was a bullet with my name on it. I was not anxious for it to find me.

"I retired from military service on May 28th, 1962, to avoid deployment. It was as simple as that. I was 46 years old. I wanted to be old someday, and I did not think that I would be that if I went to Vietnam. Already I had been in two wars, and I had all the stars on my Combat Infantry Badge that I wanted.

"I had also paid my respects to many of my officers at Arlington Cemetery. I did not want to be on the other side of a tombstone, and I felt that I would be actively seeking my own death if I were to go.

"Genevieve and I had had a taste of what it was like to have a normal family life, and I considered the effect of another deployment on my wife and children. I wanted to see them grow up. If I had grandchildren, I wanted them to know me.

"I needed to consider Genevieve as well. She never had a problem with World War II, but Korea had bothered her."

But she did, I thought. *She had a nervous breakdown.* I did not comment.

"Genevieve was worn out with it—with the waiting, the separations, the constant wondering. So I put in my papers for retirement, and here I am today—fading away. I'm about ready to ride off into the sunset, like in one of those cowboy movies. You've seen those, haven't you?"

I nodded. He smiled.

"But I've had some things to say."

And yes, I thought, *you've said them, and said them well. Now I must say them as best I can.* It wasn't long before I heard Jane's key in the kitchen door. Before I saw her, I smelled the fresh spring air and the roses, red on the trellis.

"Not dressed, Legs? We're having lunch here at home today, so it doesn't matter. Let me get my coat off, and I'll make us some Dagwoods, or would you rather have a Reuben? Legs? Mary Susan?" All this was said in rapid succession even as Jane was heading to the hall closet to hang up her cashmere Sunday coat.

"Whatever you want to fix," he said, flipping his hand in the air.

"I'll have the same," I added. It was unusual for my uncle not to express a strong preference in any matter.

Jane made Dagwoods on wheat, piled high with cheese, ham, turkey, lettuce, tomato, and pickles. They were eaten mostly in silence except for Jane's chirping on about church that morning and who had asked about Uncle Legs, as well as the meetings she would attend that afternoon.

When we were finished, I stood up and said, "I probably need to go now, Uncle Legs. You might want to rest this afternoon since you didn't sleep well last night."

My uncle did not argue with me. Instead he took out the plaid handkerchief that had somehow found its way into his pocket and wiped his eyes.

"You'll come back?"

"Of course I will."

"Then I'll see you then. Thank you so much for coming."

"Of course," I said. "I wouldn't have missed it for the world."

"All right, you two," Jane said, "break it up. Legs, you look like you're about to fall asleep at the table." But she smiled at me.

I kissed him goodbye on the cheek, and this time he kissed me back.

I stood in the driveway in the sun and took a good long look behind me before I left. I was staring straight into the sun and squinting at the house that was illuminated by it. I thought, when you open the door to pain, even a little bit, she rushes in and cleans out all the corners, gathering up whatever she finds there and sweeps it into the middle of the floor of your mind, into your consciousness, to be gathered up, dispensed with, scattered, or stepped over. But you can't ignore her or the memories she brings.

Uncle Legs was tired from his housecleaning, and he needed to rest.

Afterword

"The next best thing to being there is being told about being there."

—Lieutenant Colonel Lehman H. Johnson, Jr.

My own granite mountain call came in late April 2009. He and Jane had gone to the Presbyterian Home of Hawfields in Mebane for what his attending physician called rehabilitation — to get his heart rate and blood pressure up. The doctor wasn't fooling anybody. The brochure I picked up in the waiting room said that the facility offered long-term care, short-term rehabilitation, and end-of-life care.

"Come quick if you want to speak to him," Jane had said into the phone, her voice clear and even. "Legs is having trouble breathing and time is of the essence." There were no tears that I could hear, just calm, flowing acceptance in the stream of her characteristic serenity. "Candy is coming at once to stay for a while, and the others will be here as soon as they can. You'll probably get to see them, too."

Always the family. I knew we would wade into the stream of our family consciousness by asking about each other's children and grandchildren, my mother, and then their father.

When I arrived, Uncle Legs was sitting upright in a wheelchair with an afghan spread over his legs. "Legs, it's Mary Susan," Jane said. When he saw me, the veil of memory which now shrouded him was

391

lifted slightly. His eyes brightened and he made an attempt to sit up straight.

Jane asked him a couple of questions. "How many men are there in a company?"

His head was cocked to one side, and he could hardly speak. "One hundred ninety-two men." His voice was raspy and the words were slurred.

"What's the best job in the Army?"

My uncle's response was predictable. The tears that I felt behind my eyes were unexpected. "Company commander." I swallowed hard, knowing he would not like it if I lost control.

That Sunday the nurse's assistant had wheeled him into the on-site church service, but Candy reported that he had slept through it. When my cousin pushed her father's wheelchair up to the table for lunch, he ate nothing, nor would he eat when she tried to feed him. Her eyes, so like her father's, met mine.

I knew my uncle had his orders, and he would not resist them. When we had begun this project together, I had been drafted to serve. I had served willingly, but now that he was going home, I felt abandoned and frightened by what he had given me.

I understood why some veterans don't want to reveal their stories. The telling is like undressing in front of strangers, showing your scars and unhealed wounds. My uncle had been very brave in sharing stories with me that he had told to no one else. Could I be as willing to make myself vulnerable as a writer?

Uncle Legs had dealt with many questions throughout our time together, but he was also leaving me with one. The Zeus of Greek mythology feared he would be forgotten, so he went in search of Mnemosyne (memory). Together, they produced the muses, who sang of the greatness of Zeus, as well as the mysteries of life and death, and what takes place in between. My uncle had also searched for memory and found her. He had courted her. Their union had produced this book.

Did I understand that what he had given me wasn't mine?

I stood over him this time for my leave-taking. He did not look up; his head remained cocked to his left side as though he was listening. I knew he wasn't, even when I bent down, hoping to catch his eye. But he was not with me in that way, and I wished I could ask him how he felt about that.

On the way home, I played our last session over in my mind. It had taken place just weeks before my visit to Hawfields. "I've been fighting the Japanese all night. They were back." Exhausted, but still regal, Uncle Legs had shuffled into the kitchen in his silky, striped bathrobe that Sunday morning. He had sat down heavily at the breakfast table. I remembered that his hand had trembled as he lifted a cup of steaming coffee to his lips and sloshed it a bit as he returned it to the saucer. "Our recent sessions have caused me to have the strangest dreams."

He had been sad at times, brushing away my concerns with a sweeping motion of his bony hand. "You become who you are because of a time and a place." Again, my uncle had showed me the worn, folded copy of Psalm 91 that was always in his wallet. "You know why I carry this," he said, his hand trembling. It was not a question.

I nodded.

Uncle Legs had glanced down at the paper in his hands, but he was not reading it. "With long life will I satisfy him and show him my salvation."

Our eyes met, and I did not look away. "I've had a wonderful life," he said. "I've had certain advantages, growing up like I did, that children today don't have. I just wish my own children and grandchildren could have had those same kinds of experiences. There's Michael and Nicole, Lee's children; Wooten and Wheeler, Jule's children; Christopher, Jessica, Chance, Colton, and Cameron, Steve's children; and Jay,

Matt, and Clay, Candy's children. They need to know. The next best thing to being there is being told about being there."

I had leaned back against the couch that was my accustomed seat and sighed. I didn't know how I was going to be able to leave him, but I knew even then that memory does not require a leave-taking. The contents of the bag that my uncle had unpacked had been sorted through, aired out, and handed over to me. I would carry it.

The last time I saw my uncle, April 30, 2009, the night before his death, we—including my mother and his children—were all at the hospital. Jane had said her goodbyes, and she wanted his children to have their dad to themselves. She had gone home.

The drip that fed him had already been taken out, and the respirator was to be disconnected that night. The attending nurse lowered her eyes and said softly to me, "We don't know whether or not he can hear you, but that is a possibility. If you say anything, be sure it's something you want him to hear. He can't answer you, but he may be able to understand you." I nodded, an assent, and smiled because his nurse was very pretty. I remember that he had once said to me, "I never did carry an ugly girl to a dance. I always dated the prettiest girls." It looked like this waltz was going to be with another pretty one.

My mother went in first to see her Lehman, Jr., the big brother who had always loved and protected her whenever he could. I had known intimately what was between them up until that moment. Now there would be nothing more to know. I was stunned by the finality of it all. When she returned, I was allowed to go in next. She and I would leave together to allow his children some privacy.

I approached his bed and noticed that the sheet stretched across his chest rose and fell in perfectly measured breaths. The exhales were the wind blowing through his soul, if that was still there. I took his hand,

and it was cold in mine, the fingers flexing involuntarily. I squeezed them and whispered in his ear, "Thank you so much for all the time we had together and for the stories. I love you, and I will never forget you." I stared down at him and wished he would pierce me with those blue eyes just once again, or perhaps veil them in memory. Instead, he appeared to be dreaming, and occasionally he winced, although his eyes were already closed.

I rested my hand on his shoulder, and I was surprised when I felt him distinctly shrug it off. In an odd association that memory sometimes grants us and gives us truth, I remembered. "Excuse me," he had once said to a pretty USO girl. "I've just come off the combat zone, and I'm going to take these four aspirins that this nice stewardess just brought me, and I'm going back to sleep. Please don't disturb me anymore."

In my mind's eye, I saw that girl and her wide-eyed acceptance of his dismissal as he had turned away. Unlike her, I took his hand again and squeezed it, and I brushed his forehead with my lips. Then I, too, left him alone.

Author's Notes

"I've got some things to say to you that I haven't told anybody yet."

— Lieutenant Colonel (Retired) Lehman H. Johnson, Jr.

These were his words to me, in December of 1997, when he called me in for what I thought was a social call. It hadn't exactly been an invitation. He had called me and said for me to come. He was about to turn 82, so I took a notebook, just in case. I remembered that the subject of writing his memoir had come up at his eightieth birthday party. He had been reticent, cagey even, in responding to his family members' prompting. "I'll let you know when I'm ready," he said, turning away.

That Saturday morning, his eyes would have bored a hole in my back if I had retreated. "I've got some things to say to you that I haven't told anybody yet." He was seated in his leather chair in the den, and I was on the couch. The time had come, and there was an urgency in his voice I did not hear, but I remembered, as the weekends we spent together stretched into eleven years.

All I heard was the word "you," as he pointed his finger at me. I thought, "Me? Why, me?"

I didn't dare ask him that question. He was a man used to giving orders and having them obeyed. He had not given up that prerogative in retirement, and that was the way I knew him. It took me ten years to get around to asking, as our relationship grew—and I got bolder. He was gracious enough to tell me, and his response is in the Foreword of this book.

Over the course of time, he told me some of the stories over and over, and I came to ask myself another question. "How can I untangle these memories and make them into a memoir?" What exactly is memoir? There were several drafts of what I called a memoir over the time following his death on May 1, 2009, and the time of publication in 2020.

I learned first what a memoir is not, especially since I was writing someone else's memoir. It could not be a word for word repetition of what my uncle said. Without the immediacy of his physical presence, I came to understand that my reader couldn't, and wouldn't want to, follow that. Memoir is not an exact retelling or a transcription of the memories that person shares. Dialogue and conversation have much in common, but they are not the same thing.

Just as my subject was selective about the stories he told, I would learn to be selective for his readers. Uncle Legs did not tell me everything about everything in his life, but he told me the stories that had meaning for him. Those were the stories I would tell, and I would pay close attention to the way he associated these memories. Sometimes the kaleidoscope of memory shifted, and he told me the same stories in a different order. Occasionally, he would tell me a story one time and then refuse to talk about it again. His silence spoke volumes.

As a military memoir, *Legs Astride the World* has validity in that veterans need to tell their stories, and we need to hear them even more. My uncle was concerned about possible conflicts in perspective with other men—those he had commanded, those under whom he had served. He knew their truth might be different from his. He waited to tell his war stories until most of those men were deceased.

Two notable exceptions at the time we began were Lee Holstein, his faithful mortarman and friend, and Edward M. (Fly) Flanagan, Jr., his forward observer. "Fly," as my uncle always called him, passed away at age 98, on November 7, 2019. After his distinguished retirement as a lieutenant general, Fly became a military historian. I never met him, but his books on World War II and on the history of the 11th Airborne Division were invaluable resources for fact-checking the historical aspect of *Legs Astride the World*. In military memoirs, history and memory march together although there is variance in the cadence of each soldier's march. But dates need to be verified and the broader aspects of the story, which are the same for every man, should be accurate.

But since a memoir tells what an individual person thought and felt at the time, in reading such an account, it's best to remember that memory both recalls and represses. The best memoir writing places that experience in the context of a person's entire life, however short or long that may be. My uncle himself said, "There's a lot that happened to me before the war, and I've lived a lot since." It was important to him that the childhood stories be included because these provided the framework for every decision, every action he took on the battlefield.

Privately, I concluded that these also allowed him time to wade into the war stories, where there were still open wounds. The salt water of memory washing over them would help the healing, but the process would be painful. He could talk about his childhood with me, our shared heritage, but he wasn't comfortable discussing his experiences in World War II, during the Occupation, or in Korea. I was very much aware of the fact that he didn't get around to talking about his military career until our fourth actual interview. I think he didn't trust me yet — with his feelings — and I'm sure I was just as impatient as that little boy (Bobby) in the first part of the book, who asked him about executing Nazi war criminals.

Incidentally, that wasn't Bobby's real name, and the woman in church, who thought my name was Denise, wasn't named Alma either. But both people are real. Other names were omitted or changed, at Lee Holstein's insistence. My uncle and I had not gotten around to talking about the sensitivity of that issue, although there is one instance he thought was so shameful that he did not name the man. Lee helped me to understand that even if a person was long deceased, my uncle would not have wanted to hurt or embarrass that man's family. I respected Lee's viewpoint and agreed with him.

Because Lee was with my uncle in the Philippines, he was a wonderful primary source and an enthusiastic supporter of this project. Uncle Legs put me in touch with him during our interviews, and they talked frequently, so there was no violation of trust between them. Lee read the parts of the manuscript that applied to their time together in the military and shared his insights. Although I never met Lee in person, we enjoyed many phone conversations and corresponded until his death at age 95, in July 2018.

I am sure Uncle Legs did not tell me all his war stories because Lee Holstein told me a few more. I did not attempt to fill in the gaps in history, and I did not go outside of my uncle's story—because it was his. By the time we finished our sessions, shortly before his death, I had tremendous admiration for Lieutenant Colonel Lehman H. Johnson's courage and his willingness to undergo the painful process of self-examination that is part and parcel of a military memoir. That was more than enough reason to write the book.

If you are reading *Legs Astride the World* because you are writing a military memoir, or a memoir of any kind, you must listen with more than your ears. You must learn to listen with your heart. What that means is that you will untangle, reorder, and reconnect the stories with regard to what you will come to understand as the recurring themes of that person's life. Expect that your lives will become entwined, as mine did with my uncle's. Memory makes inroads, heads home, and then journeys on. I wish you well on your own journey. Thank you for accompanying me on the one I was so fortunate to share with my Uncle Legs.

Bibliography

Devlin, Gerard M. *Paratrooper! The Saga of U.S. Army and Marine Parachute and Glider Combat Troops During World War II.* New York: St. Martin's Press, 1970, .

Flanagan, E.M. *Airborne, A Combat History of American Airborne Forces.* New York: The Ballantine Publishing Group, 2003.

Flanagan, E.M. *The Angels, A History of the 11th Airborne Division.* California: Presidio Press, 1989.

Flanagan, E.M. *Corregidor, The Rock Force Assault.* California: Presidio Press, 1988.

Flanagan, E.M. *The Los Baños Raid, The 11th Airborne Jumps at Dawn.* California: Presidio Press, 1986.

Hart, B. H. Liddell. *History of the Second World War.* New York: G. P. Putnam's Sons, 1970.

Henderson, Bruce. *Rescue at Los Baños*. New York: Harper Collins Publishers, 2015.

Lee Holstein VHP Collection (AFC/2001/001/59529), Video Recording, Veterans History Project Collection, American Folklife Center, Library of Congress. https://memory.loc.gov/diglib/vhp/bib/59529

Nash, Grace C. *That We Might Live, A Story of Human Triumph During World War II*. Arizona: Shano Publishers, 1984.

Paine, Chris, dir. *Return to the Philippines*, "Leyte Liberation: The 40th Anniversary." 1985; Portola Valley, CA: Far West Video Productions, 1985. VHS Tape, 240p SD.

Paine, Chris, and Megan McCartney, dir. *Looking Back with George Pearson*. 1997; Portola Valley, CA: Far West Video Productions, 1997. VHS Tape, 240p SD.

"Silver Star Recipients – Foreign," Korean War Educator (website), accessed September 18, 2017, http://www.koreanwar-educator.org/topics/silver_star_foreign/.

About the Author

Mary Susan Heath, writer, lecturer, and workshop leader, is the author of *Legs Astride the World*. As a journalism teacher, she recognized the significance of her uncle's stories about the Philippine Campaign in World War II, his role after the war in executing Nazi war criminals at Landsberg Prison, Germany, and his service during the Korean War. When Lieutenant Colonel Lehman H. Johnson, Jr. tapped her to write his memoir, she was honored to accept. Now retired from teaching, Ms. Heath was certified twice as a National Board Teacher. She holds a master's degree in English from N.C. State University and published her thesis in the *CLA Journal*. It was subsequently republished in the *Journal of Modern Literature*. She has published poetry in *The Crucible* and in Wayne Community College's *Renaissance*. Currently, she serves as the Education and History Consultant for the Wayne County Historical Society, in Goldsboro, N.C. Partnering with Wayne County Public Schools, she has written two plays, *Home Grown in Goldsboro, Dorothy Cotton (1930-2018)*, and *Lady Liberty* for the newly launched traveling trunks exhibition, funded through the North Carolina Humanities Council. Ms. Heath currently resides in Goldsboro, North Carolina, and in Little River, South Carolina